# TEST AND PRACTISE YOUR ENGLISH

## Beginners to Intermediate

### BOOK 1

W. S. Fowler and Norman Coe

Nelson

# Contents

| | |
|---|---|
| **How to use this book** | vi |
| **Tests 1-30** | 1 |
| **Practice Exercises** | 46 |

## Determiners

| | | |
|---|---|---|
| 1 | **a, an** | 47 |
| 2 | **What . . . ! What a/an . . . !** | 48 |
| 3 | **all** and **every** with expressions of time | 48 |
| 4 | Use and omission of **the** | 49 |
| 5 | **this, that, these, those** | 53 |
| 6 | **much, many, a lot of** | 53 |
| 7 | **some, not any, a, one, no (there is/are)** | 54 |
| 8 | **some, any, a, (a) few, (a) little** | 55 |

## Possessives and pronouns

| | | |
|---|---|---|
| 9 | Personal pronouns: **I, me** etc. | 58 |
| 10 | **one, ones** | 59 |
| 11 | **one, it, them, some, any** | 60 |
| 12 | **another, the other, others, the others** | 60 |
| 13 | **each other/one another** | 61 |
| 14 | **everything, everybody/everyone** | 61 |
| 15 | **nobody/no one, nothing, no, none** | 62 |
| 16 | **somebody/someone, anybody/anyone, nobody/no one** | 63 |
| 17 | **something, anything, nothing, somewhere, anywhere** | 64 |
| 18 | Adjectives: **my, your** etc. | 65 |
| 19 | Adjectives: **my, your** etc; pronouns: **mine, yours** etc. | 66 |
| 20 | Adjectives and pronouns with **whose?** | 66 |
| 21 | Reflexive pronouns: **myself** etc; **each other/one another** | 67 |
| 22 | Reflexive pronoun used for emphasis | 68 |
| 23 | Alternatives to the reflexive | 69 |
| 24 | Genitive: **a boy's voice, the capital of England** | 70 |
| 25 | Double possessives: **some friends of mine** | 71 |
| 26 | Genitive | 71 |
| 27 | **belong to** | 73 |

## Adjectives

| | | |
|---|---|---|
| 28 | Comparatives: **as . . . as, -er than, the same as, the same . . . as, different from** | 74 |
| 29 | Comparatives: **-er, more** | 75 |
| 30 | Comparatives: **-er**; superlatives: **-est** | 75 |
| 31 | Comparatives: **more**; superlatives: **most** | 76 |
| 32 | Position of adjectives | 77 |
| 33 | Emphasis of adjectives with **so, such** | 78 |
| 34 | Adjectives with **too, enough** | 80 |

# Contents

## Adverbs
| | | |
|---|---|---|
| 35 | Adverbs that end with **-ly** | 81 |
| 36 | Comparison of adverbs | 81 |
| 37 | **already, yet** | 82 |
| 38 | **still** | 83 |
| 39 | **very, much** | 84 |
| 40 | **once, twice, three times** etc. | 85 |
| 41 | Frequency adverbs; **first, last, just** | 85 |

## Prepositional phrases
| | | |
|---|---|---|
| 42 | Prepositions of position | 88 |
| 43 | Prepositions of movement | 91 |
| 44 | Prepositions of time | 92 |
| 45 | Prepositional verbs | 93 |
| 46 | **until, as far as** | 94 |
| 47 | **as, like; such . . . as, such as, like** | 94 |

## Modals and auxiliaries
| | | |
|---|---|---|
| 48 | **can** | 97 |
| 49 | **can, will be able to** | 98 |
| 50 | **could** | 99 |
| 51 | **may, might** | 100 |
| 52 | **must** and **need to** | 101 |
| 53 | **must** (to express a logical deduction) | 104 |
| 54 | **had to** | 105 |
| 55 | **did you have to?** | 106 |
| 56 | **should** | 106 |
| 57 | **ought to** | 107 |
| 58 | **must have, should have, ought to have** | 108 |
| 59 | **shall, will** | 109 |
| 60 | **used to** | 110 |
| 61 | **had better** | 110 |
| 62 | **would rather** | 111 |
| 63 | Short answers | 112 |
| 64 | **so do I; I do, too** etc. | 113 |

## Verb forms
| | | |
|---|---|---|
| 65 | Present of **be** | 115 |
| 66 | Noun/verb agreement with **be** | 116 |
| 67 | Present and past of **be** | 117 |
| 68 | Present and past of **have** | 118 |
| 69 | Present Continuous | 119 |
| 70 | **going to** | 120 |
| 71 | Present Continuous, **going to** future | 120 |
| 72 | Present Simple | 121 |
| 73 | Present Simple: negative | 122 |
| 74 | Present Simple: questions | 123 |
| 75 | Present Continuous, Present Simple | 123 |
| 76 | Verbs not used in continuous forms | 124 |
| 77 | Past Simple: irregular verbs | 125 |

iii

| | | |
|---|---|---|
| 78 | Past Simple: negative | 127 |
| 79 | Past Simple: questions | 127 |
| 80 | Past Simple, Past Continuous | 128 |
| 81 | Present Perfect: regular and irregular verbs | 128 |
| 82 | **gone** and **been** | 130 |
| 83 | Present Perfect, Past Simple | 130 |
| 84 | Present Perfect Simple and Continuous | 133 |
| 85 | Present Perfect with **ever** and **never** | 134 |
| 86 | **ago** and **for** | 134 |
| 87 | Present Perfect with **for**; **since** with Past Simple | 135 |
| 88 | Past Perfect Simple | 135 |
| 89 | Second Conditional | 136 |
| 90 | **wish** with Past Simple | 137 |
| 91 | Third Conditional | 137 |
| 92 | Imperatives | 138 |
| 93 | Alternatives to the imperative | 139 |
| 94 | Imperative and **Why (not) do this?**, **Why do/don't you do this?** | 140 |
| 95 | **Don't . . .** and **Be careful not to . . .** | 140 |
| 96 | **let's** | 141 |

## Questions

| | | |
|---|---|---|
| 97 | Question tags | 142 |
| 98 | Question words | 143 |
| 99 | **Who?** and **What?** as subject | 144 |

## Introductory **there** and **it**

| | | |
|---|---|---|
| 100 | **there is/are** | 145 |
| 101 | **there is/are, it is/they are** | 146 |
| 102 | **there is/are** as alternatives | 147 |
| 103 | **its, it's, it is** | 147 |
| 104 | **It takes (two hours) to . . .** | 148 |

## Gerunds and infinitives

| | | |
|---|---|---|
| 105 | Verb + gerund, verb + infinitive | 149 |
| 106 | Verbs of the senses + infinitive or -ing | 151 |
| 107 | Preposition + gerund | 151 |
| 108 | **make** and **let** + infinitive | 152 |
| 109 | **for him to do** | 152 |
| 110 | Verb + object + infinitive | 153 |
| 111 | Question word + infinitive | 153 |

## Passive

| | | |
|---|---|---|
| 112 | **was born; is/was called** | 155 |
| 113 | **made of/from/with/by** | 155 |
| 114 | Active and passive | 156 |
| 115 | Infinitive forms | 157 |
| 116 | Double object verbs | 157 |
| 117 | Causative: **have/get something done** | 158 |

# Contents

## Reported speech
| | | |
|---|---|---|
| 118 | Direct and reported speech | 160 |
| 119 | Tense changes: Present Simple and Future | 161 |
| 120 | Reported speech: questions | 162 |
| 121 | Reported imperatives | 163 |

## Clauses
| | | |
|---|---|---|
| 122 | neither . . . nor | 164 |
| 123 | Future time clauses with **when, if, before, after, until** | 164 |
| 124 | **the more . . . the more** | 165 |
| 125 | **what, the thing that** | 165 |
| 126 | **however, whatever, whoever, wherever** | 167 |
| 127 | Infinitive of purpose and **for** | 168 |
| 128 | **so as to/in order to, so that, because; avoid, prevent** | 168 |
| 129 | **unless** | 170 |
| 130 | **in case** | 170 |
| 131 | **while, meanwhile** | 171 |
| 132 | **the reason for/why . . .** | 171 |
| 133 | **although/even though, in spite of; however, nevertheless, all the same** | 172 |
| 134 | Defining relative clauses | 173 |
| 135 | Non-defining relative clauses | 174 |
| 136 | Co-ordinating relative clauses | 176 |

## Word order
| | | |
|---|---|---|
| 137 | **all, both, the whole** | 177 |
| 138 | **enough** | 178 |
| 139 | Direct and indirect object | 178 |
| 140 | Phrasal verbs | 179 |

## Lexis
| | | |
|---|---|---|
| 141 | Nationality words | 180 |
| 142 | Mass (uncountable) nouns | 180 |
| 143 | **I'm cold, thirsty** etc. | 181 |
| 144 | **look, sound, taste, seem** | 182 |
| 145 | **make** and **do** | 182 |
| 146 | **say** and **tell** | 184 |
| 147 | **arrive, get to, reach** | 185 |
| 148 | **raise** and **rise** | 186 |
| 149 | **I (don't) think so, I hope so/not** | 187 |
| 150 | **likely, probably** | 187 |

## Structural Appendix   188

## Lexical Appendix   191

## Index   198

# How to use this book

This book is in four parts: the **Tests**, the **Test Key**, the **Practice Exercises** and the **Practice Key**.

Your results in the **Tests** show you which grammatical areas you need to revise. There are 30 multiple-choice tests. The time limit for **Tests 1-20** is twenty minutes and for **Tests 21-30** twenty-five minutes.

After the **Test**, use the **Test Key** to check your answers. If you have made a mistake, the **Test Key** will tell you where to go for help: to the **Practice Exercises**, or to the **Structural** and **Lexical Appendixes (SA** and **LA)**.

The **Practice Exercises** contain explanations, examples and exercises. First, study the examples and read the explanations, then do the exercises. Of course, if you know you need more practice for a particular area, you can find the appropriate exercise in the **Index** without first doing a test. The answers to the exercises are in the **Practice Key**.

The **Practice Key** is the main part of the **Master Key Booklet** and gives the answers to all the **Practice Exercises**.

## Notes for use in the classroom

Students should either complete a **Mark Sheet** (see page viii) or underline the correct answer in their books. Once the correct answers are known, a useful reinforcement exercise is to read the passage through aloud, since this then provides a model containing the right forms in context.

The **Tests** should be used at regular intervals during the course as the results will show both teacher and student what the common mistakes are. If they are used as part of a remedial programme, the following method of marking is recommended:

Make a set of cards labelled A,B,C and D and give one set to each of the students when they have completed a **Test** . When marking the **Test** ask the students to hold up the card which shows their answer for each question. This is a quick way of finding out which questions require remedial work.

# How to use this book

Here is a practical example of this method:

A  Tell me where it is
B  Tell me where is it
C  Say me where it is
D  Say me where is it

Answer A is correct, B shows uncertainty about indirect questions, C shows uncertainty about **say** and **tell** and D is a double error.

| e.g. | A | B | C | D |
|---|---|---|---|---|
| Class 1 | 17 | 2 | 1 | 0 |
| Class 2 | 14 | 6 | 0 | 0 |
| Class 3 | 12 | 4 | 4 | 0 |
| Class 4 | 10 | 4 | 3 | 3 |

Class 1   requires no remedial action.
Class 2   needs to be reminded of word order in indirect questions.
Class 3   must be reminded of the difference between **say** and **tell**.
Class 4   contains a number of students with difficulties and remedial work on both structures is required.

The **Tests** are not intended to compare individual students' achievements or knowledge but to find out the weaknesses of the class as a whole. Encourage students to approach them in a co-operative way so that they want to find out what they don't know and so that they can see that remedial work is necessary if a large proportion of them (more than 30%) make a mistake when answering a question.

The **Master Key Booklet** consists of two keys: the **Practice Key** and the **Test Key** (in the middle eight pages). The **Booklet**, inserted in the back cover, can be removed so that the teacher can decide when the students have access to it.

# Mark Sheet

Test_____ Name_____ Date_____

| 1 | Answer | Correct Answer | Practice Exercise |
|---|---|---|---|
| A | | | |
| B | | | |
| C | | | |
| D | | | |

| 2 | Answer | Correct Answer | Practice Exercise |
|---|---|---|---|
| A | | | |
| B | | | |
| C | | | |
| D | | | |

| 3 | Answer | Correct Answer | Practice Exercise |
|---|---|---|---|
| A | | | |
| B | | | |
| C | | | |
| D | | | |

| 4 | Answer | Correct Answer | Practice Exercise |
|---|---|---|---|
| A | | | |
| B | | | |
| C | | | |
| D | | | |

| 5 | Answer | Correct Answer | Practice Exercise |
|---|---|---|---|
| A | | | |
| B | | | |
| C | | | |
| D | | | |

| 6 | Answer | Correct Answer | Practice Exercise |
|---|---|---|---|
| A | | | |
| B | | | |
| C | | | |
| D | | | |

| 7 | Answer | Correct Answer | Practice Exercise |
|---|---|---|---|
| A | | | |
| B | | | |
| C | | | |
| D | | | |

| 8 | Answer | Correct Answer | Practice Exercise |
|---|---|---|---|
| A | | | |
| B | | | |
| C | | | |
| D | | | |

| 9 | Answer | Correct Answer | Practice Exercise |
|---|---|---|---|
| A | | | |
| B | | | |
| C | | | |
| D | | | |

| 10 | Answer | Correct Answer | Practice Exercise |
|---|---|---|---|
| A | | | |
| B | | | |
| C | | | |
| D | | | |

| 11 | Answer | Correct Answer | Practice Exercise |
|---|---|---|---|
| A | | | |
| B | | | |
| C | | | |
| D | | | |

| 12 | Answer | Correct Answer | Practice Exercise |
|---|---|---|---|
| A | | | |
| B | | | |
| C | | | |
| D | | | |

| 13 | Answer | Correct Answer | Practice Exercise |
|---|---|---|---|
| A | | | |
| B | | | |
| C | | | |
| D | | | |

| 14 | Answer | Correct Answer | Practice Exercise |
|---|---|---|---|
| A | | | |
| B | | | |
| C | | | |
| D | | | |

| 15 | Answer | Correct Answer | Practice Exercise |
|---|---|---|---|
| A | | | |
| B | | | |
| C | | | |
| D | | | |

| 16 | Answer | Correct Answer | Practice Exercise |
|---|---|---|---|
| A | | | |
| B | | | |
| C | | | |
| D | | | |

| 17 | Answer | Correct Answer | Practice Exercise |
|---|---|---|---|
| A | | | |
| B | | | |
| C | | | |
| D | | | |

| 18 | Answer | Correct Answer | Practice Exercise |
|---|---|---|---|
| A | | | |
| B | | | |
| C | | | |
| D | | | |

| 19 | Answer | Correct Answer | Practice Exercise |
|---|---|---|---|
| A | | | |
| B | | | |
| C | | | |
| D | | | |

| 20 | Answer | Correct Answer | Practice Exercise |
|---|---|---|---|
| A | | | |
| B | | | |
| C | | | |
| D | | | |

# Tests 1-30

## How to use the Tests

All the **Tests** are multiple-choice. There are four answers to each question, A,B,C or D, but only ONE is correct. Each test has twenty questions. The time limit for **Tests 1-20** is twenty minutes and for **Tests 21-30**, twenty-five minutes. The **Mark Sheet** (see page viii) is a useful way of answering the questions.

# Test 1

*Choose the correct answer. Only one answer is correct.*

A  Where are David and Janet?
B  They \_\_1\_\_ the bus stop. They're going \_\_2\_\_ school.
A  Have they got \_\_3\_\_ books?
B  Yes, Janet is reading \_\_4\_\_ book, and David \_\_5\_\_ books in his bag.

| | | | | | | | |
|---|---|---|---|---|---|---|---|
| 1 | A | are at | B | are | C | is at | D | is to |
| 2 | A | in | B | on | C | at | D | to |
| 3 | A | there | B | they're | C | their | D | they |
| 4 | A | her | B | she | C | she's | D | hers |
| 5 | A | have her | B | has her | C | have his | D | has his |

A  Is this \_\_6\_\_ car?
B  No, it's \_\_7\_\_. He is \_\_8\_\_ there.
A  Is he \_\_9\_\_?
B  Yes, but his car \_\_10\_\_ American.

| | | | | | | | |
|---|---|---|---|---|---|---|---|
| 6 | A | you're | B | you | C | your | D | yours |
| 7 | A | of Mr Brown | B | to Mr Brown | C | Mr Brown's | D | a Mr Brown |
| 8 | A | this man | B | that man | C | this men | D | that men |
| 9 | A | England | B | English | C | an English | D | a English |
| 10 | A | it | B | it's | C | is | D | its |

A  Hullo, Ann. \_\_11\_\_ you today?
B  \_\_12\_\_ fine. And you?
A  Very \_\_13\_\_, thank you.
B  \_\_14\_\_ your mother today?
A  \_\_15\_\_ London.

| | | | | | | | |
|---|---|---|---|---|---|---|---|
| 11 | A | Who are | B | How are | C | Who is | D | How is |
| 12 | A | I'm | B | Am | C | I | D | Am I |
| 13 | A | good | B | fine | C | well | D | best |
| 14 | A | When is | B | Where is | C | When are | D | Where are |
| 15 | A | On | B | At | C | In | D | Of |

A  There's a bottle \_\_16\_\_ the table. \_\_17\_\_ it?
B  It's \_\_18\_\_. Have you got \_\_19\_\_?
A  No, I haven't got \_\_20\_\_.

| | | | | | | | |
|---|---|---|---|---|---|---|---|
| 16 | A | in | B | on | C | into | D | onto |
| 17 | A | Who is | B | Whose | C | Who's | D | Whose is |
| 18 | A | of me | B | me | C | my | D | mine |
| 19 | A | drink | B | some drink | C | any drink | D | a drink |
| 20 | A | a | B | one | C | some | D | any |

# Test 2

*Choose the correct answer. Only one answer is correct.*

A  What ___1___ the girls doing?
B  ___2___ playing.
A  Where?
B  ___3___ the garden. Can you see ___4___ ?
A  Yes, they're ___5___ the big tree.

| | | | | | | | | |
|---|---|---|---|---|---|---|---|---|
| 1 | A | is | B | do | C | are | D | does |
| 2 | A | She's | B | They | C | Them | D | They're |
| 3 | A | At | B | On | C | In | D | Into |
| 4 | A | they | B | she | C | her | D | them |
| 5 | A | between | B | in front | C | over | D | near |

A  What ___6___ doing?
B  ___7___ a book. ___8___ many books?
A  No, I ___9___ books, but I like good films.
B  Yes, I like ___10___ , too.

| | | | | | | | | |
|---|---|---|---|---|---|---|---|---|
| 6 | A | are you | B | you are | C | you | D | is you |
| 7 | A | I reading | B | Am reading | C | I'm reading | D | I read |
| 8 | A | You read | B | Are you read | C | You reading | D | Do you read |
| 9 | A | no like | B | don't like | C | doesn't like | D | like not |
| 10 | A | them | B | they | C | it | D | him |

A  ___11___ my sister. She is writing a letter ___12___ new pen. She's writing ___13___ brother. He doesn't live here.
B  Oh, where does he live?
A  He ___14___ a big town. He ___15___ a good job.

| | | | | | | | | |
|---|---|---|---|---|---|---|---|---|
| 11 | A | See | B | See at | C | Look | D | Look at |
| 12 | A | by his | B | with his | C | with her | D | by her |
| 13 | A | to our | B | at she | C | at her | D | to us |
| 14 | A | work on | B | work in | C | works on | D | works in |
| 15 | A | have | B | has | C | are having | D | is having |

A  What ___16___ is it?
B  It's half ___17___ one.
A  Good. Now we ___18___ to have lunch. You ___19___ on this chair.
B  Thank you. Please ___20___ any potatoes.

| | | | | | | | | |
|---|---|---|---|---|---|---|---|---|
| 16 | A | clock | B | hour | C | time | D | watch |
| 17 | A | at | B | to | C | past | D | on |
| 18 | A | going | B | are going | C | are go | D | goes |
| 19 | A | can to sit | B | can sit | C | sitting | D | are sit |
| 20 | A | not give me | B | give me | C | don't give me | D | not to give me |

# Test 3

*Choose the correct answer. Only one answer is correct.*

A  My big brother  __1__  football.
B  Where  __2__  ?
A  In the park. We can  __3__  this afternoon.
B  I  __4__  go to the park this afternoon. I  __5__  help my mother.

| | | | | | | | |
|---|---|---|---|---|---|---|---|
| 1 | A | plays the | B | play the | C | plays | D | play |
| 2 | A | he plays | B | he play | C | does he play | D | do he play |
| 3 | A | to go here | B | to go there | C | go here | D | go there |
| 4 | A | not can | B | can't | C | don't | D | not |
| 5 | A | must | B | must to | C | go to | D | going to |

A  __6__  hot today.  __7__  a cold drink in the house?
B  I'll  __8__  my mother. Mum,  __9__  any Coca-Cola?
C  No, but you can have milk.
B  Oh, but we  __10__  milk.

| | | | | | | | |
|---|---|---|---|---|---|---|---|
| 6 | A | The sun's | B | The sun | C | A sun's | D | A sun |
| 7 | A | Are there | B | Is there | C | There are | D | There is |
| 8 | A | say to | B | ask to | C | say | D | ask |
| 9 | A | has we | B | we has | C | have we | D | we have |
| 10 | A | no like | B | don't like | C | do like not | D | not like the |

A  Jack, come over  __11__  .
B  Yes, what  __12__  ?
A  Go to the shop and buy  __13__  bread.
B  __14__  go now? I'm  __15__  my friends.
A  Yes, please go now.

| | | | | | | | |
|---|---|---|---|---|---|---|---|
| 11 | A | there to me | B | here to me | C | there to my | D | here to my |
| 12 | A | you do want | B | do you want | C | does you want | D | you does want |
| 13 | A | some | B | any | C | a | D | much |
| 14 | A | Must I | B | Do I must | C | I must | D | I must to |
| 15 | A | talk to | B | talking to | C | talk at | D | talking at |

A  Do you know Jane Smith?
B  Yes, but she  __16__  to school with me. She  __17__  a big shop.
A  Where is it?
B  It's  __18__  my house.
A  Do you see Jane at the weekends?
B  Yes.  __19__  Saturday we  __20__  play tennis.

| | | | | | | | |
|---|---|---|---|---|---|---|---|
| 16 | A | isn't go | B | goes not | C | doesn't go | D | doesn't going |
| 17 | A | walks on | B | walks in | C | works on | D | works in |
| 18 | A | between | B | near | C | at | D | in front |
| 19 | A | At | B | In | C | The | D | This |
| 20 | A | are | B | go to | C | are going to | D | are going |

# Test 4

*Choose the correct answer. Only one answer is correct.*

A   ___1___ these books?
B   They're ___2___ . This book is ___3___ .
A   I can't read it. It's ___4___ English.
B   No, but you can ___5___ the pictures.

| | | | | | | | | |
|---|---|---|---|---|---|---|---|---|
| 1 | A | Whose are | B | Who's are | C | Whose is | D | Who's is |
| 2 | A | me | B | of me | C | my | D | mine |
| 3 | A | very well | B | very good | C | much well | D | much good |
| 4 | A | in the | B | in | C | on the | D | on |
| 5 | A | to look | B | to look at | C | look | D | look at |

A   Hullo, I'm ___6___ . Is your mother ___7___ ?
B   Yes, she ___8___ in the garden.
A   Can I ___9___ her, please?
B   I think ___10___ . Come with me.

| | | | | | | | | |
|---|---|---|---|---|---|---|---|---|
| 6 | A | a police | B | police | C | a policeman | D | policeman |
| 7 | A | in home | B | in the home | C | at home | D | at the home |
| 8 | A | work | B | works | C | working | D | is working |
| 9 | A | tell | B | talk | C | tell to | D | talk to |
| 10 | A | this | B | it | C | that | D | so |

A   Have you got ___11___ ?
B   I've got one brother and one sister.
A   What does your sister do?
B   ___12___ English teacher. There are 40 pupils ___13___ her class.
A   Does she ___14___ English people?
B   Yes, she ___15___ .

| | | | | | | | | |
|---|---|---|---|---|---|---|---|---|
| 11 | A | a big family | B | the big family | C | a family big | D | the family big |
| 12 | A | He's a | B | He's an | C | She's a | D | She's an |
| 13 | A | in | B | into | C | at | D | on |
| 14 | A | know much | B | know many | C | knows much | D | knows many |
| 15 | A | does | B | does it | C | knows them | D | knows |

A   What is your teacher ___16___ ?
B   Our teacher is a tall man ___17___ . We like him ___18___ .
    He ___19___ Leeds.
A   Are there a lot of children in your class?
B   Yes, but the classroom's big. It's ___20___ this room.

| | | | | | | | | |
|---|---|---|---|---|---|---|---|---|
| 16 | A | like | B | likes | C | liking | D | does like |
| 17 | A | of long hairs | B | with long hairs | C | of long hair | D | with long hair |
| 18 | A | very good | B | very much | C | very well | D | very nice |
| 19 | A | is coming from | B | is coming of | C | comes from | D | comes of |
| 20 | A | as big as | B | as big that | C | so big as | D | so big that |

# Test 5

*Choose the correct answer. Only one answer is correct.*

A   When   __1__   your homework?
B   I usually go   __2__   early and do it there.
A   I   __3__   in bed but I   __4__   the radio. I do my homework in the morning. I   __5__   six o'clock and do it then.

| 1 | A | you do | B | do you | C | to do | D | do you do |
|---|---|---|---|---|---|---|---|---|
| 2 | A | to bed | B | to the bed | C | in bed | D | in the bed |
| 3 | A | am never reading | B | never read | C | read never | D | never am reading |
| 4 | A | hear on | B | hear to | C | listen to | D | listen on |
| 5 | A | get up on | B | get up at | C | go up on | D | go up at |

A   Where's Brighton?
B   It's   __6__   the south coast of England.
A   How many kilometres   __7__   from London?
B   About 80 kilometres. You can go   __8__   train.
A   How   __9__   does it take?
B   About 55 minutes.
A   And   __10__   many trains?
B   Yes, a lot.

| 6 | A | by | B | beside | C | on | D | in |
|---|---|---|---|---|---|---|---|---|
| 7 | A | is there | B | are there | C | is it | D | are they |
| 8 | A | by | B | on | C | in | D | with |
| 9 | A | much | B | many times | C | long | D | far |
| 10 | A | there are | B | are there | C | they are | D | are they |

A   Did you see the film on television   __11__   ?
B   No, we went to see some friends of   __12__   . We   __13__   very late.
A   Why? What   __14__   ?
B   There weren't   __15__   , so we walked and it took two hours.

| 11 | A | at night | B | in the night | C | last night | D | tonight |
|---|---|---|---|---|---|---|---|---|
| 12 | A | we | B | us | C | our | D | ours |
| 13 | A | get home | B | got home | C | get to home | D | got to home |
| 14 | A | did happen | B | have happened | C | happened | D | has happened |
| 15 | A | some bus | B | some buses | C | any bus | D | any buses |

A   Have you   __16__   to the shops?
B   No, I went this morning.
A   __17__   many things?
B   Yes, but everything   __18__   expensive. I didn't buy   __19__   fruit but I got   __20__   apples.

| 16 | A | just gone | B | just been | C | gone just | D | been just |
|---|---|---|---|---|---|---|---|---|
| 17 | A | Bought you | B | You bought | C | Did you buy | D | You did buy |
| 18 | A | was very | B | were very | C | was much | D | were much |
| 19 | A | much | B | many | C | some | D | any |
| 20 | A | any big red | B | some big red | C | any red big | D | some red big |

# Test 6

*Choose the correct answer. Only one answer is correct.*

A There __1__ bread in the house. You must __2__ to the shops.
B Give me __3__ money, please, Mum. How much bread __4__ you want?
A Hm, I don't know. I __5__ buy bread on Mondays. Buy two large loaves.

| | | | | | | | | |
|---|---|---|---|---|---|---|---|---|
| 1 | A | isn't any | B | aren't any | C | isn't some | D | aren't some |
| 2 | A | to get | B | to go | C | get | D | go |
| 3 | A | a | B | some | C | any | D | those |
| 4 | A | do | B | does | C | are | D | is |
| 5 | A | usually not | B | no usually | C | usually doesn't | D | don't usually |

A What is Mary doing __6__ her room?
B She's __7__ letters.
A __8__ often write to her?
B Yes, she has __9__ friends. She __10__ letters.

| | | | | | | | | |
|---|---|---|---|---|---|---|---|---|
| 6 | A | in | B | on | C | at | D | up |
| 7 | A | writes some | B | writing some | C | write any | D | writing any |
| 8 | A | Does people | B | Does person | C | Do people | D | Do persons |
| 9 | A | much | B | a lot of | C | every | D | many of |
| 10 | A | is often writing | B | often writes | C | writes often | D | often is writing |

A My brother is bigger __11__ .
B __12__ is he?
A He's 25. He has __13__ job.
B My brother __14__ taxi. Sometimes he works __15__ night.

| | | | | | | | | |
|---|---|---|---|---|---|---|---|---|
| 11 | A | that yours | B | that your | C | than yours | D | than your |
| 12 | A | What old | B | How old | C | What age | D | How age |
| 13 | A | very well | B | very good | C | a very well | D | a very good |
| 14 | A | drives | B | drive | C | drives a | D | drive a |
| 15 | A | on | B | at | C | during | D | in |

A Here are the books.
B Good. Give __16__ .
A What __17__ to do with them?
B Put __18__ on the table. Now look at these. Do you want to read __19__ ?
A Can't I read that one on the table?
B No, that's a present __20__ my sister.

| | | | | | | | | |
|---|---|---|---|---|---|---|---|---|
| 16 | A | it to me | B | them to me | C | to me it | D | to me them |
| 17 | A | we're going | B | are we going | C | we go | D | go we |
| 18 | A | that red | B | those red | C | that red one | D | those red one |
| 19 | A | someone | B | anyone | C | one | D | it |
| 20 | A | for | B | of | C | at | D | to |

# Test 7

*Choose the correct answer. Only one answer is correct.*

A I'm going to __1__ you some questions. What is the capital __2__ England?
B London.
A Yes. Now, where is it?
B __3__ south.
A How __4__ live there?
B About seven million.
A Now another question for you. What's fifty and fifty?
B That's easy. __5__ .

| | | | | | | | |
|---|---|---|---|---|---|---|---|
| 1 | A | ask | B | tell | C | say | D | talk |
| 2 | A | from | B | on | C | of | D | in |
| 3 | A | On | B | On the | C | In | D | In the |
| 4 | A | much people | B | much person | C | many people | D | many person |
| 5 | A | A hundred | B | Hundred | C | Thirteen | D | Thirty |

A Have you __6__ this book before?
B Yes, Tom __7__ it last week. He thought it __8__ . Have you read it?
A Not __9__ , but I want __10__ it this weekend.

| | | | | | | | |
|---|---|---|---|---|---|---|---|
| 6 | A | seen | B | saw | C | see | D | seed |
| 7 | A | read | B | reads | C | red | D | has read |
| 8 | A | were very good | B | was very good | C | were very well | D | was very well |
| 9 | A | already | B | yet | C | still | D | before |
| 10 | A | read | B | reading | C | to read | D | to reading |

A Where __11__ yesterday?
B We went to that new restaurant. We __12__ there at 8 o'clock and there wasn't __13__ in the place.
A Did you __14__ ?
B No, we stayed for half an hour, but we only __15__ a drink.

| | | | | | | | |
|---|---|---|---|---|---|---|---|
| 11 | A | have you gone | B | went you | C | did you go | D | you do go |
| 12 | A | got | B | came | C | get | D | come |
| 13 | A | nobody | B | anybody | C | no persons | D | any people |
| 14 | A | leave | B | live | C | lived | D | left |
| 15 | A | were having | B | were taking | C | had | D | took |

A When I got up this morning __16__ raining, and I haven't got __17__ umbrella.
B I haven't, __18__ , but the bus stop is __19__ my house.
A I don't go by bus. I walk __20__ .

| | | | | | | | |
|---|---|---|---|---|---|---|---|
| 16 | A | was it | B | was there | C | it was | D | there was |
| 17 | A | a | B | an | C | any | D | no |
| 18 | A | either | B | neither | C | too | D | also |
| 19 | A | very close | B | very near | C | next | D | very next |
| 20 | A | to work | B | at work | C | to the work | D | at the work |

# Test 8

*Choose the correct answer. Only one answer is correct.*

A When ___1___ born?
B In 1976. My birthday is ___2___ June. When is ___3___ ?
A It's the ___4___ December.
B How old ___5___ this year?
A Fourteen.

| 1 | A | you were | B | were you | C | are you | D | you are |
|---|---|---|---|---|---|---|---|---|
| 2 | A | in | B | on | C | at | D | of |
| 3 | A | the your | B | the yours | C | your | D | yours |
| 4 | A | third | B | three | C | third of | D | three of |
| 5 | A | shall you be | B | will you be | C | you are | D | have you |

A This is a nice park. I ___6___ here before.
B I ___7___ here. When I was young, my parents ___8___ me. Now I ___9___ here on my bike.
A My parents never come here. They ___10___ parks.

| 6 | A | don't be | B | haven't been | C | wasn't | D | didn't be |
|---|---|---|---|---|---|---|---|---|
| 7 | A | often come | B | come often | C | often go | D | go often |
| 8 | A | were bringing | B | brought | C | bring | D | have brought |
| 9 | A | am riding | B | am driving | C | ride | D | drive |
| 10 | A | doesn't like | B | don't like | C | doesn't like the | D | don't like the |

A What time did you arrive ___11___ yesterday?
B About six o'clock. Why?
A ___12___ a good film on television.
B Was the ___13___ ?
A Yes, it was about two policeman ___14___ Berlin.
B Oh yes, I remember. I watched the beginning but I ___15___ the end.

| 11 | A | home | B | go home | C | at home | D | in home |
|---|---|---|---|---|---|---|---|---|
| 12 | A | It was | B | It has been | C | There was | D | There has been |
| 13 | A | Germany film | B | German film | C | film German | D | film Germany |
| 14 | A | of | B | in | C | on | D | at |
| 15 | A | didn't see | B | didn't saw | C | haven't saw | D | haven't seen |

A I don't like winter.
B ___16___ . It's so cold today.
A Yes, ___17___ cold. Where's my ___18___ coat?
B Your coat's here, in ___19___ place. Are you going to ___20___ ?
A Yes, I am.

| 16 | A | Nor I do | B | Nor do I | C | Nor like I | D | Nor I like |
|---|---|---|---|---|---|---|---|---|
| 17 | A | I have very | B | I have much | C | I'm very | D | I'm much |
| 18 | A | long hot | B | long warm | C | tall hot | D | tall warm |
| 19 | A | its usually | B | it's usually | C | its usual | D | it's usual |
| 20 | A | put on it | B | put it on | C | take on it | D | take it on |

# Test 9

*Choose the correct answer. Only one answer is correct.*

A How ___1___ is Mary?
B About five feet.
A And ___2___ ?
B She's not very clever but she plays the guitar ___3___ .
A ___4___ lessons?
B Not from a teacher, but her brother ___5___ her.

| 1 | A | long | B | tall | C | far | D | much |
|---|---|---|---|---|---|---|---|---|
| 2 | A | what's she like | B | how's she like | C | how is she | D | what she likes |
| 3 | A | nice | B | good | C | nicely | D | better |
| 4 | A | Has she had | B | Have she has | C | Had she have | D | Had she has |
| 5 | A | teachers | B | teaches | C | teach | D | teaching |

A Hullo, Betty. What are you ___6___ ?
B A photo of a fish that ___7___ the air.
A ___8___ fly. They can't.
B ___9___ wrong. Some fish can fly. You don't know ___10___ .

| 6 | A | looking | B | watching | C | looking at | D | seeing |
|---|---|---|---|---|---|---|---|---|
| 7 | A | fly in | B | flies on | C | flies in | D | fly on |
| 8 | A | The fish don't | B | Fish don't | C | The fish doesn't | D | Fish doesn't |
| 9 | A | You're | B | Your | C | You have | D | You've |
| 10 | A | something | B | all things | C | everything | D | nothing |

A Hullo, Bill. Where were you ___11___ Saturday? ___12___ to town?
B No, I ___13___ money.
A I was there but there weren't ___14___ people.
B Where ___15___ ?
A At the football match.

| 11 | A | the | B | at | C | last | D | in |
|---|---|---|---|---|---|---|---|---|
| 12 | A | Were you | B | Was you | C | Did you go | D | Have you gone |
| 13 | A | don't have | B | didn't have no | C | didn't have any | D | hadn't |
| 14 | A | much | B | many | C | a lot | D | no |
| 15 | A | were everybody | B | was everybody | C | were all people | D | was all people |

A Are you ___16___ ?
B No, I come ___17___ Scotland.
A Is Scotland ___18___ England?
B No, but it is ___19___ .
A Oh, is it? Perhaps ___20___ there next year.

| 16 | A | an English | B | Englishman | C | English | D | English man |
|---|---|---|---|---|---|---|---|---|
| 17 | A | out of | B | in | C | of | D | from |
| 18 | A | so big that | B | as big than | C | as big as | D | as big that |
| 19 | A | much prettier | B | very prettier | C | prettiest | D | much pretty |
| 20 | A | I come | B | I go | C | I'll come | D | I'll go |

# Test 10

*Choose the correct answer. Only one answer is correct.*

A   Where do people ___1___ English?
B   ___2___ countries.
A   Yes, but where do they speak ___3___ English?
B   In this book it ___4___ in Canada.
A   Who ___5___ the book?
B   A Canadian, of course.

| 1 | A | talk | B | talk the | C | speak | D | speak the |
|---|---|---|---|---|---|---|---|---|
| 2 | A | In much | B | In many | C | On much | D | On many |
| 3 | A | better | B | best | C | the better | D | the best |
| 4 | A | say | B | says | C | tell | D | tells |
| 5 | A | wrote | B | did write | C | have written | D | was writing |

A   Hullo, Tony. Where ___6___ you been?
B   We've ___7___ back from a holiday ___8___ the country.
A   When did you go?
B   We went on the ___9___ of July.
A   ___10___ a good time?
B   Yes, it was very good.

| 6 | A | are | B | do | C | has | D | have |
|---|---|---|---|---|---|---|---|---|
| 7 | A | came just | B | come just | C | just came | D | just come |
| 8 | A | in | B | at | C | on | D | to |
| 9 | A | fifty | B | fifteen | C | fiftieth | D | fifteenth |
| 10 | A | Had you | B | Did you have | C | Have you got | D | Were you having |

A   ___11___ drive a car when you ___12___ 16 years old?
B   No, and I ___13___ can't drive a car. I go everywhere by bus.
A   Doesn't that take ___14___?
B   Not always. Sometimes it's ___15___ by car.

| 11 | A | Did you could | B | Did you can | C | Could you | D | Can you |
|---|---|---|---|---|---|---|---|---|
| 12 | A | had | B | have got | C | were | D | was |
| 13 | A | still | B | yet | C | now | D | already |
| 14 | A | many times | B | much time | C | long time | D | a long time |
| 15 | A | quickly as | B | quicker as | C | quicker than | D | quickly than |

A   In 1960 ___16___ more trees in this town.
B   ___17___ here then?
A   No, but I ___18___ my cousins. They lived in a house ___19___ a big park.
B   Is the park there now?
A   Yes, but now it's ___20___.

| 16 | A | there were | B | they were | C | were there | D | were they |
|---|---|---|---|---|---|---|---|---|
| 17 | A | Was you living | B | Have you lived | C | Did you live | D | Were you live |
| 18 | A | often visited to | B | visited often to | C | often visited | D | visited often |
| 19 | A | buy | B | at | C | beside | D | on |
| 20 | A | more smaller | B | much more small | C | much smaller | D | more small |

11

# Test 11

*Choose the correct answer. Only one answer is correct.*

A  Hullo, Sally. I ___1___ back from the shops, but I didn't ___2___ things. Everything ___3___ expensive.
B  Yes, I think the prices are ___4___ every week. Last month bread ___5___ 60 pence and now it's 65. And today the newspaper says it ___6___ be more expensive before next year.
A  I know a shop where the bread ___7___ 60 pence, but I haven't got time to go there every day ___8___ a new job.
B  Oh, yes, someone ___9___ me that you work in the mornings now. Do you ___10___ money for that?
A  Not a lot, but it's very interesting.

| | | | | | | | | |
|---|---|---|---|---|---|---|---|---|
| 1 | A | just get | B | have just got | C | just go | D | have just gone |
| 2 | A | buy many | B | buy much | C | bought many | D | bought much |
| 3 | A | are so | B | are so much | C | is so | D | is so much |
| 4 | A | more high for | B | more high | C | higher for | D | higher |
| 5 | A | was costing | B | cost | C | costs | D | has cost |
| 6 | A | will | B | shall | C | sure to | D | going to |
| 7 | A | still cost | B | cost still | C | still costs | D | costs still |
| 8 | A | because I am having | B | why I am having | C | why I have | D | because I have |
| 9 | A | talked to | B | spoke to | C | said | D | told |
| 10 | A | become many | B | become much | C | get many | D | get much |

What do you do at the weekend? Some ___11___ like to stay at home, but ___12___ like to go for a walk or play football. My friend Jack works ___13___ a factory during the week. At the weekend he ___14___ the same thing. On Saturday he ___15___ his car and on Sunday he goes with his family to a village ___16___ the country. His uncle and aunt have a farm there. It isn't ___17___ but ___18___ so much to do on a farm. The children help with the animals and give ___19___ food. Jack and his wife help in the fields. At the end of the day, they ___20___ hungry and Jack's aunt gives them a big meal.

| | | | | | | | | |
|---|---|---|---|---|---|---|---|---|
| 11 | A | one | B | ones | C | people | D | peoples |
| 12 | A | another | B | other | C | others | D | other ones |
| 13 | A | hard in | B | hardly in | C | hard on | D | hardly on |
| 14 | A | makes always | B | does always | C | always makes | D | always does |
| 15 | A | wash | B | watch | C | washes | D | watches |
| 16 | A | into | B | on | C | in | D | at |
| 17 | A | a big | B | one big | C | big one | D | a big one |
| 18 | A | it's always | B | there's always | C | always it's | D | always there's |
| 19 | A | it his | B | its there | C | they its | D | them their |
| 20 | A | all have | B | have all | C | all are | D | are all |

12

# Test 12

*Choose the correct answer. Only one answer is correct.*

Mrs Jackson is an old woman who has a small room ___1___ an old house. She ___2___ there since 1974. That was the year when her husband ___3___ . He had been ill ___4___ many years. After his death Mrs Jackson had ___5___ money at all. She found work in a factory. Her job was to clean the offices. She ___6___ get up at 5 o'clock ___7___ the morning. Last year she was ill and her doctor said: '___8___ work so hard.' Now Mrs Jackson sells newspapers ___9___ a big shop in the middle of town. She ___10___ doesn't have much money but she is happier now.

| | | | | | | | |
|---|---|---|---|---|---|---|---|
| 1 | A | in | B | on | C | from | D | of |
| 2 | A | is living | B | lives | C | lived | D | has lived |
| 3 | A | died | B | has died | C | dead | D | was dead |
| 4 | A | since | B | for | C | in | D | during |
| 5 | A | none | B | any | C | no | D | not |
| 6 | A | must | B | must to | C | had to | D | has to |
| 7 | A | of | B | at | C | in | D | on |
| 8 | A | You haven't | B | Not | C | Don't | D | Better not |
| 9 | A | outside | B | without | C | in front | D | out of |
| 10 | A | always | B | still | C | yet | D | already |

*A* Have you ___11___ been to Africa?
*B* Yes, I visited one or two African countries ___12___ .
*A* Did you go there ___13___ holiday?
*B* No, I went with a group of European teachers. We wanted ___14___ the schools there. We ___15___ in some of the big towns and then we visited little schools ___16___ villages.
*A* What was ___17___ interesting thing about your visit?
*B* Well, in some schools the children ___18___ many books, but they could often ___19___ English very well.
*A* And were the pupils happy at school?
*B* Yes, I think ___20___ .

| | | | | | | | |
|---|---|---|---|---|---|---|---|
| 11 | A | ever | B | yet | C | still | D | any time |
| 12 | A | 4 years ago | B | since 4 years | C | for 4 years ago | D | for 4 years since |
| 13 | A | as | B | on | C | for | D | by |
| 14 | A | to visit | B | visit | C | visits | D | visiting |
| 15 | A | begin | B | begun | C | begins | D | began |
| 16 | A | at | B | on | C | in | D | of |
| 17 | A | more | B | most | C | the more | D | the most |
| 18 | A | haven't had | B | didn't have | C | hadn't have | D | weren't having |
| 19 | A | speak and wrote | B | spoken and wrote | C | spoke and written | D | speak and write |
| 20 | A | that | B | this | C | it | D | so |

# Test 13

*Choose the correct answer. Only one answer is correct.*

A  Are you going to the meeting tomorrow?
B  Where ___1___ going to be?
A  At the home of some friends ___2___ .
B  ___3___ is it going to start?
A  If everyone ___4___ there on time, at about 8.30.
B  What are we going to ___5___ ?
A  Well, in this district a lot of parents have young children. They're not ___6___ school but there isn't ___7___ for them.
B  So what can we do?
A  We must find someone ___8___ a big garden. We also need someone who likes children and can ___9___ .
B  ___10___ of my friends have big gardens, but I'll still come to the meeting.
A  Good.

| | | | | | | | | |
|---|---|---|---|---|---|---|---|---|
| 1  | A | is it | B | it is | C | is there | D | there is |
| 2  | A | to us | B | of us | C | to ours | D | of ours |
| 3  | A | Which hour | B | Which time | C | What hour | D | What time |
| 4  | A | will get | B | shall get | C | get | D | gets |
| 5  | A | talk about | B | speak on | C | tell on | D | say about |
| 6  | A | old enough to | B | old enough for | C | enough old to | D | enough old for |
| 7  | A | somewhere other | B | somewhere else | C | anywhere other | D | anywhere else |
| 8  | A | which have | B | which has | C | who have | D | who has |
| 9  | A | look after it | B | looks after it | C | look after them | D | looks after them |
| 10 | A | Not any | B | Nobody | C | No one | D | None |

Brickton is a little village __11__ from Manchester. When people __12__ to go to Manchester, they usually go __13__ train. It takes about __14__ . A lot of people live in Brickton but __15__ jobs are in Manchester. In Manchester there are __16__ cinemas than in Brickton. People there are not very __17__ cinemas but if they want to see films, they can often see __18__ on television. Brickton is __19__ Manchester and so the people there __20__ use their cars so often.

| | | | | | | | |
|---|---|---|---|---|---|---|---|
| 11 | A | not far | B | not long | C | not near | D | not away |
| 12 | A | went | B | want | C | wanted | D | wants |
| 13 | A | by | B | in | C | on | D | with |
| 14 | A | an half hour | B | half an hour | C | half hour | D | half a hour |
| 15 | A | its | B | their | C | it's | D | the |
| 16 | A | many | B | more | C | much | D | most |
| 17 | A | interested on | B | interesting on | C | interested in | D | interesting in |
| 18 | A | some old | B | olds | C | old one | D | old ones |
| 19 | A | more small that | B | more small than | C | smaller that | D | smaller than |
| 20 | A | don't need to | B | aren't | C | don't must | D | mustn't |

# Test 14

Choose the correct answer. Only one answer is correct.

---

Wednesday, 4 February

Dear Sally,

Thank you very much for your letter. I am ___1___ that you've had such bad weather. Perhaps it'll be better when the spring ___2___. We have had good weather. ___3___ week it was very hot and on Sunday I ___4___ the garden all day. Now it is 8 o'clock ___5___ but I ___6___ outside to write this letter.

Yesterday I went to the cinema. The film ___7___ 'Red River'. It was about a place in the south of England ___8___ the river became red, but ___9___ was able to explain it. Then a journalist came and found that a company ___10___ some chemicals into the river. The film wasn't very good.

I hope you are very well.
Yours,
Jimmy

---

| | | | | | | | |
|---|---|---|---|---|---|---|---|
| 1 | A | sadly | B | sorry | C | unpleasant | D | unhappily |
| 2 | A | is coming | B | will come | C | is going to come | D | comes |
| 3 | A | The last | B | In the last | C | On the last | D | Last |
| 4 | A | was in | B | have been in | C | was on | D | have been on |
| 5 | A | in the afternoon | B | in the evening | C | on the afternoon | D | on the evening |
| 6 | A | am sitting still | B | am still sitting | C | sit still | D | still sit |
| 7 | A | was calling | B | has called | C | called | D | was called |
| 8 | A | where | B | there | C | in that | D | from which |
| 9 | A | none | B | no people | C | nobody | D | no person |
| 10 | A | had thrown | B | was thrown | C | did throw | D | throwing |

# Test 14

*A* Have you got a car?
*B* No, we haven't got ___11___ . You see, we haven't got ___12___ , and in our town ___13___ too many cars, anyway.
*A* Then, ___14___ at weekends?
*B* We usually ___15___ home. In my family ___16___ read a lot of books.
*A* I often read the newspaper in the evening but I never read ___17___ . You see, I read ___18___ , and I can never finish a book.
*B* Perhaps you ___19___ read short stories. They're ___20___ .
*A* Yes, that's a good idea.

| | | | | | | | |
|---|---|---|---|---|---|---|---|
| 11 | A none | B | no one | C | one | D | it |
| 12 | A much money | B | many money | C | money enough | D | so many money |
| 13 | A are there | B | there are | C | are they | D | they are |
| 14 | A which do you do | B | what do you do | C | which you do | D | what do you |
| 15 | A rest in | B | stay at | C | stay in | D | rest in the |
| 16 | A we all | B | all we | C | all us | D | us all |
| 17 | A books | B | the books | C | some books | D | no books |
| 18 | A so much slow | B | much slowly | C | very slowly | D | very slower |
| 19 | A should | B | would | C | shall | D | must |
| 20 | A very easily | B | much easily | C | very easy | D | much easy |

17

# Test 15

*Choose the correct answer. Only one answer is correct.*

A  Come into the sitting room.
B  Thank you. Oh, __1__ lovely flowers! Where did you buy them?
A  I didn't buy them. They're __2__ our garden. I can give __3__ if you like.
B  Oh, yes please.
A  I'll get them when it's __4__ to go. But now __5__ have a cup of tea.
B  Well, I mustn't __6__ home too late because we __7__ dinner at 6 o'clock. What's the quickest way home? I came __8__. Is there a bus?
A  No, __9__ bus. I __10__ you in my car.
B  Thank you very much.

| | | | | | | | |
|---|---|---|---|---|---|---|---|
| 1 | A | so | B | which | C | what | D | how |
| 2 | A | came from | B | coming from | C | come from | D | from |
| 3 | A | you some | B | some you | C | to you few | D | few to you |
| 4 | A | hour | B | time | C | the hour | D | the time |
| 5 | A | let's | B | let us to | C | will we | D | you want |
| 6 | A | to go | B | to come | C | go | D | come |
| 7 | A | have | B | take | C | have the | D | take the |
| 8 | A | on foot | B | by foot | C | with foot | D | walking |
| 9 | A | not to take | B | don't take a | C | take no | D | don't take any |
| 10 | A | may bring | B | may take | C | can bring | D | can take |

I am 30 years old. I __11__ born in 1960 in a town in the west of England. I __12__ there all my life, but I usually __13__ my holidays in London. My town is not __14__ it was in 1960 or 1965. In those days we __15__ walk from one side to __16__ in about fifteen minutes. There __17__ two schools but __18__ big factories. Then in 1968 they built two factories and a lot of new people came to our town. __19__ factories are very big and I now have a job in one of __20__.

| | | | | | | | |
|---|---|---|---|---|---|---|---|
| 11 | A | am | B | have | C | was | D | were |
| 12 | A | am living | B | have lived | C | lived | D | live |
| 13 | A | am spending | B | spend | C | am passing | D | pass |
| 14 | A | same as | B | same that | C | the same as | D | the same that |
| 15 | A | can | B | could | C | was able to | D | were able |
| 16 | A | another | B | the other | C | other | D | one other |
| 17 | A | have been | B | has been | C | was | D | were |
| 18 | A | no | B | not any | C | none | D | not |
| 19 | A | All the | B | The all | C | Both the | D | The both |
| 20 | A | they | B | them | C | their | D | this |

# Test 16

*Choose the correct answer. Only one answer is correct.*

Have you ever had to stay __1__ a long time? I have. About six months ago I __2__ very weak and so I went __3__ a doctor. He looked at me and asked a lot of questions: 'Have you been working __4__?' 'Have you __5__ anything special?' And so on. Finally he __6__ that it was not very serious but that I __7__ not to meet other people. I had to stay in bed for two weeks and take some medicine __8__. It wasn't so bad because my friends came and talked to me __9__ the window. I'm glad my bedroom is on the __10__.

| 1 | A | in the bed for | B | in the bed since | C | in bed for | D | in the bed since |
|---|---|---|---|---|---|---|---|---|
| 2 | A | felt | B | filled | C | fell | D | feel |
| 3 | A | and see | B | to see | C | for see | D | for to see |
| 4 | A | too hard | B | too hardly | C | too much hard | D | too much hardly |
| 5 | A | ate or drank | B | ate or drunk | C | eaten or drunk | D | eat or drank |
| 6 | A | told | B | said me | C | told to me | D | told me |
| 7 | A | ought | B | would | C | should | D | must |
| 8 | A | all the days | B | every days | C | all days | D | every day |
| 9 | A | through | B | along | C | though | D | across |
| 10 | A | flat ground | B | ground flat | C | floor ground | D | ground floor |

A  We __11__ in this house for eight months and we __12__ haven't got a bookcase for this room.
B  But we haven't got __13__ money to buy one.
A  All right, what do we need __14__ a bookcase?
B  We've got a hammer and things, but we haven't got any wood, and we haven't any paint, __15__.
A  Well, we'd better buy some then, __16__ we? Is there a good shop near here?
B  Well, if you __17__ the main road __18__ the centre of town, there's a big wood shop __19__.
A  All right. Let's go now. What are we __20__?

| 11 | A | are living | B | live | C | have live | D | have been living |
|---|---|---|---|---|---|---|---|---|
| 12 | A | always | B | already | C | still | D | yet |
| 13 | A | too much | B | so much | C | as much | D | enough |
| 14 | A | to do | B | to make | C | for do | D | for make |
| 15 | A | too | B | also | C | neither | D | either |
| 16 | A | won't | B | wouldn't | C | hadn't | D | aren't |
| 17 | A | get along | B | go along | C | get through | D | go through |
| 18 | A | until | B | against | C | as far as | D | at |
| 19 | A | in the right | B | on the right | C | to right | D | at right |
| 20 | A | hoping | B | waiting for | C | waiting | D | expecting |

# Test 17

*Choose the correct answer. Only one answer is correct.*

Why do people drink? Often because they ___1___ , but this can't be the ___2___ reason; there ___3___ be other reasons, too. In many countries, when friends see ___4___ , they often have a drink while they sit and talk. Many English people don't need ___5___ : they drink tea several times ___6___ day even if they are alone!

In most countries people say ___7___ when they drink together. The English ___8___ Cheers. In all countries there are many places (cafes, bars, etc) ___9___ main purpose is to sell drinks. Since there are so many of these places, it seems that many people drink more often than they really ___10___ .

| | | | | | | | |
|---|---|---|---|---|---|---|---|
| 1 | A | have thirsty | B | have thirst | C | are thirsty | D | are thirst |
| 2 | A | lonely | B | single | C | only | D | alone |
| 3 | A | shall | B | must | C | should | D | ought |
| 4 | A | each other | B | themselves | C | them | D | another |
| 5 | A | another | B | any other | C | anyone else | D | other persons |
| 6 | A | a | B | during | C | the | D | by |
| 7 | A | something specially | B | something special | C | anything specially | D | anything special |
| 8 | A | often say | B | often says | C | say often | D | says often |
| 9 | A | of which | B | where the | C | what's | D | that the |
| 10 | A | need to | B | need it | C | must | D | must it |

*Test 17*

A  Your cup is empty. __11__ you like another cup of tea?
B  Yes please, but __12__ it too strong.
A  And a piece of cake?
B  Yes please. It __13__ . Thank you. Did you hear __14__ Mary told Peter? She said that she __15__ a Rolls Royce when she was young.
A  She __16__ many stupid things. I don't believe anything she says. She isn't even a friend __17__ , is she?
B  No, I've only met her __18__ , and I don't really want __19__ her again.
A  No, nor __20__ .

| | | | | | | | |
|---|---|---|---|---|---|---|---|
| 11 | A | Will | B | Are | C | Would | D | Do |
| 12 | A | don't do | B | don't make | C | don't | D | make not |
| 13 | A | is looking nicely | B | looks nicely | C | is looking nice | D | looks nice |
| 14 | A | what | B | that what | C | which | D | that |
| 15 | A | was having | B | used to have | C | have had | D | is having |
| 16 | A | says so | B | says such | C | tells so | D | tells such |
| 17 | A | to you | B | of you | C | of your | D | of yours |
| 18 | A | once before | B | since one month | C | for one month ago | D | last Saturday |
| 19 | A | a meeting | B | meeting | C | meet | D | to meet |
| 20 | A | I meet | B | want I | C | do I | D | I don't |

# Test 18

Choose the correct answer. Only one answer is correct.

> Wednesday, 20 July
>
> Dear Fred,
>
> Thanks for your letter. It was ___1___ from you. Your new job sounds very interesting and you ___2___ with it. I am still with the same firm that I joined five years ago when we ___3___. ___4___ I am happy there, I must say that I sometimes feel that I ___5___ to move, but here in Bakewell there are only ___6___ companies.
>
> I like this town. What I like ___7___ living here is that it is quiet. Perhaps I should say it was quiet ___8___ these big lorries started coming through the town. Anyway, they only come through during the day, never ___9___ night.
>
> If you have time before the end of the summer, why don't you come and ___10___ with us one weekend? That would be very pleasant.
>
> I hope you are still well. Write again soon.
> Yours,
> Terry

| | A | | B | | C | | D | |
|---|---|---|---|---|---|---|---|---|
| 1 | A | well to listen | B | well to hear | C | good to listen | D | good to hear |
| 2 | A | look pleased | B | seem pleased | C | look pleasing | D | seem pleasing |
| 3 | A | left school | B | left the school | C | have left school | D | have left the school |
| 4 | A | Although | B | Already | C | Because | D | Through |
| 5 | A | ought | B | should | C | would | D | must |
| 6 | A | some | B | any | C | few | D | a few |
| 7 | A | more about | B | most about | C | more of | D | most of |
| 8 | A | as long as | B | as far as | C | when | D | until |
| 9 | A | during | B | at the | C | in | D | at |
| 10 | A | live | B | pass | C | stay | D | rest |

*Test 18*

A  Hullo, love. Have you had a good day at __11__ ?
B  Yes, quite good, __12__ that the manager was unpleasant __13__ day. How about you?
A  Oh, it was a quiet day. There wasn't much work __14__ so I got home early.
B  Good for you. What's for dinner?
A  Well, when __15__ dinner at a restaurant? It was __16__ time ago that I can't remember. Can't we go tonight?
B  Well, it's a good idea, but let's not __17__ tonight because I want to watch the football on the television.
A  Oh, I forgot __18__ you. There's something __19__ the television. I wanted to watch a programme this afternoon but I __20__ get a picture.
B  All right, I believe you. Which restaurant do you want to go to?

| 11 | A | work | B | job | C | office | D | factory |
| --- | --- | --- | --- | --- | --- | --- | --- | --- |
| 12 | A | but | B | expect | C | though | D | except |
| 13 | A | in the all | B | the all | C | in the whole | D | the whole |
| 14 | A | to me to do | B | for doing | C | that I did | D | for me to do |
| 15 | A | had we last | B | did we last have | C | last had we | D | did we have last |
| 16 | A | such a long | B | a such long | C | so long a | D | a so long |
| 17 | A | go away | B | go out | C | to go away | D | to go out |
| 18 | A | to say | B | to tell | C | saying | D | telling |
| 19 | A | wrong on | B | bad on | C | wrong with | D | bad with |
| 20 | A | can't | B | couldn't | C | may not | D | might not |

23

# Test 19

*Choose the correct answer. Only one answer is correct.*

I have a brother who is ___1___ me. We ___2___ . Yesterday was an important day ___3___ friends. In the morning ___4___ of us had a big exam at the technical college and then ___5___ there was a big meeting at the youth club at 9 o'clock. (That's where we usually go when we want to ___6___ ourselves.) A rich woman had given us some money and yesterday we ___7___ decide what to do ___8___ . Many people wanted to buy something new for our club, but my brother and I wanted to give the money to another club that has ___9___ . In the end we decided to give half to the poor club and ___10___ half for ourselves.

| | | | | | | | | |
|---|---|---|---|---|---|---|---|---|
| 1 | A | so old as | B | so old that | C | the same age that | D | the same age as |
| 2 | A | both are 16 | B | are both 16 | C | are 16 both | D | are 16 the both |
| 3 | A | to us and our | B | for us and our | C | to us and ours | D | for us and ours |
| 4 | A | most | B | much | C | more | D | few |
| 5 | A | last night | B | the last night | C | last evening | D | the last evening |
| 6 | A | enjoy | B | meet | C | like | D | divert |
| 7 | A | had to | B | must | C | should | D | would |
| 8 | A | with it | B | with them | C | for it | D | for them |
| 9 | A | something | B | anything | C | nothing | D | everything |
| 10 | A | keep another | B | keep the other | C | hold another | D | hold the other |

Test 19

A  Is Ann __11__ music?
B  Well, she ikes to listen to records but she's never __12__ anything. What about Tommy?
A  He'd __13__ be outside than in the house. __14__ best is to spend a whole weekend in the country. I was __15__ when I was young.
B  My husband and I __16__ walk a lot before we got married. But he's got __17__ fat stomach now that he can hardly walk to his car.
A  Perhaps he __18__ eat so much.
B  I try to help when I cook, but he __19__ the cooking and then there's enough food for ten people, and the __20__ about it is that he cooks very well so everybody eats a lot.

| 11 | A liking | B fond of | C interest in | D playing the |
| 12 | A learning to play | B learning play | C learnt to play | D learnt play |
| 13 | A rather | B prefer | C better | D like |
| 14 | A What he prefers | B What he likes | C That he prefers | D That he likes |
| 15 | A same | B like that | C so | D as him |
| 16 | A used to | B were used to | C were liking to | D liked |
| 17 | A so | B such | C such a | D a so |
| 18 | A shouldn't | B shan't | C mustn't | D hasn't to |
| 19 | A often makes | B often does | C does often | D makes often |
| 20 | A more bad | B most bad | C worse thing | D worst thing |

25

# Test 20

Choose the correct answer. Only one answer is correct.

> Thursday, 9 October
>
> Dear Christine,
>
> It was a pity that you ___1___ be here for the play last night. I think that it ___2___ very well, but I'm glad that it's over now because it was a lot of ___3___. Mrs Johnson is the leader of the theatre group so she told everyone ___4___. My sister Penny had one of the big parts (she was the queen and she ___5___) but I only had ___6___ things to say. A lot of people came to see the play and we made over one hundred pounds. Mrs Johnson asked everyone how ___7___ spend it. We have agreed to organise a trip to one of the big theatres in London, but can't go now; it'll ___8___ Christmas.
>
> In your last letter you asked ___9___ Jim's new address, but I'm afraid I don't know it. We must both wait until he ___10___ to us.
>
> I hope you are well. Write soon.
> Love,
> Brian

| | | | | | | | | |
|---|---|---|---|---|---|---|---|---|
| 1 | A | can't | B | couldn't | C | may not | D | mightn't |
| 2 | A | went | B | was going | C | was | D | has been |
| 3 | A | the work | B | work | C | job | D | the job |
| 4 | A | which to do | B | which they did | C | what to do | D | what they did |
| 5 | A | seemed very nicely | B | seemed very nice | C | looked very nicely | D | looked very nice |
| 6 | A | few short | B | a few short | C | a short few | D | short few |
| 7 | A | we should | B | should we | C | shall we | D | we shall |
| 8 | A | must be at | B | must be in | C | have to be at | D | have to be in |
| 9 | A | from me | B | me for | C | to me | D | to me for |
| 10 | A | is going to | B | is writing | C | will write | D | writes |

# Test 20

**A** Excuse me. I haven't anywhere __11__ . Can you tell me __12__ anybody's seat?
**B** I __13__ . There was a woman sitting there but she __14__ the last station.
**A** I suppose it'll be all right if I sit there then. I think __15__ hot in here but perhaps it's because __16__ this thick coat.
**B** Why don't you __17__ ? You'll be quite warm enough without it.
**A** Good idea. How long does it take this train __18__ to London?
**B** About one and __19__ , I think.
**A** Perhaps I'll be able to finish the book __20__ . Would you like to have a look at my newspaper?
**B** Thank you very much.

| | | | | | | | | |
|---|---|---|---|---|---|---|---|---|
| 11 | A | for sitting | B | that I sit | C | to sit | D | that I'm sitting |
| 12 | A | that this is | B | if this is | C | is this | D | whether is this |
| 13 | A | don't believe | B | don't believe it | C | don't think | D | don't think so |
| 14 | A | went out in | B | went out at | C | got out in | D | got out at |
| 15 | A | it's very much | B | it's very | C | there is very much | D | there is very |
| 16 | A | I wear | B | I'm wearing | C | I carry | D | I'm carrying |
| 17 | A | put it off | B | put off it | C | take it off | D | take off it |
| 18 | A | to get | B | to arrive | C | coming | D | going |
| 19 | A | half an hour | B | a half hour | C | a half hours | D | half hour |
| 20 | A | I'm reading | B | that I'm reading it | C | that I read it | D | which I read |

# Test 21

*Choose the correct answer. Only one answer is correct.*

## Interview with a Football Manager

A  Now, Mr Pye, I __1__ me what you think about your chances in the game tomorrow.
B  This time we ought __2__ Rovers.
A  But you __3__ a game for two months. What __4__ think you'll do better tomorrow?
B  Well, we have a new forward, Johnny Briggs, as you know. He __5__ the team the confidence they need.
A  I __6__ about that on the news last night. How much __7__ for Briggs?
B  I __8__ the figure exactly but you know how much __9__ these days. If I __10__ been sure he was the man we needed, I wouldn't have bought him.
A  Thank you. The best of luck tomorrow.

| | | | | | | | |
|---|---|---|---|---|---|---|---|
| 1 | A | want that you tell | B | would that you told | C | would like that you told | D | would like you to tell |
| 2 | A | to beat | B | to win | C | beat | D | win |
| 3 | A | aren't winning | B | don't win | C | haven't won | D | haven't been winning |
| 4 | A | does make you to | B | does make you | C | makes you to | D | makes you |
| 5 | A | will give to | B | shall give to | C | will give | D | shall give |
| 6 | A | have heard | B | have been hearing | C | did hear | D | heard |
| 7 | A | had you to pay | B | did you have to pay | C | must you have paid | D | were you to pay |
| 8 | A | am not remembering | B | am not reminding | C | don't remind | D | don't remember |
| 9 | A | a good player costs | B | a good player cost | C | costs a good player | D | cost a good player |
| 10 | A | hadn't | B | wouldn't have | C | shouldn't have | D | mustn't have |

## Buying a Hotel

The price of hotels in Britain is going up __11__ at any time since the war. There are a number of reasons for this but the __12__ all is the Government's economic policy. Managers in factories see __13__ so they are attracted to the idea of owning __14__ businesses. __15__ Britain's weather is often disappointing, the tourist industry is growing. Many people __16__ like to combine a __17__ holiday with the opportunity of improving their English. It is therefore not surprising that businessmen are buying hotels. The only thing __18__ worries me is the kind of treatment their guests are __19__ to receive since __20__ of them know anything about hotel management.

| | | | | | | | |
|---|---|---|---|---|---|---|---|
| 11 | A | more fast than | B | more fast that | C | faster than | D | faster that |
| 12 | A | most important of | B | more important of | C | most important from | D | more important from |
| 13 | A | to fall their standard of living | B | falling their standard of living | C | their standard of living to fall | D | their standard of living falling |
| 14 | A | his proper | B | his own | C | their proper | D | their own |
| 15 | A | In spite of | B | Although | C | Even | D | However |
| 16 | A | in the Continent | B | in the overseas | C | abroad | D | foreign |
| 17 | A | fortnight | B | fortnight's | C | two weeks | D | two week's |
| 18 | A | that | B | what | C | as | D | who |
| 19 | A | like | B | probable | C | probably | D | likely |
| 20 | A | little | B | a little | C | few | D | a few |

# Test 22

*Choose the correct answer. Only one answer is correct.*

## Telephone Call to the Office

A  Hallo, darling. What ___1___ for dinner tonight?
B  I don't mind
A  We could have steak but we ___2___ had that this week. I thought you ___3___ like a change.
B  Ask me later, ___4___ you? I'm very busy at the moment.
A  But ___5___ to the shops. It will be too late to talk about it when I ___6___ back. How about some fish? It's a long time since we ___7___ fish?
B  All right, then. Why ___8___ some fish.
A  But if you'd rather ___9___ steak, say so. Don't say you'll have fish just ___10___ me.
B  No, fish will be fine.

| | | | | | | | | |
|---|---|---|---|---|---|---|---|---|
| 1  | A | would you want | B | would you like | C | would you | D | are you wanting |
| 2  | A | already | B | yet | C | 've yet | D | 've already |
| 3  | A | could | B | can | C | might | D | may |
| 4  | A | do | B | are | C | shall | D | will |
| 5  | A | I've gone out | B | I've gone away | C | I'm going out | D | I'm going away |
| 6  | A | get | B | shall get | C | will get | D | am getting |
| 7  | A | had | B | have had | C | were having | D | are having |
| 8  | A | aren't you getting | B | don't you get | C | not to get | D | not be getting |
| 9  | A | to have | B | have | C | having | D | that we have |
| 10 | A | to please | B | for pleasing | C | please | D | so you're pleasing |

## Slimming Food

These days most people, especially young girls, like ___11___ slim. Our grandparents' tastes were different ___12___ ours but nowadays ___13___ seems to enjoy ___14___ fat people. That is why many companies have developed special foods to help people to slim. The only thing ___15___ is wrong with this is ___16___ ___17___ said to me the other day: 'I don't mind ___18___ these foods if they'll help me to lose weight but why do they taste so awful?' The reason ___19___ this is that the manufacturers have to include a lot of vitamins to satisfy the law, so the only sensible advice I could give my friend was 'Eat normal food, but ___20___ less'.

| | | | | | | | | |
|---|---|---|---|---|---|---|---|---|
| 11 | A | to look | B | to be looked | C | that they look | D | that they are looking |
| 12 | A | of | B | that | C | from | D | as |
| 13 | A | anyone | B | anybody | C | none | D | no one |
| 14 | A | looking | B | looking at | C | to look | D | to look at |
| 15 | A | it | B | that | C | what | D | as |
| 16 | A | one | B | that | C | which | D | what |
| 17 | A | a friend of mine | B | a friend of me | C | a friend mine | D | one friend of me |
| 18 | A | eat | B | to eat | C | eating | D | the eating |
| 19 | A | for | B | of | C | that | D | why |
| 20 | A | to eat | B | eating | C | be eating | D | eat |

# Test 23

*Choose the correct answer. Only one answer is correct.*

## At the Casino

A  I ___1___ in a casino before, Roger. Don't you think it's risky? We might lose all our money.
B  You ___2___ worry, darling. You'll find it easy when you ___3___ used to it. If you ___4___ my advice, you're certain to win. I never bet on the numbers, because that's silly. I bet on the same colour and ___5___ my bet. In that way, I must win. Red, please.
A  (Five minutes later) I don't understand your system, Roger. Black has won every time. ___6___ I have a go now?
B  Oh, all right. But ___7___ I say. Put it on the red again. This time it must win.
A  Twenty-four, please.
B  Darling, I ___8___ bet on the numbers. Now you've lost our last 10 francs.
C  Number twenty-four! Here you are, Madame.
A  Oh, lovely! We've won! I think we'd better ___9___ home now, Roger, while we're winning, in case you ___10___ all the money again.

| | | | | | | | |
|---|---|---|---|---|---|---|---|
| 1 | A | never am | B | am never | C | never have been | D | have never been |
| 2 | A | needn't | B | needn't to | C | haven't to | D | oughtn't |
| 3 | A | get | B | are getting | C | will get | D | got |
| 4 | A | are listening | B | are listening to | C | listen | D | listen to |
| 5 | A | follow raising | B | follow rising | C | keep raising | D | keep rising |
| 6 | A | Would | B | Can | C | Will | D | Ought |
| 7 | A | do as | B | do like | C | to do as | D | to do like |
| 8 | A | said you to not | B | told you to not | C | said you not to | D | told you not to |
| 9 | A | going | B | gone | C | go | D | to go |
| 10 | A | will lose | B | lose | C | lost | D | would lose |

## Problems of the National Health Service

The National Health Service in Britain has grown into ___11___ big organisation that it now employs more people ___12___ other in the country. ___13___ efficient an organisation like this may be, it is bound to ___14___ sooner or later but ___15___ the public can do when they occur. The Patients' Association gives ___16___ when they think they have not been properly looked after. Some time ago the Assocation fought against the Government's idea ___17___ general health centres for individual doctors. It said it did not want to tell the Health Service ___18___ do but added that it ___19___ spend more money on doctors' salaries, ___20___ would be cheaper than building health centres.

| | | | | | | | |
|---|---|---|---|---|---|---|---|
| 11 | A | a such | B | such a | C | so | D | a so |
| 12 | A | than any | B | than some | C | that any | D | that some |
| 13 | A | For | B | It doesn't mind | C | Whatever | D | However |
| 14 | A | make faults | B | do faults | C | make mistakes | D | do mistakes |
| 15 | A | there is a few | B | there is little | C | it is few | D | it is a little |
| 16 | A | to people advice | B | to people advises | C | people advice | D | people advices |
| 17 | A | of substituting | B | for substitute | C | for replacing | D | for replace |
| 18 | A | that it must | B | that it is to | C | what is to | D | what to |
| 19 | A | should have to | B | needs | C | should | D | ought |
| 20 | A | which | B | who | C | that | D | it |

# Test 24

*Choose the correct answer. Only one answer is correct.*

## Wet Holiday

A  Hallo, Jean. I ___1___ you for ages.
B  No. We were on holiday. We ___2___ back last night.
A  ___3___ a good time? You don't look very brown.
B  No, not really. We ___4___ have gone abroad again but Jack said he couldn't afford it this year. We always ___5___ the car but Jack was afraid that if we ___6___ it this year, we ___7___ run out of money somewhere and not be able to get back.
A  So what ___8___, then?
B  We went to Crofton instead but the weather was awful. We spent most of the holiday ___9___ cards in the hotel. Jack says that he ___10___ stay at home next year than go there again.

| | | | | | | | |
|---|---|---|---|---|---|---|---|
| 1 | A | don't see | B | haven't seen | C | 'm not seeing | D | haven't been seeing |
| 2 | A | have only been | B | have only got | C | only were | D | only got |
| 3 | A | Did you have | B | Have you | C | Had you | D | Were you having |
| 4 | A | should | B | ought | C | must | D | had to |
| 5 | A | were used to be taking | B | were to be taking | C | were used to take | D | used to take |
| 6 | A | take | B | have taken | C | took | D | would have taken |
| 7 | A | can | B | may | C | had better | D | might |
| 8 | A | did you do | B | did you | C | have you done | D | you have done |
| 9 | A | playing the | B | playing | C | on playing the | D | on playing |
| 10 | A | would rather to | B | would rather | C | had better to | D | had better |

## King Arthur's Round Table

One of the most interesting tourist attractions in Winchester, the Saxon capital of England __11__ , is King Arthur's Round Table. It is made __12__ wood and has places for the __13__ and twenty-four of his knights. Now experts have shown that the table __14__ King Arthur, if King Arthur, the hero of romantic legends, ever existed. __15__ interesting about this is that two completely different methods were used to prove that the table was made about 1330. X-rays suggested that it __16__ , and so __17__ measuring the size of tree rings. The reason __18__ the table was made was probably that King Edward III was very fond __19__ the stories about King Arthur and it was made for him. The results of the investigation have pleased the experts. But __20__ terrible disappointment for the romantics!

| 11 | A | it makes a long time | B | during a long time | C | at a time | D | a long time ago |
|----|---|---|---|---|---|---|---|---|
| 12 | A | of | B | from | C | by | D | with |
| 13 | A | proper king | B | personal king | C | king himself | D | king personally |
| 14 | A | was not of | B | was not from | C | did not belong | D | did not belong to |
| 15 | A | The | B | What is | C | That which is | D | That what is |
| 16 | A | was 600 years ago | B | was 600 years old | C | had 600 years | D | was 600 years |
| 17 | A | did a method | B | has a method | C | a method did | D | a method has |
| 18 | A | why | B | for | C | how | D | of |
| 19 | A | of | B | in | C | to | D | for |
| 20 | A | such | B | what a | C | how | D | so |

# Test 25

*Choose the correct answer. Only one answer is correct.*

## Making a Will

A  Good morning. I've come to see you about making a will. __1__ that if I __2__ suddenly, my wife would have a lot of problems.

B  A very sensible idea, sir. Now, __3__ to leave everything to your wife or would you like anyone else __4__ ?

A  Well, I'm fond of my sisters and my Uncle Arthur was kind to me when I was young, but I expect he'll be dead before anything __5__ to me.

B  I don't want to worry you, sir, but you __6__ be involved in an accident, and then...

A  Yes. Well, I'd rather not __7__ things difficult so just __8__ down that I leave everything to my wife.

B  I hope you don't mind __9__ me, sir, but is there much money involved in the will?

A  Oh, no. I've only got five pounds.

B  I see. Well, I must tell you that my fee for __10__ this work will be five pounds exactly.

1  A  It's been said me      B  It's been told me    C  I've been said       D  I've been told
2  A  died                   B  am dying             C  was dying           D  would die
3  A  want you               B  do you want          C  are you wanting     D  do you be wanting
4  A  to be mentioned        B  to mention           C  that they're        D  being mentioned
                                                        mentioned
5  A  will happen            B  would happen         C  happens             D  happen
6  A  had better             B  should               C  can                 D  might
7  A  to make                B  make                 C  be making           D  that I made
8  A  putting                B  be putting           C  to put              D  put
9  A  say                    B  to tell              C  telling             D  saying
10 A  do                     B  to do                C  doing               D  being done

# The Case of the Football Referee

An unusual case was heard in the High Court some time ago. A football referee asked the judge to make the Football League __11__ him again. The League stopped him refereeing __12__ after a game when he sent four players off the field. He said he had bought a shop __13__ free to __14__ necessary while he was working __15__ referee __16__ Saturdays. He had even shown more interest __17__ football than in his children, __18__ had suffered as a result. The League said they had sacked him because neither their inspectors __19__ the football clubs thought he was __20__ .

| | | | | | | | |
|---|---|---|---|---|---|---|---|
| 11 | A | that they employed | B | employing | C | employ | D | to employ |
| 12 | A | since three years | B | three years ago | C | it makes three years | D | during three years |
| 13 | A | so as to be | B | in order be | C | so that he will be | D | for being |
| 14 | A | do the long travels | B | do the long journeys | C | make the long travels | D | make the long journeys |
| 15 | A | as | B | as a | C | like | D | like a |
| 16 | A | on | B | in | C | at | D | the |
| 17 | A | to the | B | to | C | in the | D | in |
| 18 | A | that | B | which | C | who | D | what |
| 19 | A | either | B | or | C | neither | D | nor |
| 20 | A | enough good | B | good enough | C | rather good | D | so just |

# Test 26

*Choose the correct answer. Only one answer is correct.*

## At the Customs

A  Good afternoon, sir. Have you anything to declare?
B  No. I ___1___ a few days. That's why I came through the door where the notice ___2___ 'Nothing to Declare'
A  Then you ___3___ this case, will you, sir?
B  Well, it's rather a nuisance. My wife ___4___ me outside and I'm in a hurry.
A  It won't take long, sir.
B  I see. Oh, dear. I can't find the key. I ___5___ it.
A  What a pity, sir. Then we'll have to stay here until you ___6___ one. Perhaps if you ___7___ through all your pockets, you'd find it.
B  Ah, here it is. But before you open it, I ___8___ you that all the watches are presents for my family.
A  Hm. ___9___ 17 of them. You ___10___ a large family, sir.

| | | | | | | | |
|---|---|---|---|---|---|---|---|
| 1 | A | am only abroad for | B | am only abroad since | C | have only been abroad for | D | have only been abroad since |
| 2 | A | says | B | tells | C | is saying | D | is telling |
| 3 | A | don't mind opening | B | don't mind to open | C | won't mind opening | D | won't mind to open |
| 4 | A | waits for | B | is waiting for | C | waits | D | is waiting |
| 5 | A | must have lost | B | must be lost | C | had to lose | D | have had to lose |
| 6 | A | will get | B | would get | C | are getting | D | get |
| 7 | A | look | B | looked | C | had looked | D | would have looked |
| 8 | A | need tell | B | need say | C | must tell | D | must say |
| 9 | A | They exist | B | They are | C | There exist | D | There are |
| 10 | A | have to have | B | must have | C | must be having | D | have to be having |

# Test 26

## Pavement Artists

Artists ___11___ draw pictures on the pavement with chalk used to be a common sight ___12___ London, but ___13___ now. Sometimes the pictures are very good. This is proved by the fact that one of the ___14___ favourite tricks is to draw a five-pound note and see ___15___ try ___16___ . The police usually treat pavement artists kindly and ___17___ in the law against drawing on the pavement ___18___ the artist is ___19___ he gets a large crowd around him and this prevents other people ___20___ freely along the street.

| | | | | | | | | |
|---|---|---|---|---|---|---|---|---|
| 11 | A | who | B | which | C | what | D | whose |
| 12 | A | at | B | on | C | by | D | in |
| 13 | A | there are only left a few | B | there are only a few left | C | they are only left a few | D | they are only a few left |
| 14 | A | artists | B | artists' | C | artist's | D | artist |
| 15 | A | the lot of people that | B | the amount of people that | C | how many people | D | how much people |
| 16 | A | picking up it | B | picking it up | C | to pick up it | D | to pick it up |
| 17 | A | there is nothing | B | there is anything | C | it is nothing | D | it is anything |
| 18 | A | even | B | whether | C | if not | D | unless |
| 19 | A | so good as | B | as good as | C | so good that | D | as good that |
| 20 | A | that they pass | B | that they don't pass | C | from passing | D | to pass |

37

# Test 27

*Choose the correct answer. Only one answer is correct.*

## Hard Day and Night Travelling

A  Hello, Mr Fletcher. You look rather tired this morning.
B  I expect I do. I __1__ to bed until four o'clock.
A  __2__ a difficult journey back from Scotland yesterday?
B  Yes. The business trip was successful but the train arrived four hours late and I __3__ a taxi. In the end I __4__ home and found my wife __5__ the door and she didn't hear me when I rang the bell.
A  So what __6__ then?
B  I thought I __7__ to get in by breaking the kitchen window but I cut __8__ hand on the glass and fell on the dustbin. My wife woke up and rang the police, thinking I was a thief. When they came, they asked me __9__ to the police station with them. But my wife explained what had happened. The next time I __10__ in London late at night I'll go to a hotel.

| | | | | | | | | |
|---|---|---|---|---|---|---|---|---|
| 1 | A | didn't go | B | wasn't | C | haven't gone | D | haven't been |
| 2 | A | Had you | B | Did you have | C | Were you having | D | Have you had |
| 3 | A | must take | B | must be taking | C | must have taken | D | had to take |
| 4 | A | arrived in | B | arrived to | C | got | D | got to |
| 5 | A | has locked | B | had locked | C | locked | D | was locked |
| 6 | A | did you do | B | did you | C | you did | D | have you done |
| 7 | A | must | B | have | C | will have | D | would have |
| 8 | A | me the | B | myself the | C | my | D | me my |
| 9 | A | that I went | B | that I would go | C | to go | D | for going |
| 10 | A | shall arrive | B | will arrive | C | am arriving | D | arrive |

# That's Life

One of the __11__ programmes __12__ television in Britain is called 'That's Life'. It's main job is to draw attention to companies __13__ salesmen cheat the public. The programme is so popular that millions of people watch it __14__ and the team running it get 2,000 letters __15__ week from people complaining about __16__ bad products and tricks used by salesmen to make people __17__ things they do not really want. For example, salesmen offer to __18__ to pay for improvements to their houses, __19__ means that if the improvements are badly carried out, the owner still cannot __20__ . The programme helps to prevent salesmen from using such techniques.

| | | | | | | | |
|---|---|---|---|---|---|---|---|
| 11 | A | more popular | B | most popular | C | popularer | D | popularest |
| 12 | A | for | B | in | C | on | D | by |
| 13 | A | whose | B | which | C | what | D | that |
| 14 | A | the Sunday nights | B | all Sunday nights | C | all the Sunday nights | D | every Sunday night |
| 15 | A | by | B | in | C | the | D | a |
| 16 | A | such things like | B | such things as | C | things such like | D | things as |
| 17 | A | buy | B | to buy | C | buying | D | that they buy |
| 18 | A | lend people money | B | borrow people money | C | lend to people money | D | borrow money to people |
| 19 | A | what | B | that | C | which | D | it |
| 20 | A | prevent to pay | B | prevent paying | C | avoid to pay | D | avoid paying |

# Test 28

*Choose the correct answer. Only one answer is correct.*

## At the Dentist's

A  Now then, Mrs Charlton. How long ___1___ giving you trouble?
B  Well, I ___2___ last year and it was all right until last Sunday. Then it started hurting again.
A  I see. ___3___ what ___4___ when in started to give you pain?
B  Yes. I was eating some chocolate with nuts in it. I ___5___ the tooth.
A  Well, let me ___6___ a look at it. Ah, yes, I'm afraid I'll have to ___7___ . Would you like ___8___ you an injection? It ___9___ be rather painful, otherwise.
B  Yes, please. ___10___ pity I didn't think of that when I was eating the chocolate!

| | | | | | | | |
|---|---|---|---|---|---|---|---|
| 1 | A | this tooth is | B | is this tooth | C | this tooth has been | D | has this tooth been |
| 2 | A | had it filled | B | filled it | C | have had it filled | D | have filled it |
| 3 | A | Do you remind | B | Do you remember | C | Are you reminding | D | Are you remembering |
| 4 | A | were you doing | B | you were doing | C | did you do | D | you did |
| 5 | A | must have broken | B | must be broken | C | had to break | D | should break |
| 6 | A | to have | B | have | C | to make | D | make |
| 7 | A | bring it out | B | bring it off | C | take it out | D | take it off |
| 8 | A | me give | B | me to give | C | me giving | D | that I give |
| 9 | A | may | B | can | C | has to | D | shall |
| 10 | A | How | B | How much | C | What | D | What a |

## Suitcases

Many people buy suitcases to carry __11__ when they go abroad __12__ and never take the trouble to find out whether they will be __13__ to survive the journey. __14__ case you buy — and obviously __15__ you pay for it the better it is likely to be — you should be careful __16__ too much into it. A lot of passengers __17__ and then the locks break. Some people think manufacturers should say how much __18__ . But the manufacturers say it depends __19__ the quality of the case. A cheap case, __20__ has been badly made, will obviously not last as long as an expensive one.

| 11 | A | his luggages | B | his luggage | C | their luggages | D | their luggage |
| 12 | A | in holiday | B | on holiday | C | in holidays | D | on holidays |
| 13 | A | so strong | B | enough strong | C | strong enough | D | too strong |
| 14 | A | However | B | Wherever | C | Whatever | D | Which |
| 15 | A | the more | B | the most | C | how much | D | how many |
| 16 | A | for not packing | B | to not pack | C | not to pack | D | in order to not pack |
| 17 | A | do so | B | do such | C | make so | D | make such |
| 18 | A | can carry the case | B | the case can carry | C | can bear the case | D | the case can bear |
| 19 | A | for | B | with | C | in | D | on |
| 20 | A | what | B | which | C | it | D | when |

# Test 29

*Choose the correct answer. Only one answer is correct.*

## Trouble at the Factory

A  Good morning, Angela. __1__ lovely day!
B  You __2__ think so when you __3__ this, Mr Laver. The workers are having a meeting at lunch time. They say that if you __4__ their wages they'll go on strike.
A  Why __5__ that when I've arranged to play golf?
B  They __6__ see their representatives before the meeting, Mr Laver.
A  But I don't know what to say. If they __7__ harder, I could pay them more money. It's really quite simple. Anyway, I have to take the car to the garage at 11 o'clock. I __8__ for a long time.
B  What __9__ I tell them, then, Mr Laver?
A  You __10__ that I'll see them now. But only for five minutes. I'm a very busy man, you know.

| | | | | | | | | |
|---|---|---|---|---|---|---|---|---|
| 1 | A | What | B | What a | C | How | D | So |
| 2 | A | cannot | B | must not | C | may not | D | could not |
| 3 | A | shall read | B | will read | C | read | D | are reading |
| 4 | A | didn't raise | B | didn't rise | C | don't rise | D | don't raise |
| 5 | A | always they do | B | do they always | C | do always they do | D | do they always do |
| 6 | A | want that you | B | want you to | C | would that you | D | are wanting you |
| 7 | A | would have worked | B | have worked | C | worked | D | should work |
| 8 | A | haven't had it serviced | B | haven't serviced it | C | don't have it serviced | D | don't service it |
| 9 | A | shall | B | let's | C | ought | D | would |
| 10 | A | had better tell | B | had better say | C | would rather say | D | would rather say |

42

## Trouble for Fox-hunting People

The English upper classes have always enjoyed ___11___ . A hundred years ago a gentleman who did not meet his friends and neighbours to hunt after church ___12___ Sunday mornings seemed ___13___ to them. But nowadays there are many people who take an active interest in preventing hunters from enjoying ___14___ . They used to lay false trails for the dogs, ___15___ spoiled the hunt because the dogs often followed their cars along the main road ___16___ the fox watched them ___17___ from the safety of a nearby field. But now they are buying land in areas where hunting takes place. Some time ago they wrote to Princess Anne and her husband, ___18___ are keen hunters, saying they would be taken to court ___19___ if they rode across it. I wonder what ___20___ about that.

| | | | | | | | |
|---|---|---|---|---|---|---|---|
| 11 | A | to hunt foxes | B | fox hunting | C | the fox hunting | D | to hunt the foxes |
| 12 | A | in | B | on | C | at | D | the |
| 13 | A | strange | B | to be strange | C | that he was strange | D | strangely |
| 14 | A | each other | B | one another | C | theirselves | D | themselves |
| 15 | A | that | B | what | C | which | D | it |
| 16 | A | while | B | meanwhile | C | when | D | for |
| 17 | A | going passed | B | going past | C | to go passed | D | to go past |
| 18 | A | that | B | which | C | what | D | who |
| 19 | A | as other person | B | like other person | C | like anyone else | D | as anyone else |
| 20 | A | the Iron Duke would have said | B | the Iron Duke would have told | C | would have said the Iron Duke | D | would have told the Iron Duke |

Note: The Iron Duke = the Duke of Wellington

# Test 30

*Choose the correct answer. Only one answer is correct.*

## Arriving at the Office

A  Hullo, Janet. What was the film like last night? Is it worth ___1___ ?
B  I wish I ___2___ tell you, but we didn't manage to see it.
A  I thought you said you ___3___ going to the Ritz.
B  I know. But ___4___ hundreds of people outside the cinema when we got there. If we ___5___ the film was going to be so popular John would have booked the tickets in advance, but we didn't expect ___6___ .
A  So what ___7___ ?
B  We waited outside for half an hour, but it was no good, so we ___8___ home and watched the television.
A  What a pity! That ___9___ disappointing.
B  Yes. I've told John that the next time we ___10___ to the cinema, we'll get the tickets beforehand.

| | | | | | | | |
|---|---|---|---|---|---|---|---|
| 1 | A | see | B | to see | C | seeing | D | to be seen |
| 2 | A | should | B | would | C | might | D | could |
| 3 | A | are | B | were | C | have been | D | should be |
| 4 | A | there were | B | there have been | C | they were | D | they have been |
| 5 | A | had known | B | would have known | C | knew | D | should have known |
| 6 | A | so much people to come | B | so many people to come | C | to come so much people | D | to come so many people |
| 7 | A | did you | B | were you doing | C | you did | D | did you do |
| 8 | A | went to | B | were going to | C | went | D | were going |
| 9 | A | should have been | B | ought to have been | C | must have been | D | had to be |
| 10 | A | will have gone | B | shall go | C | will go | D | go |

# Test 30

## The Soil and Atmosphere of Mars

The first pictures of Mars taken by the Viking spacecraft showed that there may once have been __11__ the planet. Mars seems red from Earth and in fact __12__ . The probable reason __13__ this is that it is apparently covered with iron ore oxide, __14__ means that there must be oxygen there. Viking also carried with it a machine to collect samples of the soil. The samples contained oxygen and there is no doubt, __15__ , that nitrogen, a gas which is __16__ essential to life as oxygen, also exists in the Martian atmosphere. One of the most remarkable discoveries is that __17__ that the oxygen is being turned into carbon dioxide. This interested scientists to __18__ extent that __19__ of them began experiments in the American desert to see if Earth soils would behave in the same way __20__ from Mars.

| 11 | A | the life in | B | the life on | C | life in | D | life on |
|---|---|---|---|---|---|---|---|---|
| 12 | A | there is | B | it is | C | it's | D | its |
| 13 | A | of | B | to | C | why | D | for |
| 14 | A | which | B | what | C | that | D | it |
| 15 | A | too | B | however | C | either | D | neither |
| 16 | A | like | B | similar | C | as | D | so |
| 17 | A | there is evidence | B | there are evidences | C | it is evidence | D | they are evidences |
| 18 | A | a so great | B | a such | C | so much | D | such an |
| 19 | A | a big lot | B | a great deal | C | some | D | an amount |
| 20 | A | than the ones | B | as the ones | C | than the one | D | as the one |

# Practice Exercises 1-150

**How to use the Practice Exercises**

A wrong answer in one of the Tests has a cross-reference in the **Test Key**. This says which Practice Exercise should be done in order to avoid future error. Study the examples, read the explanations and then do the exercise.

Alternatively, you can use the **Index**, at the back of the book, to find an exercise for a particular grammar point. In this way the exercises can be used for remedial practice of a given grammatical area without doing a test.

# Determiners

## 1 a, an

**a** Look at these sentences:

**A** guide book is **a** useful thing to take on holiday.
I eat **an** apple after every meal.

We use **a** before a consonant sound,
e.g. **a book, a good apple, a job, a hill.**
Note that some words that begin with the letter **u** have a consonant sound when we say the word, and so we use **a**,
e.g. **a university, a useful idea, a union.**
We use **an** before a vowel sound,
e.g. **an egg an apple, an awful job, an umbrella.**
Note that some words that begin with the letter **h** have no **h** sound when we say the word, and so we use **an**,
e.g. **an hour, an honest worker.**

Put **a** or **an** in the following:

1 _____ friend of mine studies at _____ university in Germany.
2 _____ young man was carrying _____ umbrella.
3 He has _____ uniform that belonged to _____ American general.
4 _____ hour is _____ long time in _____ underground train.
5 She was _____ honest girl and said she wanted _____ horse for her birthday.

**b** Notice that we need **a/an** in the following expressions:

My cousin is a nurse.
Mrs Smith drives a taxi.

though not, of course, in the plural:
Both my cousins are nurses.

Put **a** or **an** in the following sentences, if it is necessary:

1 Mrs Simon isn't _____ nurse; she's _____ doctor.
2 We haven't got _____ car; we always use _____ taxis.
3 Is that the telephonist? Give me _____ line, please.
4 My brother was _____ office worker, but now he's _____ gardener.

**c  a/an** with expressions of frequency

Notice how **a** is used in the following answer:

**A** How often do you go to the theatre?
**B** About twice **a** month.

We use **a** or **an** in expressions of frequency to answer questions like **how much, how many, how fast,** etc. **Twice a month** means 'twice in one month'.

*Determiners*

*Choose the expression on the right which best answers each question on the left:*

1. How often do you shave?
2. How fast can you run?
3. How often do you have examinations?
4. How much do you smoke?
5. What is your pulse rate?
6. How often do you have English classes?

a. Twice a year.
b. Eighty beats a minute.
c. Three times a week.
d. Twenty km. an hour.
e. Thirty cigarettes a day.
f. Once a day.

## 2 What...! What a/an...!

*Notice where* **a** *is necessary and where it is not used:*

That's a lovely flower. **What a** lovely flower!
Those are lovely flowers. **What** lovely flowers!
That's lovely food. **What** lovely food!

The second sentence of each pair, e.g. **What a lovely flower!** is stronger, or more emphatic, than the first.
We need **a** (or **an**) only with a singular count noun, e.g. **a flower, an ice cream.**

*Put* **What** *or* **What a/an** *in the following:*

1. _an_ awful picture!
2. ___ pretty dresses!
3. _a_ beautiful room!
4. ___ nice tea!
5. _a_ nice cup of tea!
6. ___ delicious bread!
7. _a_ disappointing programme!
8. ___ lovely weather!
9. ___ delightful cakes!
10. _an_ obvious thing to say!

## 3 all and every with expressions of time

*Compare these sentences:*

I haven't seen him **all day.** (since I got up this morning)
He goes to work **every day** except Sundays.

# Determiners

With periods of time (day, week, etc.) **all** refers to the total period of time (duration), **every** to a period of time which is continually repeated.

**Complete these sentences with all *or* every:**

1. The neighbours had a party until five o'clock this morning. It kept me awake _____ night.
2. Each morning just before dawn, the birds start singing outside my bedroom window. They wake me up _____ morning.
3. Evergreen trees are called 'evergreen' because they keep their leaves _____ year.
4. In America, autumn is called 'fall' because it is the time when the leaves fall from the trees _____ year.
5. The programme is shown from 7.00 to 8.00 _____ Sunday evening.
6. The film was four hours long. It lasted _____ Sunday evening.
7. In London, dustmen come to collect the rubbish _____ week.
8. The shop said they were sending a man to mend the television on Monday, but we've been waiting _____ week for him and he still hasn't come.
9. _____ time we meet he says hello.
10. He has never said hello to me in _____ the time I've known him.

## 4  Use and omission of **the**

a  *Look at these sentences:*

**I drive to work** at 8.30 and **come home** at 5.30.
**I'm** usually **at home** in the evenings and **I go to bed** at 10 o'clock.

We don't usually use **the** with **school**, **work**, **bed** and **home** after verbs of motion, e.g. **go, drive,** and some others.

So we say:

| | | | |
|---|---|---|---|
| walk | | | to university |
| go | to church | | to sea |
| come | to school | go | to prison |
| get | to work | | to bed |
| travel | to market | | to hospital |
| drive | home | | |
| cycle | | | |
| | | | in prison |
| | | | in bed |
| | | | in hospital |
| | | be | at school |
| | | stay | at work |
| | | | at home |
| | | | at church |
| | | | at sea |

49

*Determiners*

Notice also: **start school, leave school, start work, leave work, leave home, take (somebody) to school, drive (somebody) to work.**

But with **office, factory, shop** we use **the**, e.g. **go to the office, work at the factory, arrive at the shop,** etc.

*Put **the** where it is necessary in the following:*

1. In my room _____ bed is in the corner.
2. I usually go to _____ bed at about 12 o'clock.
3. My wife leaves _____ home at 6.00 because she starts _____ work at 6.30.
4. Yesterday I was at _____ office all day, but today I have been at _____ factory.
5. _____ work that my wife does is hard, and she is usually tired when she gets _____ home.
6. My daughter left _____ school last year; now she takes her brother to _____ school before she goes to _____ work.
7. **A** Is your brother at _____ work?
   **B** No, he's ill, so he's at _____ home in _____ bed.
8. After I left _____ factory, first I went to _____ shops, and then I went _____ home.
9. One of their daughters is at _____ university, but the other is in _____ prison.
10. We drive to _____ market because there is so much to carry, but we always cycle to _____ church.

**b** *Look at these sentences:*

1. Games and sports

    I **play football** every week. My sister **plays tennis** and **likes swimming**, too.

    Which games or sports are the following people famous for?
    Steffi Graf, Ruud Gullit, Severiano Ballesteros, Carl Lewis, Boris Becker,
    e.g. **Steffi Graf is famous for tennis.**

2. Subjects of study

    I **studied literature** at university and now I **teach English**.

    Which subject would you study if you were interested in the work of
    Marconi, Shakespeare, Sophocles, Einstein, Mozart, Keynes, Pasteur?
    e.g. **If I were interested in the work of Marconi, I would study physics.**

## 3  Languages

Many Welsh people **speak Welsh** but most Scots **speak English**.
This book was originally written in German.

Note that we can say **the English** (noun) or **English people,** but nationality as an adjective has no definite or indefinite article,
e.g. **I'm English**.
Which language do the following speak? — the Belgians, the Austrians, the Brazilians, the Danes, the Cretans, the Swiss,
e.g. **The Belgians speak French or Flemish**.

## 4  Meals and clock time

*A* What time do you **have breakfast?**
*B* **About eight o'clock**.

## 5  Gerunds

**Horse racing** is more popular in Britain than **fox-hunting**.

*Put in a preposition where necessary and also put in* **the** *where necessary:*

1. I like _____ tennis, but I prefer _____ swimming.
2. They often play _____ cards; they are very good _____ bridge.
3. This book _____ nuclear physics was written _____ English and then translated _____ German.
4. _____ walking and _____ running are good _____ body.
5. We have _____ lunch at about _____ 1 o'clock.
6. Ms Thomson teaches _____ geography, but her hobby is painting.

## c  Use of **the**

### 1  Unique objects, points of the compass, some time expressions

**The sun** rises in **the east**.
**The past** is often more real to old people than **the present**.

We use **the** when there is only one of something, e.g. **the sun, the moon, the earth, the world**.
We use **the** with points of the compass, e.g. **the north, the south, the east, the west**. But compare these sentences:
We were travelling **north**.
We were travelling **towards the north**.

We usually use **the** when we speak of **the past, the present** and **the future**.
The exceptions are **at present** which means 'now, at this time' and **in future** which means 'from now on',
e.g. I'll drive more carefully **in future**. (from now on, from this moment)
   **In the future** (but not from now on) men may live on the moon.

*Determiners*

## 2 Plural count nouns and mass nouns

> She likes **flowers**. (general)
> She liked **the flowers** that I gave her. (specific)
> **Coffee** is expensive nowadays. (general)
> **The coffee** that you bought is very bitter. (specific)

*Put **the** where it is necessary in the following:*

1 _____ sun rises in _____ east and sets in _____ west.
2 Did you see _____ moon last night?
3 I like _____ Alsatians and _____ other big dogs, but I don't like _____ small dogs or _____ cats.
4 _____ food is more important than _____ art.

## d Noun + modifying phrase/clause

*Study these examples:*

> **Life** is always valuable.
> **Modern life** is often tiring.
> **Albert Schweitzer's life** was devoted to the sick.
> **The life of Albert Schweitzer** was devoted to the sick.
> **The life he is leading** bores him.
> **The life of our grandparents** was very different from **the life we lead** today.

**The** is used when the noun is modified by a relative clause, or by a phrase including **of**.

*Put **the** where it is necessary in the following:*

1 Tom is fond of _____ music.
2 Mozart composed _____ music in the eighteenth century.
3 She likes _____ music of the eighteenth century.
4 She likes _____ music that Mozart composed.
5 She likes _____ Mozart's music.
6 She likes _____ music of Mozart.
7 She prefers _____ classical music to _____ pop music.
8 I don't think _____ music we heard on the radio last night was really _____ jazz. It didn't sound like _____ Louis Armstrong's music, though some of _____ music of the 1920s, _____ music they played in New Orleans, was a bit like it.

# Determiners

## 5 this, that, these, those

*Compare these two dialogues:*

    *A* Is **this** hat here yours?
    *B* No, **that** hat over there is mine.

    *A* Are **those** books over there John's?
    *B* No, **these** books here are his.

We normally use:
**this** for a thing or person that is near,
**that** for a thing or person that is not near,
**these** for two or more things or people that are near,
**those** for two or more things or people that are not near.

*Put* **this, that, these** *or* **those** *in the following:*

1.  *A* Is _____ bike over there Betty's?
    *B* No, _____ bike here is hers.
2.  *A* Are _____ shoes here yours?
    *B* No, _____ shoes over there are mine.
3.  *A* Are _____ papers over there the teacher's?
    *B* No, but _____ papers here are hers.
4.  *A* Is _____ pen here yours?
    *B* No, _____ pen over there is mine.
5.  *A* Is _____ record here yours?
    *B* No, but _____ records over there are mine.
6.  *A* Are _____ photos over there Tim's?
    *B* No, but _____ photo here is his.

## 6 much, many, a lot of

*Compare these sentences:*

    There isn't **much** milk.
    There aren't **many** biscuits.

We use **much** only with mass nouns, e.g. **air, help, ink, sugar**. Note that the following are mass nouns: **bread, furniture, grass, hair, information, money, news, weather, work**. We must always use a singular verb with these nouns.

We use **many** only with plural count nouns, e.g. **apples, houses, girls, ideas**. Note that the following are plural: **people, children**.

**Many** and **much** are normal in question and negative statements,
e.g. **Have you got many records?**
    **We don't eat many potatoes.**
    **Did he drink much milk?**
    **She didn't give me much bread.**

*Determiners*

In positive statements we very often use **a lot of** instead of **many** and **much**, e.g. **We eat a lot of potatoes. She gave me a lot of bread.**

*Put* **much** *or* **many** *in the questions and negative statements; put* **a lot of** *in the positive statements:*

1. Is there _____ hot water?
2. I haven't got _____ stamps.
3. Jenny took _____ photos.
4. Do you write _____ letters?
5. There weren't _____ people in the park.
6. They haven't bought _____ furniture for the flat.
7. The girls had _____ good ideas.
8. Have you got _____ money on you?
9. Do _____ children visit the zoo?
10. We all ate _____ ice cream.

# 7 some, not any, a, one, no (there is/are)

*Look at these diagrams and read the sentences about Diagram 1:*

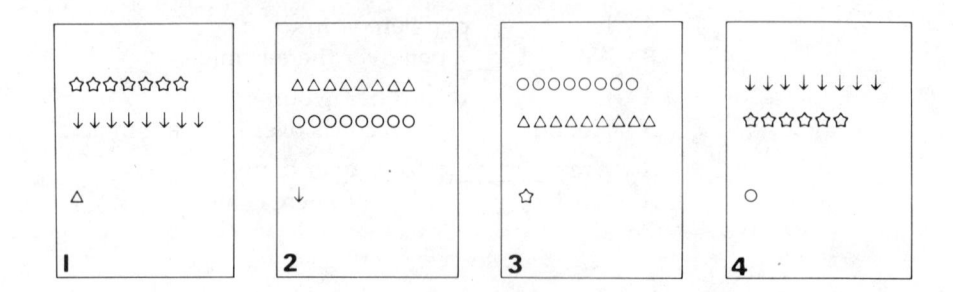

a In Diagram 1 there are **some** stars and **some** arrows, but there are**n't any** circles.
b There's **a** triangle in Diagram 1, but there isn't **one** in Diagram 4.
c There are **no** circles in Diagram 1.

*Write three sentences about the other diagrams, using* **there are some ...** *and* **there aren't any ...** *(see Sentence* **a***):*

1. In Diagram 2 _____
2. In Diagram 3 _____
3. In Diagram 4 _____

## Determiners

*Write three more sentences, using **There's a/an ...** and **there isn't one ...** (see Sentence **b**):*

    4 _____ in Diagram 2, but _____ in Diagram 3.
    5 _____ in Diagram 3, but _____ in Diagram 2.
    6 _____ in Diagram 4, but _____ in Diagram 1.

*Now write three more sentences, using **There are no ...** (see Sentence **c**):*

    7 _____ in Diagram 2.
    8 _____ in Diagram 3.
    9 _____ in Diagram 4.

## 8 some, any, a, (a) few, (a) little

### a some, any, a

*Notice where **some**, **any** and **a** are used:*

We bought **some** books.
We did**n't** buy **any** books.
We bought **a** book.
Did you buy **any** books?
Did you buy **some** books?

We use **some** and **any** with plural count nouns,
e.g. **some books, any books, some friends, any friends.**

Note that the singular of these expressions is **a book, a friend;** we do not use **some** and **any** here.

We also use **some** and **any** with mass nouns,
e.g. **some milk, any milk, some cloth, any cloth.**
We use **some** in positive statements and positive commands,
e.g. **Give me some milk.**

**Any** is not negative, but with **not** it is used in negative statements and negative commands,
e.g. **Don't give me any milk.**

In questions **any** is more usual than **some**,
e.g. **Did she give you any milk?**

Sometimes, when we are sure the answer will be 'yes', we ask a question with **some**,
e.g. **Did she give you some milk?**

*Put **some**, **any** or **a(n)** in the following. If **some** and **any** are both possible, what is the difference?*

    1 There are _____ good programmes on TV tonight.
    2 There's _____ good programme on TV tonight.
    3 Can you lend me _____ money?

## Determiners

4   The tyre hasn't got _____ air in it.
5   They gave us _____ cakes and _____ cup of tea.
6   I didn't take _____ nails out of the box.
7   I didn't take _____ nail out of the box.
8   Bring me _____ paint and _____ good brush.
9   For this cake we need _____ eggs and _____ milk.
10  For this cake we don't need _____ eggs or _____ milk.

### b  (a) few, (a) little

*Notice where* **a** *is used:*

There were only **a few** visitors.
There were very **few** visitors.
There was only **a little** time.
There was very **little** time.

Notice that **some** and **any** indicate an indefinite quantity, and so they cannot answer the questions **how many?** or **how much?** We can answer these questions with, for example, **a lot (of)** and, for a small quantity, **few** or **a few** with countable nouns (**few books, a few apples**) and **little** or **a little** with mass nouns (**little butter, a little milk**). We often use **a few** or **a little** with **only**, and **few** and **little** with **very**. **Few** and **little** have a negative meaning, so **few** means 'not many' and **little** means 'not much'.

*Put* **few, a few, little** *or* **a little** *in the following:*

1   We expected a lot of people, but only _____ came.
2   We'll have to go to the shops, because there's very _____ food in the house.
3   I'm sorry to say that we've only got _____ food.
4   There were very _____ people on the beach.
5   A  How many lamps have they sold?
    B  Only _____ .
6   A  How much cheese have they sold?
    B  Very _____ .

c  **few, a few, little, a little**

*Compare these sentences:*

I **don't think** there's **much** use trying to persuade him; he's already made up his mind.

I **think** there's **little** use trying to persuade him; he's already made up his mind.

I'd like **some** milk, please.

I'd like **a little** milk, please.

*Rewrite these sentences, using* **little, a little, few** *or* **a few,** *as in the example above:*

1  She worked hard, although her boss didn't give her much encouragement.
2  Not many people voted for him; he's not popular.
3  Would you like some sugar in your tea?
4  There have been some cases of stealing in the firm but not many workers were involved, and there is not much reason to be alarmed.
5  A  You look as though you need some help.
   B  Yes, there are some problems I don't understand.
6  Not many teachers think that students can learn English without much effort, though some suggest this to give the students some encouragement. Personally, I don't see much sense in saying this.

# Possessives and pronouns

## 9 Personal pronouns: **I, me** etc.

a   *Notice the pronouns in this sentence:*
   I don't like **him,** and **he** doesn't like **me.**

   The subject personal pronouns are:
   **I, you, he, she, it, we, they.**
   They are used as the subject of a sentence,
   e.g. **I can swim.**
       **She doesn't like fruit.**
       **We went home.**

   The object personal pronouns are:
   **me, you, him, her, it, us, them.**
   We use these as the object of a sentence and after a preposition,
   e.g. **The dog bit me.**
       **The policeman spoke to him.**
       **The medicine will be good for her.**

*Put a personal pronoun in each of the following spaces:*
1   You sold that pen to me. _____ gave _____ £2 for _____ .
2   I sold that book to Jim. _____ gave _____ £4 for _____ .
3   Mary sold the chairs to Mr and Mrs Scott. _____ gave _____ £20 for _____ .
4   We sold our old car to Victoria. _____ gave _____ £300 for _____ .
5   Mr Smith sold his stamps to us. _____ gave _____ £50 for _____ .

b   *Notice the pronouns in these sentences:*
   I'm worried about my hair. **It's** going grey.
   I'm worried about my teeth too. I clean **them** every day, but **they** are full of holes.

   Note that **it** goes with the following words (they are singular): **hair, money, tooth, foot, news, furniture.** Note that **they** and **them** go with the following words (they are plural): **feet, teeth, scissors, glasses, jeans, pyjamas, trousers, people, police.**

*Put **it, they** or **them** in the following:*
1   I've brought the money; I've got _____ in this bag.
2   The news was interesting but we didn't have time to watch _____ .
3   A   Where have you put my glasses?
   B   _____ are on the television.
4   We've paid for the new furniture, and the shop is going to bring _____ round tomorrow.

## Possessives and pronouns

    5  *A*  Can we ask the police about our problem?
        *B*  Yes, but it's not really a problem for _____ .

**C**  *Notice how the person who asks the question in this dialogue gets everything the wrong way round:*

    *A*  Did John shout at Mary?
    *B*  No, **she** shouted at **him**.

*Complete these sentences in the same way:*

    1  *A*  Have Mr and Mrs Brent invited Peter?
        *B*  No, _____ has invited _____ .
    2  *A*  Did you and your husband work for Mr and Mrs Foster?
        *B*  No, _____ worked for _____ .
    3  *A*  Did you make a cake for your sister?
        *B*  No, _____ made a cake for _____ .
    4  *A*  Do I owe Peter some money?
        *B*  No, _____ owes _____ some.
    5  *A*  Is Mrs Patrick going to come and see you?
        *B*  No, _____ am going to go and see _____ .
    6  *A*  Did we beat you and your husband last year?
        *B*  No, _____ beat _____ last year.

## 10  **one, ones**

*Look at these sentences:*

    I don't know the tall girl, but I know **the short one.**
    They didn't have any big apples, so I bought **some small ones.**

These sentences would not be complete without the words **one** and **ones** because we cannot say **the short** or **some small** alone.

*Put* **one** *or* **ones** *in the following:*

    1  He gave me two French stamps and a Japanese _____ .
    2  There are six small cakes and two large _____ .
    3  *A*  Did you buy a big cabbage?
        *B*  No, I got some small _____ instead.
    4  *A*  Would you like the expensive map or the cheaper _____ ?
        *B*  I think I'll take the cheaper _____ .

Possessives and pronouns

## 11   one, it, them, some, any

*Notice the use of* **one, it, them, some** *and* **any** *in these dialogues:*

    *A*  Did you buy **a newspaper?**
    *B*  No, I didn't buy **one.**

    *A*  Have you got **any stamps?**
    *B*  Yes, I've got **some.** (or: No, I haven't got **any.**)

In the first dialogue the speakers are not talking about a particular newspaper; in the second, **any** and **some** don't refer to any special stamps.

    *A*  Have you posted **the letter?**
    *B*  Yes, I've posted **it.**

    *A*  Did you ask for **the books?**
    *B*  Yes, I asked for **them.**

Here the speakers are talking about a letter and a number of books which they know about.

*Put* **one, it, them, some** *or* **any** *in the following:*

1  *A*  Have you got any sisters?
    *B*  No, I haven't got _____ .

2  *A*  Can you give me the books now?
    *B*  No, I haven't got _____ here.

3  *A*  Have you seen some in here?
    *B*  Yes, there are _____ on that chair

4  *A*  Can you touch the ceiling?
    *B*  No, I can't touch _____ .

5  *A*  Did you see a big dog in the park?
    *B*  Yes, I saw _____ near the lake.

## 12   another, the other, others, the others

*Notice the way* **another, the other, others,** *and* **the others** *are used in the sentences below:*

    ☆  ○  △△  □  ◊◊◊

Here are **some** shapes. **One** is a star; **another** is a circle.

    ☆  ○

Here are two shapes. **One** is a star; **the other** is a circle.

    ☆☆☆☆  ○○○○○○  ◊◊◊◊◊◊◊  □□□□□□□  △△△△

Here are **several** shapes. **Some** are stars; **others** are circles.

    ☆☆☆☆  ○○○○○○

Here are **several** shapes. **Some** are stars; **the others** are circles.

Put **another, the other, others** or **the others** in the following:

1 △△△△△  ☐☐☐☐☐  ◊◊◊◊◊◊◊◊◊  ☆☆☆☆  ○○○

Here are several shapes. Some are triangles; _____ are squares.

2 ☆  △  ☐  ◊◊◊  ○

Here are some shapes. One is a star; _____ is a triangle.

3 ◊  ☐

Here are two shapes. One is a diamond; _____ is a square.

4 ◊◊◊◊◊◊◊◊  △△△△△△△△△

Here are several shapes. Some are diamonds; _____ are triangles.

## 13 each other/one another

Compare these sentences:

Tom helps Kate and Kate helps Tom.
Tom and Kate help **each other/one another**.

Both sentences have the same meaning, but we usually use the second sentence pattern with **each other** or **one another**.

Change the following in the same way:

1 Brenda often writes to Paula, and Paula often writes to Brenda.
2 David sometimes makes cakes for Neil, and Neil sometimes makes cakes for David.
3 Cathy never argues with her sister, and her sister never argues with Cathy.
4 Fred respects me, and I respect Fred.
5 Mrs Rowe admires Mrs Webb, and Mrs Webb admires Mrs Rowe.
6 Ben often complains about Sara, and she often complains about him.
7 The Smiths hate the Tomlinsons, and the Tomlinsons hate the Smiths.
8 Alan loves Pauline, and she loves him.

## 14 everything, everybody/everyone

Notice the verbs in these sentences:

**Everything is** dirty.
**Everybody goes** home at 5 o'clock.
**Everyone** in the office **knows** James.

**Everything** means 'all the things'.
**Everybody** and **everyone** mean 'all the people'.
They are all singular and take a singular verb.

*Possessives and pronouns*

*Put **everything**, **everybody** or **everyone** and the correct form of the verb in the following:*
1 _____ in their bedroom _____ blue. (be)
2 Almost _____ young children. (like)
3 Nowadays _____ too much money. (spend)
4 _____ in the house _____ to her parents. (belong)

## 15 nobody/no one, nothing, no, none

**Nobody** or **no one** is used for people and **nothing** for things:
**Nobody** answered the phone. There was **nothing** in the box.
I saw **no one** in the corridor. **Nothing** happened.

**No** must go with a noun; **none** is not followed by a noun:
**No** children came. We've got **no** clean towels.
**None** of the children came. We've got **none**.

The negative words that answer the question **who?** are **nobody** and **no one** (two words),
e.g. A  Who's there?
     B  Nobody. (or: No one.)

The negative word that answers the question **what?** is **nothing**,
e.g. A  What have you done?
     B  Nothing.

The negative words that answer the questions **how much?** or **how many?** are **no** and **none**.
**No** must go with a noun, e.g. **no books, no interesting books, no milk, no fresh milk**, but **none** is not followed by a noun,
e.g. A  How many books are there?
     B  There are no books.
     (or: There are none.)
     A  How much milk is there?
     B  There is no milk.
     (or: There is none.)

*Put the correct negative word in the following:*
1 A  What have you got in your mouth?
  B  _____ .
2 A  How many sweets have you eaten?
  B  _____ . I've eaten _____ sweets at all today.
3 A  Who have you been talking to?
  B  _____ .
4 Peter has _____ interest in sports.
5 Most of the students passed the exam, but _____ of them got really good marks.
6 There are _____ good theatres in our town.

## 16 somebody/someone, anybody/anyone, nobody/no one

**a** Look at these sentences:

I saw **somebody** in the garden.
I didn't see **anybody** in the garden.
I saw **nobody** in the garden.

**Somebody** is used in a positive statement.
**Anybody** is used in a statement with a negative word (**not, never,** etc.).
**Nobody** is negative and is not used with another negative word.

**Somebody** and **nobody** can be the subject of the sentence,
e.g. **Somebody was in the garden.**
  **Nobody was in the garden.**
We cannot use **anybody** as the subject of the sentence.

Note that:  instead of **somebody** we can use **someone** with the same meaning;
  instead of **anybody** we can use **anyone** with the same meaning;
  instead of **nobody** we can use **no one** with the same meaning.

Put **somebody, anybody** or **nobody** in the following sentences:

1 _____ from the post office brought this for you.
2 _____ came to see me at the weekend, so I was all alone.
3 I don't know _____ who speaks Chinese.
4 A _____ telephoned this morning.
  B Oh, who was it?
5 I wanted to talk to _____ about my problems, but _____ wanted to listen because they were all watching television.
6 Please don't tell _____ my secret.
7 _____ is talking because everybody has a lot of work.
8 _____ is talking, but I don't know who it is.

**b someone/somebody, anyone/anybody**

Compare these sentences:

Listen! There's **someone** at the door.
It's not a difficult job. **Anyone** could do it.

**Someone** means 'a particular person', although perhaps we do not know his name; **anyone**, in an affirmative sentence, means 'a person, any person, whoever he is and whatever he is like'.

*Possessives and pronouns*

Complete these sentences using **someone/somebody** and **anyone/anybody** where appropriate:

| | | |
|---|---|---|
| Doris | He's an impossible man, and ___1___ should tell him so. | |
| Flo | Ssh! ___2___ may hear you. | |
| Doris | I don't care. ___3___ would say the same in my situation. | |
| Doris | Oh, ___4___ rang while you were out. | |
| Mr Cross | Who was it? | |
| Doris | I don't know. I didn't ask him. | |
| Mr Cross | Good heavens! ___5___ with a little common sense would have taken a message. It may have been ___6___ important. | |
| Doris | Well, if it was, I expect he'll ring back. | |
| Mr Cross | Miss Smith, ___7___ but you would have asked him his name. That's what I pay you for. ___8___ could do a simple job like yours. | |
| Doris | Well, you'd better look for ___9___ then, Mr Cross, because I'm leaving. But your wife might like to know that you took ___10___ out to lunch today, ___11___ called Gloria from the accounts office. | |
| Mr Cross | Now, Miss Smith, er, Doris, don't get upset. ___12___ can lose his temper, you know. | |

# 17 something, anything, nothing, somewhere, anywhere

a *Notice which sentences are positive and which are negative:*

There's **something** in that box.
There isn't **anything** in that box.
There's **nothing** in that box.

There's a cafe **somewhere** near here.
There isn't a cafe **anywhere** near here.

**Something** is used in a positive statement.
**Anything** is used in a statement with a negative word **(not, never, etc.)**.
**Nothing** is negative and is not used with another negative word.

**Somewhere** is used in a positive statement.
**Not . . . anywhere** is used in a negative statement.

We can use an adjective after these words (**something,** etc.),
e.g. **There's something heavy in that box.**
  **There isn't anything heavy in that box.**
  **There's nothing heavy in that box.**

## Possessives and pronouns

*Put* **something, anything, nothing, somewhere** *or* **anywhere** *in the following:*

1. I didn't see _____ about the fire in the newspaper.
2. My pen must be _____ in this room.
3. We saw _____ very unusual this morning, didn't we?
4. The children haven't _____ to play games.
5. There was _____ in the case. It was completely empty.

**b** *Notice the use of the infinitive,* **to eat, to sit,** *after* **anything** *and* **anywhere:**
I'm hungry, but I haven't got **anything to eat**.
They're tired, but they haven't got **anywhere to sit**.

*Put* **anything** *or* **anywhere** *and an infinitive in the following:*

1. I'm thirsty, but I haven't got _____ .
2. We'd like to go somewhere, but we can't think of _____ .
3. He'd like to read something, but he hasn't got _____ .
4. They'd like to play football, but they haven't got _____ .

## 18 Adjectives: **my, your** etc.

*Look at these sentences:*

**My** sisters and I are very different. **My** hair is blonde but **their** hair is very dark.

**My** and **their** are possessive adjectives.
The possessive adjectives are:
**my, your, his, her, its, our, their.**

*Look at the example below and then complete the other sentences in the same way:*
e.g. If it belongs to David, it'll have **his** name in it.

1. If it belongs to me, it'll have _____ name in it.
2. If it belongs to Paula, it'll have _____ name in it.
3. If it belongs to you, it'll have _____ name in it.
4. If it belongs to Mr and Mrs Turner, it'll have _____ names in it.
5. If it belongs to Frank's sister, it'll have _____ name in it.
6. If it belongs to us, it'll have _____ names in it.
7. If it belongs to the school, it'll have _____ name in it.
8. If it belongs to you and your husband, it'll have _____ names in it.

## 19 Adjectives: **my, your** etc; pronouns: **mine, yours** etc.

Compare these sentences:

**My sister's house** is very different from **my house**.
**Her house** has three small rooms but **my house** is very large.

**My sister's house** is very different from **mine**.
**Hers** has three small rooms but **mine** is very large.

**Her** and **my** are possessive adjectives.
**Hers** and **mine** are possessive pronouns.

The possessive adjectives are:
**my, your, his, her, its, our, their.**

We use possessive adjectives with a noun, e.g. **my book, your trousers, her mother, our house, your idea, their problem.**

The possessive pronouns are:
**mine, yours, his, hers, its, ours, theirs.**
We use possessive pronouns without a noun,
e.g. A  Which hat is **yours**?
      B  **Mine** is the green one.

Complete the following, with one word only in each space:
1  I think that's my book. Yes, it's certainly _____ .
2  I think those are _____ socks. Yes, they are certainly hers.
3  I think that's their car. Yes, it's certainly _____ .
4  I think those are our coats. Yes, they're certainly _____ .
5  I think those are _____ boots. Yes, they are certainly his.

## 20 Adjectives and pronouns with **whose?**

Look at these sentences:

A  **Whose** book is this?
B  It's **my book.** (possessive adjective)

A  **Whose** is this book?
B  It's **mine.** (possessive pronoun)

A  **Whose** shoes are those?
B  They're **her shoes.** (possessive adjective)

A  **Whose** are those shoes?
B  They're **hers.** (possessive pronoun)

The question word that is answered by a possessive adjective (see Practice 18) is **whose.**
The question word that is answered by a possessive pronoun (see Practice 19) is also **whose.**

*Put one word only, either* **whose** *or a possessive adjective or pronoun, in each space:*

1 A _____ are those books?
  B They're _____ . They've got my name in them.
2 A _____ shirt is this?
  B It's Peter's. It's got _____ name in it, so it must be _____ .
3 A _____ are those records?
  B They're mine and Jane's. They've got _____ names on them, so they must be _____ .
4 A _____ dog is that?
  B It's Mr and Mrs Smith's. It's got _____ name on _____ collar, so it must be _____ .
5 A _____ is this wallet?
  B It's Veronica's. It's got _____ name inside, so it must be _____ .
6 A All these caps are the same. _____ is that one?
  B I think it belongs to you. Yes, it's got _____ name in it, so it must be _____ .

## 21 Reflexive pronouns: **myself** etc; **each other/one another**

### a Reflexive verbs

*Notice the reflexive verbs in these sentences:*

He didn't have a guitar teacher. He **taught himself.**
I **looked** at **myself** in the mirror this morning and **said to myself,** 'You need a holiday.'
The children **enjoyed themselves** very much.

The following verbs are often found in reflexive constructions:
a verbs connected with action, pain or danger,
  e.g. **burn, cut, defend, drown, hurt, kill, shoot,**
b verbs connected with behaviour or emotion,
  e.g. **amuse, behave, blame, control, deceive, enjoy, be ashamed of, be sorry for, feel sorry for,**
c verbs connected with thought or speech,
  e.g. **consider, count, express, say to, talk to, tell, think,**
  **Count** and **think** are often reflexive when they have the meaning of 'consider',
  e.g. **Count/Think yourself lucky that you escaped.**
d verbs indicating actions which are not normally reflexive,
  e.g. **congratulate, educate, introduce, invite, teach,**
e other verbs,
  e.g. **can't help, prevent, stop, weigh**

## Possessives and pronouns

Use each of the following verbs in the correct form once only followed by a suitable reflexive pronoun to complete these sentences:

be ashamed of, behave, enjoy, feel sorry for, introduce, talk to, teach, weigh

1. She's frightened of getting fat so she _____ every morning.
2. When people _____ , they say it's a sign that they are going mad.
3. I _____ very much at the party. I had a wonderful time.
4. He speaks several languages. He's _____ Portuguese now.
5. Daddy says we can stay up to watch the programme on TV if we _____ .
6. Oh, do stop _____ . A lot of other people in the world are unhappy, too.
7. No one spoke to her so she went up to various people and _____ .
8. You ought to _____ . I've never seen such badly behaved children.

### b  myself, yourself etc. and each other/one another

Compare these sentences:

When you look in a mirror you see **yourself**.
You and your friend can talk to **each other/one another** on the telephone.

**Alan sees himself in a mirror** means that Alan sees Alan.

**Alan and Bill talk to each other** means that Alan talks to Bill, and Bill talks to Alan.

Complete the following sentences with a reflexive pronoun or **each other/one another**:

1. Parents often complain that television stops children amusing _____ with creative games.
2. They told _____ jokes to pass the time.
3. The two sisters are very fond of _____ and if anyone criticises either of them they always defend _____ .
4. The three of us were attacked by a group of thugs in the street so we had to defend _____ .
5. Don't blame _____ for what happened. It wasn't your fault, Tony, and it wasn't Joan's fault, either. I don't want you to argue with _____ about it.
6. I've always wanted to meet you but we've never had the chance to talk to _____ until now. Let me introduce _____ . My name's Alan.

## 22  Reflexive pronouns used for emphasis

Look at these sentences:

I'm not going to do it for you. Do it **yourself**!
The Queen **herself** gave it to me.

The reflexive pronouns here emphasise the words they go with.

## Possessives and pronouns

*Use the appropriate reflexive pronoun to make the sentences below emphatic, in the same way as the examples above:*

1 I wouldn't take any notice of you even if you were the king _____ .
2 Why should they expect us to do it for them? They ought to do it _____ .
3 Would you mind taking these letters to the post? I haven't got time to do it _____ .
4 Cynthia Jones is getting married. Mrs Jones told me _____ .
5 They have no right to take any credit for the success of the project: we did it all _____ .
6 You must answer the questions _____ . I'm not going to help any of you.
7 She broke it _____ and then tried to blame me.
8 It was a terrible play. The actors _____ didn't understand it.

## 23  Alternatives to the reflexive

*Compare these sentences:*

I've cut **myself**!
I've **cut my hand**!

We generally use the reflexive to describe injuries we receive by our own actions,
e.g. **I hurt myself while I was playing squash.**
     **He burned himself with his cigarette.**

But we do not use the reflexive if we mention the part of the body,
e.g. **I hit my elbow on the chair.**
     **She cut her hand on the edge of the tin.**

Where the verb only refers to that part of the body, the reflexive is impossible,
e.g. **I broke my leg.** (not **myself**)

*Complete these sentences with one of the injuries listed below. Use the correct form of the verb and an appropriate possessive (**my, your,** etc.):*

e.g. I was lighting the barbecue and **I burned my hand.**

**break/leg, burn/mouth, cut/hand, stub/toe, bite/tongue, break/nose, bang/head, burn/fingers**

1 Don't pick up that broken glass! You'll _____ .
2 He's so tall that every time he goes through a low doorway, he _____ .
3 If you touch that hot iron, you'll _____ .
4 Almost everyone I know who goes skiing _____ sooner or later.
5 A  He looks like a boxer.
  B  Yes, he _____ when he was young and it didn't set properly.

*Possessives and pronouns*

    6   A   Why are you jumping about on one foot?
           B   Who left that heavy box in the doorway? I've _____ .
    7   That soup's too hot. You'll _____ .
    8   A   Ow! I've _____ .
           B   Well, you shouldn't eat so fast.

## 24   Genitive: **a boy's voice, the capital of England**

### a  People

Look at these sentences:

**A boy's voice** is much higher than **a man's voice**.
**Shakespeare's plays** are famous all over the world.

These mean the same as:
The voice of a boy is much higher than the voice of a man.
The plays of Shakespeare are famous all over the world.

Look at these details of the horses in a certain race:

| Horse | Owner | Jockey |
| --- | --- | --- |
| Red Star | The Queen | Fred Barrow |
| Morning Mist | Sir Harry Wright | Ted Long |
| Happy Girl | Mr Truman | Johnny Porter |
| All My Love | Dina Dore | Sam Silk |

From this information we can say:
**Red Star is the Queen's horse.**
**Sam Silk is Dina Dore's jockey.**

Write similar sentences for the other horses and jockeys.

### b  Things and places

Compare this sentence with those in **a** above:

London is **the capital of England.**

We do not usually use the form with an apostrophe (') for things and places. For these we usually use a phrase with **of**.

Write similar sentences about Paris, Washington DC, Warsaw, Athens, Madrid and Rome.

## 25 Double possessives: **some friends of mine**

Notice the use of possessive pronouns in these sentences:

**Some friends of mine** are buying that house.
Is she **a cousin of yours?**

Put a possessive pronoun in each of the spaces:

1 I know Terry very well. He's a friend of _____ .
2 These photos are all of Margaret's family. These girls here are cousins of _____ .
3 He's borrowed several records of _____ , but he's never given them back to us.
4 They must know Peter. He's a colleague of _____ .
5 Do you know Mike Rolls? Is he a friend of _____ ?
6 I've never met Michael Jackson, but I once met a cousin of _____ .

## 26 Genitive

### a Punctuation

Look at the punctuation of these sentences:

The **artist's** pictures were so good that they were all sold.
The **artists'** pictures were so good that they were all sold.

In the first case, there was only one artist; in the second, more than one.

Note that **the picture of the artist** refers to a picture painted by another person where the artist was the subject. Similarly, **the pictures of the artists** refers to pictures painted by other people where the artists were the subjects.

When a noun has an irregular plural, not ending in **s**, the apostrophe comes before the **s**, e.g. **men's, women's, children's, people's,**

In these sentences the words in brackets should end in **s'** if plural or **'s** if singular. Write out these words in the correct form:

Charles and Molly have four children, Edward and Henry, aged 18, who are twins, Carol, 17, and Mary, 16.

1 Edward and Henry played together in the school tennis championship and won the doubles. Their parents saw the (boy) victory.
2 Molly says: The (twin) clothes are no problem. Edward can always wear his (brother) clothes and vice versa. But I spend a lot of money on the (girl) clothes. They always want to look different.

*Possessives and pronouns*

3 The twins are in the same class but the girls are in different classes. Charles says to the (twin) teacher: I'm worried about my (son) exam results. They've both done badly. He says to (Carol) teacher: What can you tell me about my (daughter) progress? Her results were not as good as her (sister).

4 Henry says: I don't agree with all my (parent) ideas. For instance, my (father) views on politics are very right-wing, and my (mother) attitude towards my (sister) boy-friends is sometimes a bit intolerant. Still, they're both more reasonable than some of my (friend) parents.

b  Genitive with expressions of time

*Compare the following sentences, studying the punctuation:*

I'll see you in **a week's time.**
I'll see you in **three weeks' time.**

Note that **a fortnight's time** is two weeks' time.
The genitive, with **'s**, is used for people, animals and periods of time, but not for things, except in a few phrases.

*In these sentences the words in brackets should end in* **s'** *if plural or* **'s** *if singular. Write out these words in the correct form:*

1 I'm going away for a (fortnight) holiday.
2 He gets a (month) holiday every year.
3 The doctor says he needs a few (week) rest.
4 This (year) students are better than last (year).
5 The town will be completely different in a few (year) time.
6 I couldn't get (today) newspaper, so I've brought (yesterday).
7 In six (month) time, he is going to retire, and after forty (year) work in the same firm, he deserves a gold watch.
8 In a few (minute) time, the race will begin.

c  **the grocer's**

*Look at this sentence:*

Susan, would you go to **the grocer's** and get me some flour?

**The grocer's** means 'the grocer's shop'. Shops are sometimes referred to as **the grocer's, the baker's, the butcher's,** when we do not use the actual name of the shop.

Where, in Britain, would you expect to buy: meat, bread, vegetables, fish, cigarettes, medicine, flowers, nails, sugar, newspapers?

## 27 belong to

Compare the forms in these sentences:

The table was **King Edward's**. It wasn't **King Arthur's**.
It was **King Edward's table**. It wasn't **King Arthur's**. (table)
The table **belonged to King Edward**. It **didn't belong to King Arthur**.

Rewrite these sentences, using the alternative forms, as in the examples above:

1 That car is Fred's.
2 That house over there is my sister's.
3 The factory isn't her father's. It's her uncle's.
4 It's my cousin's farm. It's not my brother's.
5 That's Jack Smith's car, isn't it?
6 It was my grandfather's watch.
7 The castle was the duke's at one time, wasn't it?
8 When he dies, it will be his son's land.

# Adjectives

## 28 Comparatives: **as...as, -er than, the same as, the same...as, different from**

### a  as...as, -er than

*Look at these sentences:*

Alan is **taller than** Bob, but he isn't **as tall as** David.
David is **older than** Clive.
Clive's shoes are **as big as** Bob's.

The information in these sentences comes from this table:

|       | Height (m) | Age | Shoe size |
|-------|------------|-----|-----------|
| Alan  | 1.78       | 19  | 46        |
| Bob   | 1.69       | 18  | 45        |
| Clive | 1.78       | 17  | 45        |
| David | 1.81       | 18  | 43        |

*Using the table, make more sentences about the boys. Use these phrases:*

taller than, shorter than, as tall as;
older than, younger than, as old as;
bigger than, smaller than, as big as.

### b  the same...as, different from

*Look at these sentences:*

This is **the same as** mine.
Your coat is **the same** colour **as** my gloves.
Their view is **different from** mine.

When we use **the same** to make comparisons, we also use **as**.

*Put **as**, **than** or **from** in the following:*

1  His name is the same _____ our teacher's.
2  This is a very different size _____ that.
3  London is bigger _____ Paris.
4  Tom isn't _____ clever _____ Kate.
5  She's about the same age _____ my sister.
6  Her ideas are completely different _____ yours.

# Adjectives

## 29  Comparatives: -er, more

Look at these sentences:

Mount Everest is **higher than** Mont Blanc.
Gold is **more expensive than** silver.

We make the comparative of short adjectives with **-er**,
e.g. **smaller than, higher than, hotter than.**

We make the comparative of long adjectives with the word **more**,
e.g. **more expensive than, more dangerous than.**

Complete the following with **-er than** or **more...than** using the adjectives in brackets:
e.g. She is **fatter than** her sister. (fat)
1   This book is _____ that one. (interesting)
2   The air here is _____ in a big town. (clean)
3   A  Was her ring _____ yours? (expensive)
    B  Yes, mine was much _____ hers. (cheap)
4   Fred is _____ his father. (slim)
5   Mosquitoes are _____ flies. (small)
6   A  I think motorbikes are _____ cars. (dangerous)
    B  I agree. Cars are much _____ motorbikes. (safe)

## 30  Comparatives: -er; superlatives: -est

Look at these sentences and notice the difference in use between **taller than** and **the tallest**:
Roger is **taller than** all the other boys; he is **the tallest**.
Roger is **the tallest boy**; he is **taller than** all the others.

Notice that we say **the tallest** but just **taller**.

Complete the following in the same way as the examples above:
1   Sylvia is the prettiest girl; she is _____ all the other girls.
2   Elephants are bigger than all other animals; they are _____ animals.
3   Fred is the fastest runner; he is _____ all the other runners.
4   That house is bigger than all the other houses; it is _____ house.
5   Fiona is fatter than all the other girls; she is _____ girl.
6   This is the tallest tree; it is _____ all the other trees.

Notice the irregular forms:
**good, better than, the best;**
**bad, worse than, the worst.**

# Adjectives

*Use these forms in the following:*

7 Tina is a very good student. In fact she is _____ student; she is _____ all the other students.

8 The cowboy film was very bad. It was _____ all the other films; in fact it was _____ film of all.

## 31 Comparatives: **more**; superlatives: **most**

### a more...than, the most...

*Look at these sentences and notice the difference in use between* **more expensive than** *and* **the most expensive:**

This car is **more expensive than** all the other cars; it is **the most expensive**.
This is **the most expensive** car; it is **more expensive than** all the other cars.

*Notice that we say* **the most expensive** *but just* **more expensive**.

*Complete the following in the same way as the examples above:*

1 Sylvia is _____ intelligent girl; she is _____ the other girls.
2 This exercise is _____ the other exercises; it is _____ difficult.
3 Mrs Johnson was _____ interesting speaker; she was _____ all the other speakers.
4 This machine is _____ efficient _____ all the other machines; it is _____ .

### b much, more

*Look at these sentences:*

A Do you eat **much** butter?/Do you eat **a lot of** butter?
B No, we eat **more** margarine **than** butter.

There are **many/a lot of** cinemas in Manchester, but there are **more** in London.

**More** is the comparative form for **much** and **many**; it can also correspond to **a lot (of)**.

*Complete the following with* **more** *or* **than** *or* **more than**:

1 A Have you had much trouble at school recently?
  B Yes, in fact this year we've had _____ last year.
2 A I see that you have a lot of birds in your garden.
  B Yes, and there are even _____ here in the spring.
3 _____ men _____ women have serious car accidents.
4 Fred smokes a lot, but Tony smokes even _____ .

## Adjectives

### c  most of us/you/them

*Look at this sentence:*

There weren't enough seats for all of us, but **most of us** managed to sit down.

We can use **most** to mean 'the majority' (more than 50%) in phrases like **most of us, most of you, most of them.**

*Put one of these three phrases in each of the following:*
1. We can't all swim but _____ can.
2. Some of you will perhaps fail the exam, but _____ will pass.
3. A few of the students are boys, but _____ are girls.

### d  Comparatives: more; superlatives: most, more...than, the most...

*Look at this example of how* **more** *is always used when making a comparison between two people or things, with* **than** *if the other people or things are mentioned, while* **the most** *indicates that one person or thing is exceptional:*

Bruce Springsteen is **the most** popular singer who has come here. Young people here buy **more** of his records **than** of any other artist. The concert he gave last month was one of **the most** successful we have ever had.

*Complete the passage with* **more, most** *or* **than:**

When I was young the _____ popular singer in the world was Bing Crosby. _____ records of *White Christmas* were sold _____ of any other song. Apparently, he made _____ recordings in a session _____ other singers because he was _____ experienced, and never had to sing the song again. He was the _____ relaxed of all artists.
He also took part in the _____ successful comedy films of those days with Bob Hope. Hope had _____ amusing lines _____ Crosby but Crosby always had the _____ romantic part, and finished up with the girl. Perhaps the _____ surprising thing about his career was that he won the Oscar for the best actor one year in the part of a priest, because he was always _____ famous as a singer _____ as an actor.

## 32  Position of adjectives

### a  *Compare these sentences:*

Their car is **expensive**. They have an **expensive car**.
His hands are **dirty**. He has **dirty hands**.

When we use an adjective (**expensive, dirty**) together with a noun (**car, hands**), the adjective goes before the noun.

## Adjectives

*Complete the following in the same way:*

1. Our flat is small. We have a _____ .
2. His shoes are brown. He has _____ .
3. My family is big. I have a _____ .
4. Her garden is pretty. She has a _____ .
5. His daughter is clever. He has a _____ .

*Notice the word order in the questions:*
**Is their car new?**
**Are those trees old?**

*Now put the words in brackets in the correct order:*

6. *A* Was the _____ ? (book, expensive)
   *B* Yes, it was a very _____ . (book, expensive)
7. *A* Is your _____ ? (English, teacher)
   *B* No, we have a _____ . (Canadian, teacher)
8. *A* They have a _____ . (Japanese, car)
   *B* Is their _____ , as well? (Japanese, television)

b  *Notice that* **(a) few** *comes before adjectives, and that adjectives of size, e.g.* **big, small, long, short,** *etc. go before colour adjectives, e.g.* **big red roses, long green leaves.**

*Now put the words in brackets in the correct order:*

1. Have they got a _____ dog. (big, black)
2. We saw _____ boats. (a few, new)
3. They found a lot of _____ shells. (pink, small)

## 33  Emphasis of adjectives with **so, such**

a  *Compare these sentences:*

That flower is **so** lovely.           That's **such a** lovely flower.
Those flowers are **so** lovely.        Those are **such** lovely flowers.
That food is **so** lovely.             That's **such** lovely food.

We use **such (a)** with an adjective and a noun; we need **a** (or **an**) only with a singular count noun, e.g. **a flower, an ice cream.**

We use **so** with an adjective alone, and we also use **so** with **much** or **many**, e.g. **There were so many flies.**
**There was so much food.**
Here we use **so** to emphasise something.

*Put* **so, such, such a** *or* **such an** *in the following:*

1. She's _____ clever girl.
2. They're _____ clever girls.
3. She's _____ clever.

# Adjectives

4 Roger's got _____ many shirts.
5 Their children are _____ helpful.
6 They're _____ helpful children.
7 There's _____ much dirt on the windows.
8 It was _____ interesting book.

**b** *Look at these sentences:*

They were **such lovely flowers (that)** I took a photo of them.
There were **so many flies (that)** we couldn't have our picnic.

We can continue the sentences with **so** and **such** (with or without **that**) to show what happens as a result.

*Add each of these results to one of the sentences 1-8:*

a (that) they pass all their exams easily.
b (that) you can't see through them.
c (that) I read it in one day.
d (that) he doesn't know which to wear.

## c so...that, such (a/an)...that

*Compare these sentences:*

The organisation is **so big that** it employs a million people.
It's **such a big organisation that** it employs a million people.

The students are **so intelligent that** they hardly need a teacher.
They're **such intelligent students that** they hardly need a teacher.

This bread is **so good that** I could eat it all day.
It's **such good bread that** I could eat it all day.

*Rewrite these sentences, using the alternative form, as in the examples above:*

1 He's such a tall man that he has to have all his clothes specially made.
2 The film was so successful that it ran for two years.
3 The music was so beautiful that I listened to it for hours.
4 The secretaries are so efficient that they could get a job anywhere.
5 She had to go to bed because her headache was so bad.
6 He plays so well that a professional team has offered him a contract.
7 He was such a kind man that she trusted him completely.
8 The weather was so good that we lay on the beach all day.
9 It was such a long journey that they felt tired at the end of it.
10 The owner and his wife were such pleasant people that we've decided to stay there again next year.

Adjectives

## 34 Adjectives with **too, enough**

*Compare these sentences:*

This book is too big { **for** my pocket
**to go** in my pocket.

This book isn't small enough { **for** my pocket.
**to go** in my pocket.

We use **for** when we mention the person or thing alone, e.g. **my pocket**.
We use **to** when there is a verb, e.g. **to go in my pocket**.

*Put* **for** *or* **to** *in the following:*
1  My grandfather is too old _____ walk very far.
2  Are these cases strong enough _____ the long journey?
3  This cupboard isn't big enough _____ hold all my things.
4  This parcel is too big _____ send by post.
5  Is Peter old enough _____ drive a car?
6  These shoes are too expensive _____ me.

# Adverbs

## 35 Adverbs that end with -ly

*Look at these sentences:*

She is a **quick** worker. (adjective)
She works **quickly**. (adverb)

To an adjective, e.g. **quick,** we can often add **-ly** to make an adverb, e.g. **quickly.** But note the common exceptions:

| Adjective | Adverb |
|---|---|
| good | well |
| fast | fast |
| hard | hard |

Note also the change of **y** to **i** in **pretty - prettily, happy - happily,** etc.

*Complete the following with either an adjective or an adverb:*

e.g. She has a loud voice; she talks **loudly.**
1  They are hard workers; they work _____ .
2  It's a _____ train; it goes very fast.
3  They are happy children; they play _____ together.
4  She was wearing a pretty dress; she was dressed very _____ .
5  He did a bad job. In fact, he did the job very _____ .
6  She's got a sweet voice; she sings very _____ .
7  He's a slow worker; he works very _____ .
8  The car is in its _____ place; I usually park it there.
9  She's a _____ painter; she paints very well.
10  They're good singers; they sing very _____ .

Note that **well** ('in good health') is an adjective,
e.g. A  **How's your mother?**
     B  **She's very well, thank you.**

## 36 Comparison of adverbs

Adverbs ending in **-ly** can make the comparative with more:
e.g. **Fred worked as quickly as I did.**
     **Fred and I worked more quickly than anyone else.**

*Complete these sentences using a form of the word in brackets:*

1  These days Albert is writing _____ than he did when he was young. (careful)
2  Nobody can tell jokes as _____ as Peter. (amusing)
3  Rubens painted _____ than other painters. (accurate)
4  No one deals with difficult customers more _____ than Mrs Beverley. (polite)

*Adverbs*

### b Comparatives: adverbs

*Note the irregular forms:*

| | |
|---|---|
| well | better than |
| badly | worse than |
| much | more than |
| little | less than |
| fast | faster than |
| hard | harder than |
| far | further than |

The regular forms are formed with **-ly** (careful, more carefully)

*Complete the sentences with an appropriate comparative form:*

1  I did not play badly, but Jack won because he played _____ me.
2  I don't earn much money. My boss earns a lot _____ me. He says he earns _____ because he works _____ .
3  She won the race because she ran _____ the other girls.
4  My stomach hurts _____ it did yesterday, probably because I have eaten _____ , but this medicine tastes _____ the other one. It's horrible!
5  We had a competition to see how far we could walk in an hour. Susan walked _____ me because she has longer legs and walks _____ .

### c like most/best

*Notice the use of* **most** *or* **best** *with a verb:*

John has many hobbies, but he **likes** tennis **most.**
My parents like all kinds of food, but they **like** fish **best.**

We can also say this in a different way:

John has many hobbies, but **what he likes most** is tennis.
My parents like all kinds of food, but **what they like best** is fish.

*Complete the following sentences in a similar way:*

1  My brothers listen to all kinds of music, but _____ is jazz.
2  Mrs Lawson watches lots of different sports, but _____ is football.
3  I like all sorts of food, but _____ is Indian curry.
4  Ted plays several instruments, but _____ is the piano.

## 37  already, yet

*Look at these sentences:*

A  Has the plane left **yet**?
B  Yes, it left two hours ago.

My little boy is only four, but he has **already** started school.

# Adverbs

**Already** and **yet** mean 'before now'.
We normally use **already** in positive statements (compare **yet**). It goes after **am, is, are, was** and **were**,
e.g. **Mrs Jones is already here.**

With compound verbs (auxiliary verb + participle), **already** goes between the auxiliary (e.g. **has, is**) and the participle (e.g. **written, waiting**),
e.g. **Mrs Jones has already arrived.**
   **Those boys are already making trouble.**

With simple verbs, **already** goes before the verb,
e.g. **Lucy has only been in Spain for two months, but she already speaks good Spanish.**

**Yet** usually goes at the end of the sentence, and it is normally found only in questions and negative statements (compare **already**),
e.g. A   Has Mrs Jones arrived yet?
   B   No, not yet.
   **Mrs Jones hasn't arrived yet.**

Put **already** or **yet** in the correct place in the sentences below:
1   Your friends are in the hall.
2   The 8 o'clock train hasn't come.
3   It's only 10 o'clock but they've prepared lunch.
4   Has the boss come back?
5   Haven't you written those letters?
6   My mother has bought all her Christmas presents.

# 38   still

a   *Look at these sentences:*

Ten years ago Charlie was living in Bristol. He hasn't moved; he **still** lives there.
Five years ago Olive was interested in jazz. She hasn't changed; she is **still** interested in jazz.

**Still** says that something is the same as before.
**Still** usually goes after **am, is, are, was, were**,
e.g. **She is still ill.**

With compound verbs (auxiliary + participle) **still** goes between the auxiliary **(is, are)** and the participle **(raining, sitting)**,
e.g. **It is still raining.**

With simple verbs, **still** goes before the verb,
e.g. **He still lives there.**

Adverbs

*Complete the sentences in the same way as the examples above:*

1 Kay was a good chess player when she was young. Nothing has changed. She _____ a good player.
2 Years ago Kim liked cowboy films. He hasn't changed. He _____ cowboy films.
3 When he was a boy, Alan was a good photographer. He hasn't changed. He _____ a good photographer.
4 Years ago Chris painted very well. Nothing has changed. She _____ very well.

**b** Look at these sentences:

He **still doesn't** play.
I **still haven't** seen her.
Sam **still can't** type.

**Still** goes before a negative auxiliary (**don't, hasn't**).

*Complete these sentences with **still** and a suitable negative auxiliary:*

e.g. I didn't read the newspaper this morning, and I **still haven't** read it.
1 Sheila didn't work hard at school, and she _____ work hard.
2 Kay couldn't ski well last winter, and she _____ ski well.
3 I didn't see the exhibition last month, and in fact I _____ seen it.
4 When they were young the children didn't like the dark, and they _____ like it.

# 39  very, much

*Compare these sentences:*

An Alfa Romeo is **very** expensive.
A Rolls Royce is **much** more expensive than an Alfa Romeo.

We can use **very** (but not **much**) with the base form of adjectives and adverbs, e.g. **very good, very expensive, very slowly.**

We can use **much** (but not **very**) with the comparatives of adjectives and adverbs, e.g. **much better, much more expensive, much more slowly** (or **much slower**).

*Put **very** or **much** in these sentences:*

e.g. He walks **much** more slowly than he used to.
He plays football **very** well.
1 They think the film was _____ interesting.
2 Is this flat _____ smaller than yours?
3 Stella was driving _____ fast.
4 She was driving _____ faster than I was.

Adverbs

## 40 once, twice, three times etc.

Look at these sentences:

I usually eat meat **once** a day, in the evening.
He goes on holiday **twice** a year, at Christmas and in the summer.
I telephoned him **five times** last weekend but he was never in.

Note that we usually say **once** for 'one time' and **twice** for 'two times'.

Look at the sentences and table below:

The following four people have difficult illnesses; they must take medicine, have injections, and also go to the doctor's regularly.

|  | Doctor | Medicine | Injections. |
|---|---|---|---|
| Mr Jackson | 1/ week | 2/ day | 3/ week |
| Mrs Thomas | 1/ month | 3/ day | 1/ day |
| Miss Bloom | 2/ month | 4/ day | 2/ week |
| Mr Potter | 1/ week | 1/ day | 6/ week |

Mr Jackson must go to the doctor's **once a week**.
He must take medicine **twice a day**.
He must have injections **three times a week**.

Complete the following, using the information in the table:

1 Mrs Thomas must go to the doctor's _____ .
2 She must take medicine _____ .
3 She must have injections _____ .
4 Miss Bloom must go to the doctor's _____ .
5 She must take medicine _____ .
6 She must have injections _____ .
7 Mr Potter must go to the doctor's _____ .
8 He must take medicine _____ .
9 He must have injections _____ .

## 41 Frequency adverbs; first, last, just

a Notice the position of the frequency adverbs in these sentences:

A Is he **ever** on time? }
B No, he is **always** late. } (after **am, is, are, was, were**)

A Does she **often** work overtime? } (before the main verb: **work, goes**,
B No, she **usually** goes home at 5.00. } etc.)

85

*Adverbs*

    A  Have they **ever** eaten curry?     } (before the main verb, here the
    B  No, they have **never** eaten Indian food. } the past participle **eaten**)

The most common frequency adverbs are: **always, usually, normally, generally, often, frequently, sometimes, seldom, rarely** and **never**. **Ever** is used in questions.

*Put the adverb in brackets in the correct position in the following:*

1  A  Do you work at the weekend? (ever)
    B  Yes, I work on Saturdays. (sometimes)
2  Paul was ill when he was young. (rarely)
3  They have given noisy parties. (frequently)
4  Mr Watson takes his dog for a walk after dinner. (usually)
5  We are interested in new ideas. (always)
6  They have dinner quite late. (normally)
7  I stay in bed late. (never)
8  Do you see Ron at work? (often)

## b  first, last

*Notice the position of* **first** *in the question and the answer:*

    A  When did you **first** hear about the fire?
    B  I **first** heard about the fire yesterday morning.

**First,** which means 'the first time', and **last,** which means 'the last time', go in the same position as frequency adverbs. These two words go with the Past Simple.

*Put* **first** *or* **last** *in the correct position in the following:*

1  A  When did you meet Polly? (first)
    B  I met her in 1976. (first)
2  A  When did you see your brother? (last)
    B  I saw him a month ago. (last)
3  A  When did Barry go to Italy? (first)
    B  He went to Italy when he was a student. (first)
4  A  When did you have a headache? (last)
    B  I had a headache on Friday. (last)

## c  just

**Just** also goes in this position,
e.g. **Have you just started?**
      **No, we are just finishing.**

**Just** means 'at this moment' in these sentences. With this meaning it is not used with the present simple or past simple tenses.

*Adverbs*

*Put* **just** *in the right place in the following sentences:*
1   She has set off for the station.
2   What have they decided?
3   I was going to help you.

**Just** means 'at this moment' in these sentences. With this meaning it is not used with the present simple or past simple tenses.

# Prepositional phrases

## 42 Prepositions of position

a *Notice the prepositions in this sentence:*

I've left all my money **at** home **on** the table **in** the kitchen.

When we are talking about the position of somebody or something: we use **in** for a volume, e.g. **in a shop, in a factory, in a room, in a house, in a cinema, in a car, in the air**, and also for an area, e.g. **in a town, in London, in a village, in the country, in a garden.**
Note also: **in the south, in the north,** etc. and **in the class, in the group.**

The opposite is usually **outside**, e.g. **outside a shop, outside the cinema.**

We use **on** for a surface or line, e.g. **on a table, on the floor, on a wall, on a roof, on a line, on the coast.** We also use **on** for: **on a bus, on a bike, on a train, on holiday, on the left, on the right.**

We use **at** for other cases, e.g. **at home, at school, at work, at the bus stop, at the station.**

*Put one of these prepositions in each of the spaces:*

1. She works _____ a big shop _____ Bristol.
2. There's a book _____ the floor. Put it _____ the table.
3. I often see Mrs Price _____ the station, waiting for her train.
4. Brighton is _____ the coast _____ the south of England.
5. My daughter isn't _____ work today; she has stayed _____ home because she doesn't feel well.
6. There were several people _____ the bus stop.
7. Mr and Mrs Briggs were _____ the shop, talking to the assistant; their children were waiting _____ the car that was standing _____ the shop.
8. Yesterday we spent the day _____ the country; we had lunch _____ a pretty little village.
9. When I was _____ the bus this morning, I saw two boys _____ the church roof.
10. The children are playing _____ their bikes _____ the park.
11. There are only 12 students _____ my class. The girl who sits _____ the left of me is from Spain; the boy who sits _____ my right is a Dane.
12. My mother teaches _____ a school _____ Oxford.

*Prepositional phrases*

**b** *Look at the drawing and read the text that goes with it.*

This is a picture of a small town. The church is **opposite** the bank. The bookshop is **between** the bank and the post office. There is a woman **in front of** the bank, and there is a dog **beside** her. There is a van **behind** the post office, and a man is working **under** the van. There is a bird **on top of** the church. **Near** (or **Not far from**) the church there is a bridge over the river.

*Now put in the correct preposition in the sentences below:*

1. There is a car _____ the post office.
2. A bird is flying _____ the church.
3. The church is _____ the school and the park.
4. The post office is _____ the park.
5. There is a tree _____ the bank.
6. The bookshop is _____ the bank.
7. There is a flag _____ the school.
8. A boat is going _____ the bridge.

*Prepositional phrases*

c   Prepositions and adverbs: **in, out (of), on, off, into, onto**.

**In, into** and **out (of)** relate to volumes, e.g. **in the room, in the box, in his mouth; into the room, into the box, into his mouth; out of the room, out of the box, out of his mouth.**

Note that we say **in the air, in the water, in the mountains.**

**On, onto** and **off** relate to surfaces and lines, e.g. **on the table, on the planet, on the floor; onto the table, onto the planet, onto the floor; off the table, off the planet, off the floor.**

Note that we say **on Earth, on an island, on the coast.**

**In** is the opposite of **out (of); on** is the opposite of **off,** e.g. If it's **in** your pocket, take it **out (of** your pocket.) If it's **on** the table, take it **off** the table.

**Into** and **onto** and **out of** are used for movement only,
e.g. They moved the chairs **into** the room.
   They moved the books **onto** the table.
   They moved the chairs **out of** the room.

*Complete the following sentences with* **in, out (of), on, off, into, onto**:

1   The bread is _____ the table _____ the kitchen.
2   He lives _____ that house, _____ the second floor.
3   They took the chairs _____ the rooms and carried them _____ the garden.
4   The Mars expedition spent 23 days _____ the rocket; they stayed _____ the planet for almost a week.
5   This tooth is bad. It mustn't stay _____ your mouth a moment longer; we must take it _____ straightaway.
6   They managed to live _____ a hut _____ an island for almost a year.
7   It wasn't difficult getting all these things _____ the lorry, so it'll be easy to get them _____ .
8   What are those children doing _____ the roof? Tell them to get _____ immediately.
9   A   Can I speak to Ms Tomlinson, please?
    B   I'm afraid she isn't _____ . She went _____ about half an hour ago.
10  In the old days the trouble with keeping your money _____ the bank was that you couldn't take it _____ at weekends. Now you can get money _____ a cash dispenser at any time.
11  There are stones _____ the track; we must get them _____ before the train comes.
12  When we went _____ the caves, it was raining, but by the time we came _____ , the weather was much brighter.

# 43 Prepositions of movement

a *Notice the prepositions in this sentence:*

You can easily go **by** car **from** Italy **to** Greece; drive **through** Yugoslavia **along** the Adriatic coast road.

For movement we often use **to**, e.g. **go to school, go to the shops, fly to Canada, drive to work, go to the beach, walk to town, write to your sister, post a letter to a friend.**

The opposite of **to** is **from**, e.g. **We walked from Brighton to Hastings. These flowers are from our garden.** Note also: **I come from Leeds** means 'Leeds is my home town'.

For movement that follows something that is long, we use **along**, e.g. **along the road, along the river, along the coast.**

For movement from one side to the other of, for example, a door or a window, we use **through**, e.g. **through the door, through a window, through a tunnel, through the wood.**

For means of transport, we use **by**, e.g. **by train, by bus, by bike, by plane, by boat,** but notice the phrase **on foot**.

*Put one of these prepositions in each of the spaces:*

1. They go _____ work _____ bus.
2. We walked _____ the road _____ the village because it was too wet to go _____ the wood.
3. In the morning the young couple sailed _____ the coast _____ Torquay _____ Plymouth; in the afternoon they went back _____ Torquay _____ train.
4. Sometimes we can't open the door, and then we have to climb _____ the window.
5. I've written a letter to my cousin. Can you take it _____ the post office, please?
6. I'm not English. I come _____ Scotland.

b **home, at home**

*Compare these sentences:*

A Is Mr Jones **in**? (the house)
B No, I'm afraid he's **out**.
A Is Mr Jones **at home**?
B No, I'm afraid he's **not at home**.

**At** is the only preposition used with **home**.

*Prepositional phrases*

No preposition is used with verbs of movement,
e.g. **A  What time did he arrive home?**
(What time did he arrive at his house?)
  **B  He got home at ten o'clock,**
(He got to his house at ten o'clock.)

*Complete the sentences with the appropriate preposition, when one is required:*
1  If I stayed _____ home all day, like you, I'd be bored.
2  When you invite people _____ the house, you must be polite.
3  When you invite people _____ home, you must be polite.
4  Come _____ home with me.
5  The President drove back _____ the White House.
6  I called _____ his house and knocked at the door but there was no one _____ home.
7  When I arrived _____ home, my son and daughter were both _____ .

# 44  Prepositions of time

a  *Notice the prepositions in this sentence*:
President Kennedy died **in** 1963. He was shot at 12.30p.m. **on** Monday the 22nd November.

We use on with days, e.g. **on Monday, on Monday afternoon** (but **in the afternoon**), **on Christmas Eve, on your birthday, on 5th September.**
Note that we do not use **on** with **next, this** or **last: next Saturday, this Thursday, last Friday.**

We use **in** for months, e.g. **in June**, for seasons, e.g. **in summer** or **in the summer**, and for years, e.g. **in 1987.**
Note also: **in the morning, in the afternoon, in the evening,** (but **on Monday morning, on Wednesday afternoon,** etc.)

*Put one of these prepositions in each space if one is necessary:*
1  Sara was born _____ 2 o'clock _____ 17th July.
2  She was born _____ 1979.
3  Our daughter came to see us _____ last Friday, and she's going back to university _____ next Saturday.
4  We often go for a drive _____ Saturday. We leave home early _____ the morning, and we come back late _____ the evening.
5  My birthday is _____ May, and my wife's is _____ Christmas Day.
6  I sometimes have to work _____ night.

*Prepositional phrases*

7   I often see her _____ the morning, but Jack met her _____ last Saturday afternoon.
8   We will leave _____ Tuesday morning _____ 6 o'clock; we will probably catch the boat early _____ Wednesday and get to London _____ the evening.

**b**   *Look at the clocks and the times:*

1   three o'clock     2   half past six     3   quarter to ten     4   quarter past five

Now write the time that goes with each clock:

1 _____
2 _____
3 _____
4 _____

# 45   Prepositional verbs

*Compare these sentences:*

Everyone was **talking** loudly.
I **talked to** some nice people at the party.

We can use the verbs **look, talk, listen** and **wait** without an object,
e.g. **He was looking.**
   **They talked.**
   **They are listening carefully.**
   **We waited a long time.**

But if these verbs have an object, then they must have a preposition:
**look at something, talk to someone, talk about something, listen to someone, wait for something,**
e.g **He was looking at the stars.**
   **They talked to everybody.**
   **They are listening carefully to the story.**
   **We waited a long time for the bus.**

93

*Prepositional phrases*

Note that **ask someone, tell someone** and **visit someone** do not have a preposition before the object.

*Put a preposition in each space if one is necessary:*
1. A  Are they still talking _____ ?
   B  Yes, they are talking _____ the football match.
2. A  Why is she waiting _____ ?
   B  I don't know. I think she's waiting _____ her husband.
3. Wait a moment. I'm just looking _____ these pictures.
4. We visited _____ our grandparents last weekend.
5. A  Did you talk _____ the manager?
   B  Yes, I asked _____ him for more money.
6. Tell _____ Florence that I'm in a hurry.
7. A  Was Marjory listening _____ her records?
   B  No, she was looking _____ her stamp collection.
8. We talked _____ a very nice young girl while we were waiting _____ the train.

# 46  until, as far as

*Notice the use of* **until** *and* **as far as** *in these sentences:*
I won't be able to finish it **until** the end of the month.
Go **as far as** the station and then turn right.
**Until** relates to time, **as far as** to distance.

*Use* **until** *or* **as far as** *to complete the following sentences:*
1. The restaurant does not open _____ seven o'clock.
2. We went _____ the castle, but then we felt tired and turned back.
3. We walked _____ we got tired. Then we sat down and had a rest.
4. I don't think you'll get _____ the village before it gets dark.
5. We played tennis _____ it got dark.
6. We could see _____ the sea from the top of the mountain.

# 47  as, like; such...as, such as, like

a  **as** and **like** to describe the way in which actions are done

*Compare these sentences:*
Do **as** I say.
Do it **like** this.
He's been very ill. He walks and talks **like** an old man.
**As** I said last week, we must do something about the rubbish in our streets.

We use **as** + clause (subject and verb) and **like** + noun, pronoun or adverb.

## Prepositional phrases

*Complete these sentences with* **as** *or* **like**:

1. A  I can't understand why he behaved _____ that.
   B  Well, you never know if people are going to behave _____ you expect them to.
2. You should pay attention to the teacher, _____ me.
3. You should pay attention to the teacher, _____ the rest of us do.
4. _____ I was saying, he stays in bed all morning, just _____ his father. If I'd known he was going to grow up _____ that, I wouldn't have let him do _____ he liked when he was younger. _____ you know, I've always been soft with him because he's the youngest. I should have brought him up _____ his brothers and sisters.

### b  as a referee, like a monkey

*Compare these sentences:*

He works **as a referee** on Saturday afternoons. (It is his job; he really is a referee.)
He can climb **like a monkey**. (but he isn't a monkey)

We use **to work as** or **to have a job as** to talk about someone's actual job, profession or social position.

When we say X is **like** something or someone, we mean that X is similar to that thing or that person.

*Complete these sentences with* **as** *or* **like**:

1. I worked _____ a waiter during the summer holidays. It was awful. We had to work _____ slaves and some of the customers treated us _____ dirt.
2. A  He's hoping to get a job _____ a racing driver.
   B  Well, he'll be better _____ a Grand Prix driver than he is on the road. He drives _____ a lunatic.
3. A  I don't think you should marry him, Kathy. I don't want to interfere; I'm speaking _____ a friend.
   B  Well, you talk _____ my father.
4. A  He works _____ a lorry driver.
   B  Does he? Well, the only thing I know about him is that he eats _____ a horse and drinks _____ a fish.
5. He started collecting stamps _____ a hobby but he's since developed it _____ a full-time job. It's the only thing he does.

### c  such . . . as, such as, like

**Such as** and **like** can be used to mean 'of the same kind as', usually when giving an example. The word order can be varied with **such . . . as**.

*Prepositional phrases*

*Look at these examples:*

People **like/such as** my aunt Elizabeth are very fussy about food.
**Such** people **as** my aunt Elizabeth are very fussy about food.
They **came** back from their holiday with typical souvenirs, **like/such as** Mexican hats and guitars.
They came back from their holiday with **such** typical souvenirs **as** Mexican hats and guitars.

*Rewrite the following sentences, using* **like** *or* **such . . . as:**

1. He has stayed at such expensive hotels as the Ritz and the Savoy.
2. Such well-known actresses as Sofia Loren and Joan Collins advertise products on TV.
3. They're arguing about things like the taxes and the cost of living.
4. I don't want to invite such strange people as Tony and Angela.
5. You're lucky to have neighbours like the Browns.

# Modals and auxiliaries

## 48 can

Look at these sentences:

I'm good at running. I **can** run 100 metres in only 12.5 seconds.
I'm not a good long-jumper. I **can't** jump more than 3 metres 90.

The negative of **can** is **can't** or **cannot**.

Look at the passage and table below:

Maria, Peter, Sally and Joe are teenagers who are interested in athletics, especially running and jumping. These are their best times and distances this year.

|  | **Running** | **Running** | **Jumping** |
|---|---|---|---|
|  | 100 metres | 800 metres | Long jump |
| Maria | 14.5 secs | 2 mins 15 secs | 5 metres 30 cm |
| Peter | 13.0 " | 2 " 50 " | 4 " 90 " |
| Sally | 13.5 " | 2 " 30 " | 5 " 20 " |
| Joe | 15.5 " | 2 " 20 " | 5 " 50 " |

Maria **can** run 100 metres in 14.5 seconds, but Joe **can't**.
Peter **can't** jump 5 metres 20, but Sally **can**.
Peter **can** run 800 metres in 2 minutes 50, but Joe **can't**.

Notice that in **5 metres 20** we do not need to say 'centimetres', and in **2 minutes 50** we do not need to say 'seconds'.

Complete the following, using the information in the table:
1. Joe _____ 100 metres in 14.5 seconds, but Maria _____ .
2. Sally _____ 800 metres in 2 mins 30 but Peter _____ .
3. Joe _____ 100 metres in 13 seconds, but Peter _____ .
4. Maria _____ 5 metres 50, but Joe _____ .
5. Sally _____ 100 metres in 13.5 seconds, but Joe _____ .
6. Joe _____ 800 metres in 2 minutes 20, but Sally _____ .
7. Maria _____ 100 metres in 13.5 seconds, but Sally _____ .
8. Peter _____ 5 metres 30, but Maria _____ .

*Modals and auxiliaries*

## 49 can, will be able to

*Compare these sentences:*

**Can** I have an ice-cream please?
**Will** your grandfather **be able to** climb the stairs?
**Can** you come/**will** you **be able to** come to my party next week?

In the first sentence, the speaker is asking for permission. In the second sentence, the speaker asks if it will be possible for the old man to climb the stairs. We also use **can** for present possibility, and sometimes future possibility as in the third sentence.

*Look at this dialogue:*

Terry broke his leg playing football yesterday. Now he is in hospital and his leg is in plaster.

*Terry*   Can I get up this afternoon?
*Doctor*  Of course you **can't**.
*Terry*   **Can** my friends come to see me?
*Doctor*  Yes, they **can** come this evening.
*Terry*   When **will** I **be able to** get up?
*Doctor*  Quite soon. You **won't be able to** walk immediately but you'll **be able to** go round on crutches.

*Complete these dialogues with* **can, can't** *or* **will/won't be able to** *and a main verb. The first letter of each main verb is given:*

a   Terry is talking to the doctor.

*Terry*   __1__ I t__1__ the radio on?
*Doctor*  Yes, of course you __2__ .
*Terry*   __3__ I g__3__ downstairs and watch the football match on TV?
*Doctor*  No, I'm sorry. You __4__ .
*Terry*   __5__ my girlfriend c__5__ to see me this evening?
*Doctor*  Yes, she __6__ .
*Terry*   __7__ she s__7__ the night here?
*Doctor*  Of course she __8__ . This is a hospital, not a hotel.
*Terry*   When __9__ I w__9__ ?
*Doctor*  I don't know yet. I __10__ t__10__ you when we take the plaster off.

Modals and auxiliaries

b  Terry is talking to his girlfriend Karen.

Karen  Hello, Terry. __1__ I w__1__ my name on your plaster?
Terry  You __2__ if you like.
Karen  When are they going to take it off?
Terry  The doctor thinks they __3__ t__3__ it off next week. But I __4__ p__4__ football again for two months.
Karen  Oh! __5__ you d__5__ ? There's a dance at the club next weekend.
Terry  Of course I __6__ d__6__ ! I can't walk yet, so I __7__ d__7__ , __7__ I?
Karen  Oh. __8__ I g__8__ to the dance without you?
Terry  With Johnny Bradshaw? No, you __9__ .
Karen  That's not fair. You say I __10__ d__10__ because you've got a broken leg. You're selfish.
Terry  All right, Karen. You __11__ g__11__ to the dance. But I __12__ g__12__ too, because the doctor says I __13__ w__13__ on my crutches. So I __14__ t__14__ you to the dance and w__14__ you dancing, and if Johnny Bradshaw dances too close, I __15__ h__15__ him with my crutch, __15__ I?

# 50  could

*Look at this sentence:*

I **couldn't** ride a bicycle when I was six, but now I can.

The Past tense of **can** is **could**.

*Look at the passage and table below:*

Maria, Peter, Sally and Joe are teenagers who are interested in athletics, especially running and jumping. They are all better this year than last year. Here are their best times and distances for this year and last year.

*Modals and auxiliaries*

|  | Running | Running | Jumping |
|---|---|---|---|
|  | 100 metres | 800 metres | Long Jump |
| Maria | last year 15.5 secs | 2 mins 40 secs | 5 metres 10 cm |
|  | this year 14.5 " | 2 " 15 " | 5 " 30 " |
| Peter | last year 13.5 " | 3 " 05 " | 4 " 40 " |
|  | this year 13.0 " | 2 " 50 " | 4 " 90 " |
| Sally | last year 14.0 " | 2 " 40 " | 5 " 00 " |
|  | this year 13.5 " | 2 " 30 " | 5 " 20 " |
| Joe | last year 17.0 " | 2 " 50 " | 5 " 30 " |
|  | this year 15.5 " | 2 " 20 " | 5 " 50 " |

Last year Maria **could** run 100 metres in 15.5 seconds; now she can run it in 14.5 seconds.

Last year Peter **couldn't** jump 4 metres 90, but now he can.

Last year Joe **could** run 800 metres in 2 minutes 50, but now he can run it in 2 minutes 20.

Notice that in **4 metres 90** we do not need to say 'centimetres', and in **2 minutes 50** we do not need to say 'seconds'.

Complete the following, using the information in the table:

1. Last year Sally _____ 5 metres; now she _____ 5 metres 20.
2. Last year Joe _____ 100 metres in 15.5 seconds, but now he _____.
3. Last year Maria _____ 5 metres 10; now she _____ 5 metres 30.
4. Last year Peter _____ 100 metres in 13 seconds, but now he _____.
5. Last year Sally _____ 800 metres in 2 minutes 40; now she _____ it in 2 minutes 30.
6. Last year Joe _____ 5 metres 50, but now he _____.

# 51 may, might

Notice the use of **may** and **might** in these sentences:

Roger and Carol are at the casino.

*Roger*   I'm going to bet on the red. It **may** win. (Perhaps it will win – the chances are about 50/50.)

*Carol*   But it **may not**. The black **may** win. I'm going to bet on one of the numbers, number 11.

*Roger*   Then you're almost certain to lose. You have only one chance in 36.

*Carol*   I might not. Number 11 **might** win. (It's possible, but unlikely.)

*Modals and auxiliaries*

Note that **can** is only used for possibility when we are talking about what is possible at all times, not one particular time,
e.g. **Accidents can happen,**

But in giving a particular person advice, whether or not he is driving at the time, we would say,
e.g. **Drive carefully, You may (might) have an accident,**

Complete these sentences with **may (not)** or **might (not)**. Choose **might (not)** if you think the possibility is more remote:

Mr Pryor, an insurance salesman, knocks on Adam's door one morning, trying to sell insurance.

*Mr Pryor* Good morning. I represent the Beacon Insurance Company. You ___1___ be fully insured, so I'd like to talk to you about our policies.
*Adam* Well, I'm not insured, actually.
*Mr Pryor* Ah, well, you _may_ be sorry about that one day. For instance, your wife and children _may_ be left in difficult circumstances.
*Adam* But I'm not married.
*Mr Pryor* But you're still young, sir. You _may_ get married quite soon. You _might_ even meet the lady on your way to work this morning.
*Adam* Well, I _might_, but it's not very likely, is it? On the other hand, I _may_ miss my train if I stand here talking to you.
*Mr Pryor* You _may_ be sorry if you don't sir. You say this flat isn't insured?
*Adam* Well, no, it isn't.
*Mr Pryor* Good heavens: Thieves ___9___ break in while you're out. They ___10___ even break in today. Of course, they _might not_, but it's better to be safe than sorry.
*Adam* Well, you _might_ be right. I'd better take your telephone number.
*Mr Pryor* I'd rather make an appointment to see you, sir. I travel a lot in my job, so I _may not_ be at the office when you ring.

## 52 **must** and **need to**

### a **must**

*Look at these sentences:*

I've got toothache. I **must** go to the dentist.
In England, you **must** drive on the left-hand side of the road.

Remember, do not use **to** after **must**.

## Modals and auxiliaries

Look at this. It's your diary for the week. Today is Sunday 21st April.

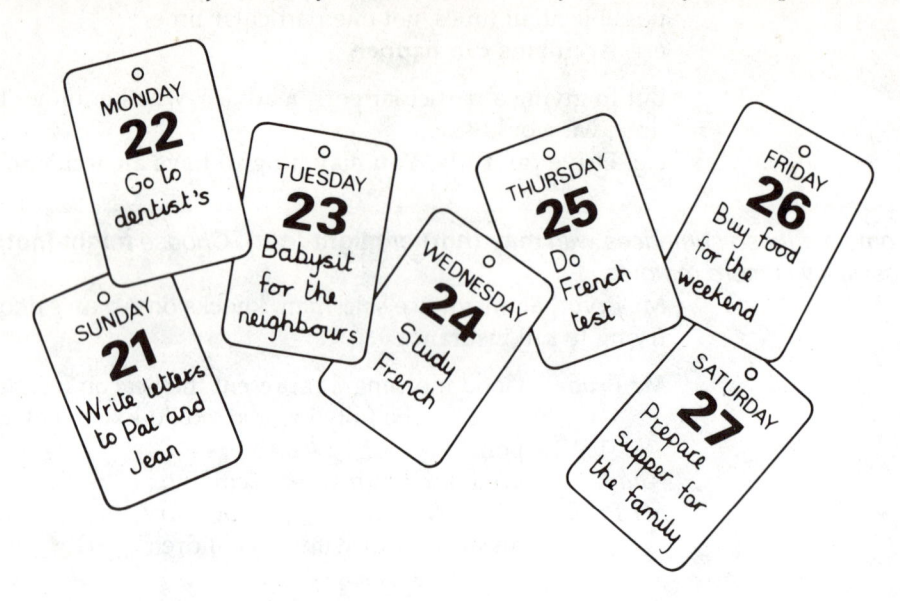

**MONDAY 22** Go to dentist's
**TUESDAY 23** Babysit for the neighbours
**WEDNESDAY 24** Study French
**THURSDAY 25** Do French test
**FRIDAY 26** Buy food for the weekend
**SATURDAY 27** Prepare supper for the family
**SUNDAY 21** Write letters to Pat and Jean

*Write down the things that you must do this week:*

    e.g. Today I **must write** letters to Pat and Jean.
1  Tomorrow I _____ to the dentist's.
2  On Tuesday I _____ for the neighbours.
3  On Wednesday I _____ French.
4  On Thursday I _____ the French test.
5  On Friday I _____ food for the weekend.
6  On Saturday _____ supper for the family.
    And on Sunday I can relax!

Questions have **must** in front of the subject,
    e.g. **Must I go to the dentist's tomorrow?**
    **When must I go to the dentist's?**

*Put* **must** *and a subject and a verb in the following:*

    e.g. When **must I do** my French test?
7  What _____ on Tuesday?
8  _____ French on Wednesday?
9  When _____ food for the weekend?
10  _____ supper on Saturday?

## b  need to, don't/doesn't need to, needn't

*Look at these sentences:*

A  I **need to** go to the bank.
B  I've got plenty of money. I **don't need to** go till next week (or: I **needn't** go till next week).

The verb **need** is usually a main verb; it then goes with an object, e.g. He needs some new shoes, or a verb with **to**, e.g. We need to tell everybody. Main verb **need** forms questions and negative with **do**, e.g. Does he need some new shoes?, We don't need to tell everybody.

Occasionally, **need** is used as an auxiliary in a negative sentence; it must then be followed by a verb without **to**, e.g. We needn't tell everybody.

| **Positive Statement** | **Negative Statement** | **Question** |
| --- | --- | --- |
| I need to go | I don't need to go | Do I need to go? |
| She needs to go | She doesn't need to go | Does she need to go? |

*Put the correct form of* **need** *and the appropriate pronoun in these sentences:*

A  I want to go to Mexico. What _____ to do before I go?
B  You _____ to book your aeroplane ticket. You _____ to buy some summer clothes. You _____ to get some travellers' cheques.
A  _____ to get a visa?
B  Oh yes, I forgot that.
A  Do I need to take any special medicines?
B  Well, you _____ to take something for malaria if you're going to the coast. If you're only going to Mexico City, you needn't to.

*Rewrite the following sentences changing* **don't need to** *or* **doesn't need to** *into* **needn't**, *and make any other necessary changes:*

1  Joan doesn't need any new winter clothes.
2  We don't need to phone Mick until tomorrow.
3  Bob doesn't need to bring both his guitars.
4  We don't need any potatoes this week.
5  We don't need to buy any potatoes this week.

## c  must and don't/doesn't need to

*Look at this sentence:*

Fred **must** go but I **don't need to** (go).

We don't need to repeat the second **go**, because we know what the sentence means without it.

There are ten people in an office. Everybody works from Monday to Friday, but on Saturday only five work. These five are different people on different Saturdays. On this list the names <u>underlined</u> are the people who must work next Saturday.

Modals and auxiliaries

**BROWN & PARTRIDGE**
SATURDAY WORKING

| Mr Brown | Mr Walters |
| <u>Miss Partridge</u> | <u>Miss Jenkins</u> |
| Mrs Thomas | <u>Miss Towers</u> |
| <u>Mr Lucas</u> | Mr Proctor |
| Miss Peabody | <u>Mr Bull</u> |

Mr Lucas **must** work next Saturday, but Miss Peabody **doesn't need to**.
Miss Peabody **doesn't need to** work, but Mr Lucas **must**.

Complete the following, using the information above:
1 Mr Brown _____ work, but Miss Jenkins _____ .
2 Mr Bull _____ work, but Mr Walters _____ .
3 Mr Proctor _____ work, but Miss Towers _____ .
4 Miss Partridge _____ work, but Mrs Thomas _____ .

# 53 ✓ must (to express a logical deduction)

## a must

Look at these sentences:
It's getting dark. **It must be about seven o'clock**,
You've been working hard all day. **You must feel tired**,

**Must** (not **have to**) is used when we are almost certain something is true because our logic tells us so.

Use **must** and the words in brackets to make a sentence, as in the example, about each of these sentences:

e.g. Brian has a good job. He's got a big house and an expensive car.
(earn . . . money)
**He must earn a lot of money,**

1 The ashtrays in Colin's house are always full of cigarette ends. (smoke . . . cigarettes)
2 Dora wears different clothes every day. (have . . . clothes).
3 Eric spends every evening in the pub. (drink . . . beer)
4 Flora plays tennis very well. (win . . . matches)
5 Gordon is a translator at the United Nations. He translates for people from different countries. (speak . . . languages)
6 Harry is a car salesman. His firm is very pleased with him. (sell . . . cars)
7 Ingrid goes to cocktail parties every week. (meet . . . people)
8 Julian's car is very big and old. (use . . . petrol)

## b must have

Look at the following:

A He couldn't find it when he arrived at the office.
B He **must have dropped** it on the way.

**Must have** + past participle is the past tense form of **must** when it expresses a logical conclusion about a past action.

The negative is formed with **can't have** (normally Present Perfect) and **couldn't have** (normally Past Simple) + past participle,
e.g. A He says he's lost it.
B He **can't have lost** it. I've only just given it to him.

Read the following and make sentences, using **must have,** as in the example below:

Mrs Cooper has a new cleaning lady. Before she left the house in the morning, Mrs Cooper told Doreen:
'You mustn't smoke, play any records or open the drinks cupboard. And please don't invite your friends in or use the telephone.' When Mrs Cooper came home, Doreen was not there, but the house was in a mess. Doreen had done everything she wasn't allowed to do.
e.g. There were a lot of cigarette ends in the ashtray.
   **She must have smoked** a lot of cigarettes.
1  One of the records was scratched.
2  The whisky bottle was empty.
3  There were four dirty glasses on the table.
4  There were some telephone numbers written down next to the telephone.

## 54 had to

Look at these sentences:

I **must** go to the dentist. My teeth are very bad.
I **had to** go to the dentist seven times last year.

The Past tense of **must** is **had to.**

Look at the diary in Practice 52a:

It is now Sunday 28 April, and you have done all the things that are in the diary. A friend asks you why you didn't go to the club last week.

e.g. A Why didn't you go to the club on Sunday?
   B **Because I had to write letters to Pat and Jean.**

Answer the following in the same way:
1  Why didn't you go to the club on Monday?
2  Why didn't you go to the club on Tuesday?
3  Why didn't you go to the club on Wednesday?

*Modals and auxiliaries*

4 Why didn't you go to the club on Thursday?
5 Why didn't you go to the club on Friday?
6 Why didn't you go to the club yesterday?

## 55 did you have to?

*Notice the verb form in this question:*
   **Did you have to** go to hospital?

*Complete the conversation, using the correct question form* **did you have to;** *put in an appropriate verb where one is not given:*

Bill Lord has just come home from work. He tells his wife, Betty, he's had a terrible day. He's had to deal with one problem after another.

**BETTY**

e.g. What did you have to do?
Did you have to go by car?
1 Where _____ ?
2 Who _____ ?

3 How long _____ ?


4 _____ move it?


5 _____ go back upstairs?
6 What _____ do?


7 _____ go there to collect it?
8 _____ pay a fine?


9 _____ push the car to a garage?
10 How far _____ ?
11 _____ walk back, too?

**BILL**

First I had to visit a customer.
Yes.
To Walton.
Mr Black. But he was busy. So I had to wait.
About half an hour. And after the interview, I went down to the car and there was a policeman there. The car was blocking the entrance.
Yes, but then Mr Black's secretary came down, so I had to leave it. The policeman was very annoyed.
Yes.
I had to see the Advertising Manager. And when I got back, they had taken the car to the car pound.
Yes.
Yes, £20. But that wasn't the end of it. On the way back to the office I ran out of petrol.
No. I left it on the road and walked.

Two miles.
Yes. Four miles altogether. My feet are killing me.

## 56 should

*Look at these sentences:*

A   I really enjoy watching tennis, but I don't often get the chance.
B   You **should** go to Wimbledon. You'll see first-class tennis there.
A   I'd like to play tennis, too, but I don't know where to play.
B   You **should** join a club. Then you can use their tennis courts.

In these examples **you should go, you should join** mean. 'It would be a good idea for you to . . .'

*Look at the passage and timetable below:*

Some young people want to see some of the European Games, but they want to go on the days when there is something that they really like.
This is the timetable for the Games:

| EUROPEAN GAMES | | | |
|---|---|---|---|
| MONDAY<br>TUESDAY<br>WEDNESDAY | Running<br>Boxing<br>Shooting | THURSDAY<br>FRIDAY<br>SATURDAY | Swimming<br>Jumping<br>Diving |

Fred likes diving, so **should** he go on Saturday? Yes, he **should**.
Sara likes jumping, so **should** she go on Saturday? No, she **shouldn't**.
She **should** go on Friday.

*Complete the following, using the information above:*

1 Jim likes jumping, so should he go on Friday? Yes, _____ .
2 Bill likes swimming and diving, so should he go on Tuesday? No, _____ . He _____ .
3 Beryl likes boxing, so should she go on Tuesday? Yes, _____ .
4 Tom likes shooting, so should he go on Thursday? No, _____ . He _____ .
5 Ann likes running and swimming, so should she go on Wednesday? _____ .
6 Tina likes running and jumping, so should she go on Monday and Friday? _____ .

# 57 ought to

*Look at these sentences:*

He's too fat. He **ought to** eat less.
He **ought to** visit his old mother more often.

**Ought** goes with **to** and an infinitive, e.g. **ought to go, ought to pay, ought not to eat.**

**You ought to go** means 'It is your duty to go', or 'I strongly recommend you to go'. Note that it does not mean 'You are obliged to go'.
If you have received a present by post, someone could say to you,
e.g. **You ought to write and thank him/her.**
and this means 'It is your duty to write.'

## Modals and auxiliaries

**Ought to** is something that a doctor often says to a patient,
e.g. **You ought to take more exercise, and you ought not to smoke.**
and this means that the doctor strongly recommends the patient to take more exercise, but warns him that smoking is bad for him.

Put **ought to** or **ought not to** in the following and complete each sentence with one of the suggestions below:

a  eat so much          c  go and see her      e  disturb her
b  smoke so much        d  pay me back         f  eat more

1  You are too thin. You _____ .
2  Tom is too fat. He _____ .
3  I lent John £5 two months ago. He really _____ .
4  Jill is in hospital. We _____ .
5  Mary is preparing for her exams. We _____ .
6  He has a very bad cough, so he _____ .

# 58  must have, should have, ought to have

*Compare these sentences:*

He's late. He **must have missed** the train.
Oh, no! I've missed the train! I **should have/ought to have left** home five minutes earlier.

**Must have** + past participle is the past tense form of **must** when it expresses a logical conclusion about a past action.
**Should have** or **ought to have** + past participle are used when we talk about what we were going to do, or were supposed to do, but for some reason did not do.

1  Read the story below about Harry's Monday morning. Find a reason why different things went wrong, and imagine what Harry said to himself about the things he was supposed to do, using **must have**:

e.g. **I must have forgotten to set the alarm last night.**
I had a terrible morning today. Everything went wrong. First, I was going to get up at 7.00, because a customer was coming to the office at 9.00. But I didn't wake up in time. I suppose I forgot to set the alarm last night. Then I was going to shave. But I couldn't find my razor. I suppose I left it at Jack's yesterday. I intended to catch the 8.00 train, so I ran to the station, but when I got there I hadn't got my season ticket. I suppose I put it in my other jacket. So I was going to buy a ticket, but I hadn't brought my wallet, either. I suppose it was in my other jacket, too. In the end I borrowed some money from a neighbour who was at the station and caught the 8.30 train. I was due to see the customer at 9.00 but when I got to the office he wasn't there. I suppose he thought I wasn't coming.

*2 Now read the story again. Notice the things which Harry intended to do, was going to do, or was due to do but which he didn't do. Write them down, using* **should have** *or* **ought to have***:*
> e.g. **He should have got up at 7.00.**

## 59 shall, will

*Look at these sentences:*
> I **shall/will** clean the car this weekend. (I'll clean the car ...)
> Fred **will** go to his parents' at Christmas. (Fred'll go ...)
> **Shall** we go home now?
> **Will** you visit us again next week?

In statements about the future we can use **will** or **shall** after **I** or **we**,
e.g. **I will go** or **I shall go, we will come** or **we shall come.**

We use **will** after all other subjects, e.g. **you will stay, she will be, they will sing, Peter will go.**
Note that 'll is used for **will** or **shall** except in questions.

In questions we use **shall** with **I** and **we** to make an offer or a suggestion,
e.g. **Shall I open the door for you?**
**What shall we do now?**

These questions with **shall** ask the listener to decide something for the speaker. We use **will** for all other subjects,
e.g. **Will you still be here on Saturday?**
**What will she do if it rains?**

*Put* **will** *or* **shall** *in the following:*
1. Mike _____ be 19 next birthday.
2. A  Where _____ I put the cases?
   B  Put them over there, please.
3. If they give me some more money, I _____ take a holiday.
4. When _____ the dinner be ready, Dad?
5. A  _____ we have a game of cards?
   B  No, let's just watch TV.
6. How many people _____ come, do you think?
7. A  Where _____ you be next year at this time?
   B  I don't know. Perhaps I _____ be in England.
8. If the weather's fine at the weekend, we _____ come and see you.

*Modals and auxiliaries*

## 60 used to

*Compare these sentences:*

I **used to play** tennis,
I often played tennis, but I don't play now.

These sentences are very similar in meaning.
**Used to** always talks about past time, never present time.
**Used to** does not talk about one time in the past, but about something that happened a lot or continued for a long time.

But look at these sentences:
**I often go to Indian restaurants.**
(**Used to** is not possible, because the sentence is in the present.)
**Ten years ago he visited Italy.**
(**Used to** is not possible, because he did not visit Italy again and again, but only once in the past.)

*Rewrite these sentences with* **used to** *only if the meaning remains the same:*
1 Now Larry often writes short stories.
2 My brother played bridge a lot when he was at university.
3 Last summer my uncle and aunt went to Greece.
4 Years ago I swam almost every day.
5 Ron smoked cigarettes when he was a young man.
6 Now Ron almost always smokes a pipe.
7 My mother once met the King when she was a little girl.
8 My cousins spent every summer in the country until they were about 18.
9 I liked jazz a lot when I was a teenager.
10 Ray very often works late.


## 61 had better

*Look at this conversation:*

A I've got a cold.
B Then you**'d better** stay in bed, **hadn't** you?

**You'd better** is short for **you had better**. We use **had better** to say what is a sensible thing to do in a situation. **Had** is the past form of **have**, but **had better** refers to future time.

*Use* **had better** *and a suitable verb to reply to the following and complete the question tags:*
e.g. **You'd better go** to the doctor's, **hadn't** you?
1 A I've got a lot of work to do tomorrow.
   B _____ early, _____ you?
2 A I've got toothache.
   B _____ to the dentist's, _____ you?

3 A I've got a headache.
  B _____ an aspirin, _____ you?
4 A My shoes are dirty.
  B _____ them, _____ you?
5 A We've got no food in the house.
  B _____ shops, _____ we?

# 62 would rather

## a I'd rather

*Notice the use of **I'd rather (I would rather)** in these sentences:*

A Would you like some tea?
B **I'd rather** have coffee, if it's no trouble.

A Would you like an apple?
B **I'd rather** have an orange, if you don't mind.

*1 Make questions and answers in the same way with the following:*

1 wine/beer  2 red wine/white wine  3 a glass of milk/a glass of beer
4 a boiled egg/an omelette  5 strawberries/raspberries

Here is another example of **I'd rather:**
A Would you like to play tennis on Saturday?
B Well, **I'd rather** play on Sunday, if you don't mind.

*2 Make questions and answers in the same way with the following:*

1 go to the theatre with me on Friday (Saturday)
2 go to the circus with me next week (to the zoo)
3 listen to some records (watch the TV)
4 play chess (play cards)
5 ride my motor-bike (sit on the back)

## b Would you rather?

*Notice the question form:*

A **Would you rather** have tea or coffee?
B Tea, please.

*Make questions and answers in the same way with the following:*

1 cheese/cake  2 ice cream/fruit salad  3 boiled potatoes/chips
4 grapefruit/yogurt  5 (listen to) a classical record/a jazz record

*Modals and auxiliaries*

### c  I'd rather not

Notice that we don't need to repeat the main verb after **I'd rather not**:

 A Would you like to play tennis on Saturday?
 B Well, **I'd rather not** (play) if you don't mind. I'd like to watch the football match on TV. How about Sunday?

Make questions and answers in the same way with the following:

1 go to the cinema with me tomorrow — have got to do some work — Wednesday
2 come round for a drink this evening — am very busy — tomorrow
3 watch the game on TV — don't like football much — the play this evening
4 go for a walk — feel tired — playing chess.
5 have lunch with me on Tuesday — have got to go to the dentist — Friday

Note If we make a comparison about what we **would rather have** at any one moment, we say,
e.g. **I'd rather have coffee than tea,**

If we are talking in general terms, we can either use the same form or say,
e.g. **I prefer coffee to tea,**

## 63  Short answers

Note the following short answers to the question:

| Questions | Short answers | |
|---|---|---|
| Are they coming? | Yes, they are. | No, they aren't. |
| Was she happy? | Yes, she was. | No, she wasn't. |
| Can John swim? | Yes, he can. | No, he can't. |
| Could he do it? | Yes, he could. | No, he couldn't. |
| Do they dance? | Yes, they do. | No, they don't. |
| Does she like them? | Yes, she does. | No, she doesn't. |
| Did he stay? | Yes, he did. | No, he didn't. |

Note that in short answers the only possible verb is an auxiliary or a modal, e.g. **can, could, am, is, are, was, were, do, does, did.** (We cannot use a main verb, e.g. **come, swim, dance, like, stay,** in these short answers.)

Complete the following short answers in the same way as above:

1 A Must we go now?
  B Yes, we _____ .
2 A Did they see him?
  B No, they _____ .

3 A Can Fred ski?
  B No, he _____.
4 A Does Linda like you?
  B Of course she _____.
5 A Are you leaving England?
  B Yes, we _____.
6 A Do you know the answer?
  B Yes, I _____.
7 A Could you swim five years ago?
  B No, I _____.
8 A Was he there?
  B No, he _____.
9 A Do the girls live here?
  B Yes, they _____.
10 A Were they playing tennis?
  B No, they _____.

# 64 so do I; I do, too etc.

## a so, too

Compare these sentences:

Chris can ski. Ian can ski, too.
**Ian can, too.**
**So can Ian.**

Instead of the complete sentence **Ian can ski, too** we can say: **Ian can, too** or **So can Ian,** and these mean the same thing.
Look at these other examples:

They've got a colour TV.      **So have** we or **We have, too.**
Fred is in London.            **So is Louise** or **Louise is, too.**
Molly plays chess.            **So does Kay** or **Kay does, too.**
Sally wrote to the paper.     **So did Bill** or **Bill did, too.**

Note that the only verb in these expressions is an auxiliary or a modal, e.g. **can, could, will, would, am, is, are, was, were, have, do, does, did.**

Complete the following, using **so...or ..., too:**
1 Alice can speak German, and _____ her brother.
2 We live in a small flat, and they _____ , _____ .
3 Mother is still in bed, and _____ my sister.
4 Mother is still in bed, and my sister _____ , _____ .
5 Joy went to the match, and Helen _____ , _____ .
6 My wife plays the piano, and _____ her sister.
7 My wife plays the piano, and _____ her sisters.

*Modals and auxiliaries*

    8  Robin was very hungry, and I _____ , _____ .
    9  Robin was very hungry, and we _____ , _____ .
  10  My boss has gone to the festival, and _____ her assistants.

## b  neither/nor, either

*Compare these sentences:*

        Brian can't swim.    Terry can't swim, either.
                                **Terry can't, either.**
                                **Neither can Terry.**
                                **Nor can Terry.**

Instead of the complete sentence **Terry can't swim, either** we can say: **Terry can't, either** or **Neither can Terry** or **Nor can Terry** and these mean the same thing.

*Look at these other examples:*

| | | |
|---|---|---|
| We haven't seen their new car. | { **Neither has Paul**<br>  **Nor has Paul** | or **Paul hasn't either.** |
| Mrs Webb isn't there. | { **Neither is Ray**<br>  **Nor is Ray** | or **Ray isn't either.** |
| Colin doesn't like the book. | { **Neither do we**<br>  **Nor do we** | or **We don't either.** |
| Dick didn't touch it. | { **Neither did I**<br>  **Nor did I** | or **I didn't either.** |

Notice that the only verb in these expressions is an auxiliary, e.g. **can could will, would, am, is, are, was were have do does** did

*Complete the following, using* **neither/nor** ... *or* ..., **either:**
    1  Jack can't speak French, and _____ his sister.
    2  We don't live near the shops, and they _____ , _____ .
    3  Pam isn't in the garden, and _____ your brother.
    4  Pam isn't in the garden, and your brother _____ , _____ .
    5  Nick didn't come to see me, and Mary _____ , _____ .
    6  My husband doesn't play bridge and _____ I.
    7  My husband doesn't play bridge, and _____ our daughter.
    8  Robin wasn't at the dance and Sara _____ , _____ .
    9  Robin wasn't at the dance, and his sisters _____ , _____ .
  10  I haven't said anything, and _____ Bob.

# Verb forms

## 65 Present of be

a   Notice the verb forms in these sentences:
   A   **Are** you English?
   B   No, **I'm** American, but my parents **are** from Scotland. And my husband**'s** Australian.

|                           | Singular |         |       |        |       | Plural  |          |           |
|---------------------------|----------|---------|-------|--------|-------|---------|----------|-----------|
| Full forms                | I am     | you are | he is | she is | it is | we are  | you are  | they are  |
| Short forms               | I'm      | you're  | he's  | she's  | it's  | we're   | you're   | they're   |

We also use **is** with a singular noun, e.g. **the house is, Mary is**.
We use **are** with a plural noun, e.g. **the houses are**, and when the subject is two or more people or things, e.g. **John and Mary are, the dog and the cat are**.

In the following put **am, is** or **are** in the questions; put **I'm, you're, he's, she's, it's, we're** or **they're** in the answers:

1   A   _Are_ you Spanish?
    B   No, _I'm_ from Portugal.
2   A   Where _is_ Peter?
    B   _He is_ in the kitchen
3   A   _are_ we in the right room?
    B   Yes, _we're_ in this class.
4   A   _are_ the girls in bed?
    B   Yes, _they're_ very tired.
5   A   When _are_ you and your husband at home?
    B   _We're_ always at home in the evenings.
6   A   _Is_ Mrs Cross away?
    B   Yes, _she's_ in Paris this week.
7   A   _am_ I ill, doctor?
    B   No, _you're_ perfectly all right.

b   Short answers

Look at these questions and answers:
   A   Are you a doctor?
   B   **Yes, I am**.
   A   Is he a good swimmer?
   B   **No, he's not./No, he isn't**.

You can answer a question with 'Yes' and a short answer. **Yes, I am** here means 'Yes, I am a doctor'. You cannot use short positive forms, (**I'm, you're, he's, she's, we're, they're**) at the end of a sentence. You can answer a question with 'No' and a short answer. **No, he's not** and **No, he isn't** here

115

## Verb forms

mean 'No, he is not a good swimmer'. You can use short negative forms (**isn't, aren't**) at the end of a sentence.

*Complete the short answers below:*

1. A Am I in the first team?
   B Yes, _you are_.
2. A Are my socks dry?
   B No, _they aren't_.
3. A Is Dublin in England?
   B No, _it isn't_.
4. A Are you and your sister Arsenal fans?
   B Yes, _we are_.
5. A Is Mrs Hurst in?
   B Yes, _she is_.
6. A Excuse me. Are we near the station?
   B No, _we aren't_.
7. A Are you a policeman?
   B Yes, _I am_.
8. A Is Brian in the office?
   B No, _he isn't_.

## 66 Noun/verb agreement with be

*Look at these sentences:*

The **girl is** here.
The **girls are** here.

A singular noun goes with a singular verb, and a plural noun goes with a plural verb.

Note that the following are singular: **foot, tooth, man, woman, child, news, everyone, everything, everybody**.

Note that the following are plural: **feet, teeth, men, women, children, scissors, glasses, jeans, pyjamas, trousers, people, police**; and also **the English (people), the Chinese**, etc.

*Put **is** or **are** in the following:*

1. The women _are_ getting on the bus.
2. The news _is_ very interesting.
3. The English _are_ usually fond of tea.
4. Everybody _is_ in the garden.
5. The people _are_ all asleep.
6. Your new trousers _are_ in your bedroom.

7 The children _are_ playing chess.
8 Everything _is_ very expensive.
9 The police _are_ looking for two young girls.
10 His teeth _are_ hurting.
11 There _is_ nobody here. Where _is_ everybody?
12 Where _are_ my pyjamas?

# 67 Present and Past of **be**

*Notice the word order in these statements and questions:*

**I am** right.                              **Am I** right?
**Bristol is** in the west.                  **Is Bristol** in the west?
**Your friends are** coming.                 **Are your friends** coming?
**Terry was** at the match.                  **Was Terry** at the match?
**They were swimming** in the sea.           **Were they swimming** in the sea?

In statements, **am, is, are, was** and **were** go after the subject.
In questions, **am, is, are, was** and **were** go before the subject.

*Put* **am, is, are, was** *or* **were** *and a subject (where necessary) in the following:*

1 A Where _____ studying English?
  B I'm studying at home.
2 A _____ raining?
  B Yes, very hard.
3 A _____ at the meeting?
  B Fanny was, but Gerry wasn't.
4 A How many apples _____ there in the bag?
  B There are four.
5 A _____ the next customer?
  B Yes, you are.
6 A Where _____ at 10 o'clock?
  B I don't know, but she wasn't here.

*Change the following into questions:*

e.g. His grandfather was a farmer.
   **Was his grandfather a farmer?**

7 The visitors were teachers.
8 I am late.
9 The second book was interesting.
10 The red jacket is expensive.
11 Those little cakes are very sweet.
12 The German film was good.

117

*Verb forms*

# 68 Present and Past of **have**

*Notice the different forms of* **have** *in these questions and answers:*

    A  **Have you (got)** any brothers or sisters?
       (**Do you have** any brothers or sisters?)
    B  I **have (got)** two sisters, but I **haven't (got)** any brothers.
    A  **Did you have** breakfast this morning?
    B  Yes, I **had** orange juice and toast, but I **didn't have** any coffee.

The Present of **have** is:

| Singular | Plural |
|---|---|
| I have (got) | we have (got) |
| you have (got) | you have (got) |
| he/she/it has (got) | they have (got) |

We often use **got** after **have**, but **got** does not change the meaning. The question form is **have...got?** or **has...got?** and the negative is **haven't got** or **hasn't got**.

Without **got** we can form the questions in two ways,
e.g. **Have you . . .?** or **Do you have . . .?**
     **Has she . . .?** or **Does she have . . .?**

In the same way, we can form the negative in two ways,
e.g. **you haven't**...or **you don't have** ...
     **she hasn't**...or **she doesn't have** ...

The Past of **have** is **had**; we use **did...have?** in questions and **didn't have** in negatives.

Complete the following with the correct form of **have**:

1. Cats _____ nine lives.
2. A cat _____ nine lives.
3. _____ Mary _____ green eyes? Yes, she _____ .
4. _____ you _____ an interesting trip last weekend?
5. _____ we _____ enough milk for the children?
6. I _____ one of your books, and Jack _____ the other.
7. Last Saturday I _____ dinner with Molly and Simon.
8. Ian often _____ a shower before he goes to bed.

Note: When **have** means 'possess' it does not have continuous tenses; however, when **have** is used as a verb of action, e.g. **have a bath**, **have breakfast**, **have a drink**, it has the range of tenses of all verbs of action,
e.g. A  Where's Teresa?
     B  She's **having** lunch in the canteen.

# 69 Present Continuous

## a Statements

*Notice the verb forms in these sentences:*

Oh, no! It**'s raining** again.
Wait for me! I**'m coming,** too.

We make the Present Continuous with the Present of **be** and a Present Participle, e.g. **going, walking, cooking**.

| Singular | Plural |
|---|---|
| I am going | we are going |
| you are going | you are going |
| he/she/it is going | they are going |

*Put the Present Continuous of the verb in brackets in the following:*

1. Sheila _____ ready now. (get)
2. I can't come now. I _____ lunch. (have)
3. Look! Those boys _____ over the wall. (climb)
4. Can you see the postman? I think he _____ here. (come)
5. Open the curtains, I think it _____ . (snow)
6. Excuse me! You _____ on my foot. (stand)

## b Questions

*Notice the word order in these questions:*

**Are** we **leaving** now? I'm not quite ready.
What**'s** Sue **wearing** today? She's always so smart.

In Present Continuous questions the subject **(she, you, I)** and the auxiliary **(am, is, are)** change places, e.g. **She is (going)** becomes **is she (going)?**

| Singular | Plural |
|---|---|
| am I going? | are we going? |
| are you going? | are you going? |
| is he/she/it going? | are they going? |

*Put the Present Continuous of the verb in brackets in the following:*

1. What _____ the children _____ now? (do)
2. It's very late. _____ Joan still _____ ? (study)
3. Why _____ you still _____ ? It's six o'clock. (work)
4. Hello, Sara. Oh, _____ it _____ ? (snow)

*Verb forms*

## 70 going to

*Look at these sentences:*

> A   What **are** you **going to** do this evening?
> B   I**'m going to** paint my bathroom.

We use **am, is, are** and **going to** when we are talking about the future. We use it when someone has already decided something that he/she is going to do in the future,

e.g.  A  **What are you going to do on Saturday?**
(This question expects that B has decided something.)
B  **I'm going to work in the garden.**
(This means that B has decided to work in the garden on Saturday.)

*Complete the following with a form of* **be going to:**

1  A  What _____ you _____ do this summer?
   B  I _____ visit my cousins.
2  A  How _____ your parents _____ travel?
   B  They _____ travel by car.
3  A  What _____ Tina _____ do with her motorbike?
   B  She _____ sell it.
4  A  When _____ your husband _____ take the children to the circus?
   B  He _____ take them on Friday.
5  A  What _____ we _____ have for lunch?
   B  We _____ have beef stew.
6  A  When _____ Milly _____ take her holiday?
   B  She _____ take it in July.

## 71 Present Continuous, going to future

*Look at this conversation:*

> Angela   We**'re having** a party on Saturday.
> Jean     Oh, who**'s coming**?
> Angela   I don't know yet, but we**'re going to invite** all our friends. Would you like to come?
> Jean     I'd love to, but I**'m going away** this weekend.

We prefer to use the Present Continuous tense in future time instead of **going to** when we have already planned something and it is not just an intention. In such cases there is usually a future time expression in the sentence (e.g. **next week, tomorrow**). We also prefer the Present Continuous tense with verbs like **come** and **go** (to avoid saying 'going to come').

## Verb forms

*Put the verb in brackets into the Present Continuous tense if the action has already been arranged. If the action is not obviously planned, use the **going to** form:*

a **Mary** Jack and Jill (1. get) married on Saturday. Her brother Andrew (2. come) all the way from Scotland for the wedding. He (3. leave) Edinburgh on Friday. It's a long drive so he (4. look for) a hotel near Birmingham. He (5. spend) the night there and (6. finish) the journey the next morning. I (7. buy) the wedding present this afternoon. Would you like to come with me?

**Paula** All right. I (8. go) into town this afternoon. What (9. buy) you?

**Mary** I'm not sure. Something useful. Jack and Jill haven't got much money so they (10. need) a lot of things for the house.

b **Paul** We (1. go) to the New Forest for a picnic on Sunday. We (2. look for) a nice place under the trees. Then we (3. sit down) and eat our lunch.

**Linda** Are you (4. take) all the food with you?

**Paul** Yes. Mum (5. make) some sandwiches and my Uncle Jack (6. bring) all the drinks. He (7. come), too, with my cousins, Peter and Jenny. We (8. play) games in the forest. I (9. be) Robin Hood. Would you like to come with us? You can be Maid Marian.

**Linda** Oh yes. But my Aunt Rachel (10. arrive) on Saturday. We (11. meet) her at the station. She's awful. She (12. spend) all weekend talking about her illnesses. She always does. She (13. have) an operation next month, Mum says.

**Paul** Is it serious?

**Linda** No. She only (14. have) her tonsils out. I (15. go) home now. I (16. ask) my mother if she'll let me come with you.

## 72 Present Simple

*Notice the verb forms in these sentences:*

I **like** wine, but my brother **prefers** beer.
They all **live** in Liverpool except for John, who **lives** in London.

In the Present Simple we use the form of the verb without **-s** for **I, you, we, they** and a plural subject, e.g. **I go, you stay, we think, they play, Tom and Gerry live, the glasses break.**
We use the form with **-s** for **he, she, it** and a singular subject, e.g. **he stays, she thinks, it plays, Tom lives, the glass breaks.**

*Verb forms*

Look at the following table about four people:

|        | Home town | Sport   | Favourite music | Newspaper       |
|--------|-----------|---------|-----------------|-----------------|
| Laura  | Bristol   | squash  | pop             | *Daily Mirror*  |
| Tony   | Cardiff   | rugby   | jazz            | *The Guardian*  |
| Sheila | Leeds     | squash  | classical       | *Daily Telegraph* |
| Donald | Leeds     | football| jazz            | *The Guardian*  |

Laura **lives** in Bristol.
Laura and Sheila **play** squash.
Laura **likes** pop music.
Laura **reads** the *Daily Mirror*.

Complete the following, using the information in the table:

1. Tony _____ Cardiff.
2. Sheila and Donald _____ Leeds.
3. Tony _____ rugby.
4. Donald _____ football.
5. Tony and Donald _____ jazz.
6. Sheila _____ classical music.
7. Tony and Donald _____ *The Guardian*.
8. Sheila _____ the *Daily Telegraph*.

# 73 Present Simple: negative

Notice the verb forms in these sentences:

I like Mr Suzuki, but he **doesn't speak** English and I **don't speak** Japanese.
James and Anna **don't live** in Leeds; they live in Hull.

In the Present Simple we make the negative with **don't** for **I, you, we, they** and a plural subject, e.g. **I don't go, you don't listen, we don't live, they don't like, Martin and Rose don't see. Don't** is short for **do not**.

We use **doesn't** with **he, she, it** and a singular subject, e.g. **he doesn't go, she doesn't listen, it doesn't live, Martin doesn't see. Doesn't** is short for **does not**.

Put a suitable negative in each space in the following:

1. They _____ in an office; they work in a factory.
2. Mr Proctor _____ by bus; he goes by train.
3. I _____ cigarettes; I smoke a pipe.
4. Geoff and Penny _____ French; they teach German.

5 My mother _____ coffee; she drinks tea.
6 We _____ our holiday in the summer; we take it in the winter.
7 The sun _____ in the west; it rises in the east.
8 Ann _____ meat; she only eats vegetables.

## 74 Present Simple: questions

*Notice the verb forms in these questions:*

**Does he speak** English?
**Do you live** near here?

In the Present Simple we make questions with **do** when the subject is **I, you, we, they** or a plural subject, e.g. **Do you go? Do we talk? Do the newspapers come?**

When the subject is **he, she, it** or a singular subject we use **does**, e.g. **Does he go? Does she talk? Does the newspaper come?**

*Complete the following questions with* **do** *or* **does** *and a suitable subject:*

1 A _____ live alone?
  B Yes, I do.
2 A _____ sell stamps?
  B No, not that shop. Try the supermarket over there.
3 A _____ earn a lot of money?
  B Well, they earn a lot more than teachers.
4 A Where _____ live?
  B Well, her official home is Buckingham Palace.
5 A _____ want to be a painter?
  B Yes, but his parents don't like the idea.
6 A Where _____ come from?
  B From Germany. Would you like to try one?

## 75 Present Continuous, Present Simple

*Notice the tense of the verbs in these sentences:*

You **are practising** English at the moment.
The sun **rises** in the east.
I usually **sleep** for seven or eight hours.

We use the Present Continuous, e.g. **I am working, he is sitting**, for actions that are in progress at the moment of speaking. Often the words **now** or **at the moment** go with the Present Continuous,
e.g. **Now you are doing an English exercise.**

*Verb forms*

We use the Present Simple, e.g. **I work, he sits,** for statement of facts, e.g. **Wood floats on water.**
**I live in Barcelona.**

We also use the Present Simple for things that are true in general about the present, but not necessarily at the moment of speaking. Words and phrases such as **always, often, sometimes, never, every day** go with the Present Simple, e.g. **My sister often visits us on Sundays, but she's ill in bed at the moment.**

*Use the Present Continuous or the Present Simple in these sentences:*

1. A  Would you like to go out?
   B  I can't go out now. I _____ the supper. (prepare)
2. I never _____ during the day, but I sometimes _____ in the evening. (smoke)
3. A  I think I can hear a hammer.
   B  Yes, you can. My sister _____ up some shelves. (put)
4. Elephants often _____ longer than humans. (live)
5. In England people _____ on the left; in most countries people _____ on the right. (drive)
6. A  Look! The lights are still on in that office block.
   B  Yes, it's usually dark at this time, but tonight they _____ late. (work)
7. A  Can I speak to Mr Brown, please?
   B  Not at the moment, I'm afraid. He _____ to a client. (talk)
8. Water _____ at 0 degrees Centigrade and _____ at 100 degrees Centigrade. (freeze, boil)

# 76  Verbs not used in continuous forms

*Look at these sentences:*

**Listen!** I **hear** bells ringing.
**Do** you **remember** her name?
No meat, thank you. I **don't like** pork.

Note that the Present Simple is used here although these sentences refer to the present moment, when we would normally use the Present Continuous. A number of common verbs are not usually used in continuous (progressive) tenses; the Present Simple will be used when we refer to the present as well as when we refer to general truths.

Here is a list of these verbs:
**hear, see, smell, taste** (these are often used with **can**);
**notice, recognise, believe, feel (that), think (that);**
**forget, remember, know, mean, suppose, understand;**
**dislike, hate, like, love, want, wish;**
**appear** (when it means 'seem'), **seem;**
**belong to, contain, matter.**

Note that **think** meaning 'have in one's mind', can also be used in combination forms,
e.g. **What do you think?** (What is your opinion?)
**Do you think (that) he's good-looking?** (Is it your opinion that he's good-looking?)
but:
**What are you thinking about?** (What is in your mind at this moment?)

Use one of the verbs from the list above to complete each space in this dialogue, but do not use any of them more than once; in a few cases, more than one verb would be possible. Use negative and question forms where indicated. The first letter of each verb is given to help you:

*Steele*     I'm sure I r\_\_1\_\_ you. I never f\_\_2\_\_ a face and yours s\_\_3\_\_ very familiar.

*Robb*     I b\_\_4\_\_ (negative) we've ever met. I t\_\_5\_\_ you've made a mistake.

*Steele*     I s\_\_6\_\_ you're right. But I u\_\_7\_\_ (negative) it. I r\_\_8\_\_ your face. I w\_\_9\_\_ (negative) to be a nuisance because I h\_\_10\_\_ annoying people but have you ever been in prison?

*Robb*     What? What m\_\_11\_\_ you (question)? I k\_\_12\_\_ (negative) what you're talking about.

*Steele*     Well, it m\_\_13\_\_ (negative). Naturally you l\_\_14\_\_ (negative) people reminding you of it. But before you go, that watch b\_\_15\_\_ me.

*Robb*     Which watch?

*Steele*     The one you took out of my pocket when we started talking. A thief like me n\_\_16\_\_ these things. And I recognise another thief when I see one.

# 77 Past Simple: irregular verbs

*Notice the verb forms in this passage:*

Yesterday **was** a terrible day. I **woke up** late and **cut** myself shaving. At breakfast I **broke** the teapot. I **missed** my usual train, so I **arrived** at work late. Then I **forgot** about an important meeting and the Managing Director **told** me that I **was** a fool.

All the verbs in these sentences are Past because everything happened yesterday.

## Verb forms

There are many common irregular past forms:

| Present | Past | Present | Past | Present | Past |
|---|---|---|---|---|---|
| begin | began | get | got | say | said |
| break | broke | give | gave | see | saw |
| bring | brought | go | went | sell | sold |
| buy | bought | have | had | shut | shut |
| come | came | hear | heard | sing | sang |
| cost | cost | hit | hit | sit | sat |
| cut | cut | know | knew | sleep | slept |
| do | did | leave | left | speak | spoke |
| drink | drank | lend | lent | stand | stood |
| eat | ate | let | let | take | took |
| fall | fell | make | made | teach | taught |
| feel | felt | meet | met | tell | told |
| find | found | put | put | think | thought |
| fly | flew | read | read | wake | woke |
| forget | forgot | run | run | write | wrote |

Regular past forms are made with **-ed**,
e.g. **play, played; watch, watched; look, looked.**

Verbs that end with **e** add **-d** only,
e.g. **like, liked; love, loved; agree, agreed.**

Verbs that end with a consonant and **y** lose the **y** and add **-ied**,
e.g. **carry, carried; study, studied; try, tried.**

We use the past form to talk about things in past time, often with phrases like: **yesterday, last week, two years ago, in August 1980**, etc.

Complete the following using the verb in brackets in the Past Simple:
1. Last week Mr Emery _____ to Rome. (go)
2. Penny _____ the guitar a lot when she was young. (play)
3. Several years ago the Queen _____ our village. (visit)
4. Last summer we _____ lots of photos. (take)
5. They _____ their house in 1977. (buy)
6. We _____ a very interesting programme last night. (watch)
7. My brother _____ a lot when he was young. (cry)
8. Shakespeare _____ many famous plays. (write)

*Verb forms*

## 78 Past Simple: negative

*Notice the verb forms in these sentences:*
>I **didn't leave** school last year; I **left** the year before.
>I **didn't study** German at school; I **studied** French.

We make the negative of the Past Simple with **didn't** and the infinitive of the verb. Note that the negative statements above have **didn't leave** and **didn't study,** but the positive ones have **left** and **studied.**

*Make one part of each sentence negative and one part positive, using the verb in brackets:*
1. Beethoven _____ drama; he _____ music. (write)
2. They _____ married in June; they _____ married in July. (get)
3. We _____ the fire; we only _____ some smoke. (see)
4. Sheila _____ the guitar to Philip; she _____ it to Phyllis. (give)
5. Socrates _____ in Rome; he _____ in Athens. (live)
6. This camera _____ £50; it _____ £30. (cost)

## 79 Past Simple: questions

*Notice the verb forms in these questions and statements:*
>A When **did you leave** school?
>B I **left** school last year.
>A **Did you study** French?
>B Yes, I **studied** French at school.

We form questions in the Past Simple with **did** and the infinitive of the verb. Note that the questions above have **did...leave** and **did...study,** but the statements have **left** and **studied.**

*Complete these questions with the appropriate verb in the Past Simple:*
1. A When _____ that film?
   B I saw it years ago.
2. A _____ to the Prime Minister?
   B No, they wrote to the President.
3. A When _____ ?
   B I think Chaplin died in 1977.
4. A Where _____ that lovely scarf?
   B I bought it in Portobello Road.
5. A What time _____ to work yesterday?
   B We got there at about half past eight.
6. A What _____ you for your birthday?
   B Lew gave me a brooch, and Beryl gave me a bag.

*Verb forms*

## 80 Past Simple, Past Continuous

*Notice the tense of the verb in these sentences:*

Hitchcock **made** the film *Psycho* in 1960.
One of the cameramen **died** while Hitchcock **was making** *Psycho*.

We use the Past Simple when we talk about a complete event, or a number of complete events, in past time, e.g. **Brian phoned me yesterday.**

We use the Past Continuous when we talk about an event that was in progress and incomplete at a particular moment in the past, e.g. **When Brian phoned, I was washing my hair.**

Notice that we can use the Past Simple and the Past Continuous to talk about the same event (the production of the film *Psycho*). When we use the Past Simple tense, e.g. **Hitchcock made *Psycho* in 1960**, we are thinking of the film as a finished thing. When we use the Past Continuous, e.g....**while Hitchcock was making *Psycho***, we are seeing the event while it is still happening, before it is finished.

*Complete the following, using the Past Simple or Past Continuous of the verb(s) in brackets:*

1. Jazz bands quite often _____ on boats on the Mississippi. (play)
2. I couldn't answer the phone because I _____ lunch ready. (get)
3. A  Where were you at 8 o'clock yesterday evening?
   B  I was at home. I _____ cards with some friends; we _____ at about 7 o'clock and _____ at about 11. (play, start, finish)
4. When Peter _____ to the station, his train _____ at Platform 2. (get, stand)
5. I _____ on the beach when suddenly I _____ a shout from someone who _____ in the sea. (lie, hear, swim)
6. As a young woman she _____ two or three books every week. Sometimes she _____ three or four just between Friday evening and Sunday evening. (read, finish)

## 81 Present Perfect: regular and irregular verbs

*Notice the verb forms in these sentences:*

**Have you taken** my dictionary?
No, I **haven't taken** it, but I **have borrowed** your grammar book.

We make the Present Perfect with **have** or **has** and the Past Participle of the verb, e.g. **I have been, she has taken. Have** and **has** make questions, e.g. **Have I been? Has she taken?**, and also negatives, e.g. **I haven't been, she hasn't taken.**

Regular past participles are made, like regular past forms, with **-ed, -d** or **-ied**, e.g. **play, played; like, liked; carry, carried** (see Practice 77)

# Verb forms

There are many common irregular past participles:

| Present | Past Participle | Present | Past Participle | Present | Past Participle |
|---------|-----------------|---------|-----------------|---------|-----------------|
| begin   | begun           | get     | got             | say     | said            |
| break   | broken          | give    | given           | see     | seen            |
| bring   | brought         | go      | gone            | sell    | sold            |
| buy     | bought          | have    | had             | shut    | shut            |
| come    | come            | hear    | heard           | sing    | sung            |
| cost    | cost            | hit     | hit             | sit     | sat             |
| cut     | cut             | know    | known           | sleep   | slept           |
| do      | done            | leave   | left            | speak   | spoken          |
| drink   | drunk           | lend    | lent            | stand   | stood           |
| eat     | eaten           | let     | let             | take    | taken           |
| fall    | fallen          | make    | made            | teach   | taught          |
| feel    | felt            | meet    | met             | tell    | told            |
| find    | found           | put     | put             | think   | thought         |
| fly     | flown           | read    | read            | wake    | woken           |
| forget  | forgotten       | run     | run             | write   | written         |

*Complete the following with the Past Participle of the verb in brackets:*

1. Someone has _____ a cup. (break)
2. I haven't _____ any new clothes for years. (buy)
3. Have you ever _____ kangaroo meat? (eat)
4. Peter says he has never _____ in a jumbo jet. (fly)
5. I'm sorry, I've _____ your name. (forget)
6. They haven't _____ any money for me. (leave)
7. Has Beryl _____ her umbrella today? (take)
8. We haven't _____ to your parents since Christmas. (write)

*Complete the following, using the Present Perfect of the verb in brackets:*

1. A   What _____ today? (do)
   B   I _____ some letters. (write)
2. A   _____ the plans? (send)
   B   No, they _____ them. (send)
3. A   _____ much this week? (rain)
   B   No, it _____ at all. (rain)
4. A   How many cakes _____ the children _____ ? (eat)
   B   I think they _____ two each. (have)

*Verb forms*

## 82 gone and been

*Compare the use of* **gone** *and* **been** *in these dialogues:*

    A  Where's Fred?
    B  He's **gone** to Canada.

    C  Where have you been, Fred?
    D  I've **been** to Canada.

Fred Smith lives in England. If we say **Fred has gone to Canada,** then Fred is on a visit to Canada and has not yet returned home. He is in Canada now.

If we say **Fred has been to Canada,** then Fred has at some time in his life visited Canada, but this sentence does not say where Fred is now.

*Put* **gone** *or* **been** *in the following:*

1  A  Is Mrs Allen here?
    B  No, she's _____ to Frankfurt. She'll be back next week.

2  A  Have you ever _____ to Moscow?
    B  Yes, I've _____ there twice on business.

3  A  Are the bosses away this week?
    B  Yes, they've _____ to a trade fair.

4  A  Would you like to go to a pop festival next weekend?
    B  Oh, yes, I've never _____ to one before.

## 83 Present Perfect, Past Simple

### a Indefinite and definite past time

*Compare the verbs in these sentences:*

    I've **stayed** at the Seaview hotel three times. (Present Perfect)
    I **stayed** at the Seaview hotel last summer. (Past)
    He isn't here; he's **gone** to London. (Present Perfect)
    I **went** to Paris last weekend. (Past)

We use the Present Perfect **(you have flown, she has been)** when we are interested in a fact, not in the time when it happened. The words **ever** and **never** often go with the Present Perfect in this use, and there is no other time expression,

    e.g. **Have you ever flown in a jumbo jet?**
          **Norman has never been to London, but Barbara has.**

We also talk about how many times someone has done something in his or her life in the Present Perfect,

    e.g.  A  **How many times have you won a big prize?**
          B  **I've won a big prize only once before.**

## Verb forms

When we talk about when something happened in the past, we cannot use the Present Perfect; for this we use the Past Simple (**I flew, she went**),
e.g. **Last year I flew to New York in a jumbo jet.**
**Barbara went to London for a holiday three years ago.**
**I won a big prize when I was a little girl.**

(For the question forms of the Past Simple, see Practice 79)

*Put the verb in brackets in either the Present Perfect or the Past Simple:*

1. A  _have_ you ever _eaten_ oysters? (eat)
   B  Yes, I _ate_ them several times. (eat)
2. Last week they _____ a new car. (buy)
3. A  When _____ Marilyn Monroe _____ ? (die)
   B  She _____ in 1962. (die)
4. A  _____ she ever _____ any books by Tolstoy? (read)
   B  No, she _____ never _____ any Russian authors. (read)
5. Ten years ago I _____ school and _____ work. (leave, start)
6. The Wimbledon tennis championships _____ more than one hundred years ago. (start)
7. A  I _____ never _____ a bullfight before. (see)
   B  I _____ only _____ a bullfight twice before. (see)
8. A  _____ they ever _____ you any money? (give)
   B  Yes, last year they _____ me £100. (give)

### b  **this week, last week** etc.

*Notice the time words used with each tense:*

**Have** you **seen** Laura **this week**?
**This year** there **have been** several good football matches.

**Did** you **see** Laura **last week**?
**Last year** there **were** several good football matches.

We use the Present Perfect with a period of time that includes the present moment, such as **today, this week, this month, this year, this century**.
We use the Past Simple with a period of time that does not include the present moment, such as **yesterday, last week, last month, last year, last century**.

*Put either the Present Perfect or the Past Simple in the following:*

1. I _____ not _____ television at all this week. (watch)
2. Last week I _____ several interesting programmes. (watch)
3. _____ you _____ busy at work this month? (be)
4. In the last century Britain _____ a rich country; in this century Britain _____ gradually _____ poorer. (be, become)
5. A  Hullo, dear. _____ you _____ an interesting day? (have)
   B  No, not really. Yesterday _____ much more interesting. (be)

## Verb forms

6  How many customers _____ they _____ this morning up to now?
   And how many customers _____ they _____ yesterday morning?
   (serve, serve)

### c  Duration and past event

*Notice which sentences tell you **how long** and which tell you **when**:*

(It is now 1990.)

Julia **has worked** here since 1986.
1986 was the year when Julia **started work** here.
Julia **has worked** here for 4 years.
Julia **started** here in 1986.

We use the Present Perfect with a period of past time that continues up to the present moment. In the sentence **Julia has worked here for 4 years,** we know that she still works here, and also for how long (the duration) she has worked here. **Julia has worked here since 1986** has the same meaning (i.e. from 1986 to the present).

If we talk about when Julia started work, we use the Past Simple, because that was one event in the past. It happened and it is now finished.

*Complete these sentences with **started (work)** or **has worked** and the appropriate time or date:*

Remember that the number of years the person has worked will depend on what year it is now.

1  Alice started here in 1988.
   1988 was the year when Alice _____ here.
   She _____ here since _____ .
   She _____ here for _____ .
2  Barry has worked here for 10 years.
   He _____ here since 198__ .
   He _____ here in 198__ .
3  Cecil has worked here since 1983.
   1983 was the year when Cecil _____ here.
   He _____ here for _____ .
   He _____ here in _____ .
4  1984 was the year when Doris _____ here.
   Doris _____ here in _____ .
   She _____ here since _____ .
   She _____ here for _____ .
5  Esther has worked here since 1977.
   She _____ here in _____ .
   She _____ here for _____ .
   1977 was the year when Esther _____ here.
6  Florence _____ here for 9 years.
   198__ was the year when Florence _____ here.
   Florence _____ here since _____ .
   Florence _____ here in _____ .

*Verb forms*

# 84 Present Perfect Simple and Continuous

*Compare these sentences:*

Leighton City **have been playing** badly   this season.
　　　　　　　　　　　　　　　　　　　　for two months.
　　　　　　　　　　　　　　　　　　　　since the season started.

They **have lost** five games and **have** only **won** one.
They **haven't won** a game   for two months.
　　　　　　　　　　　　　　　since August.

Notice that the Present Perfect Continuous, **have been playing** is used for an action that has continued for a period of time.

*Look at these tables which give the playing record of the forward line and the football club's playing record this season:*

| Name | Joined club | In first team | Goals this season |
|---|---|---|---|
| ALLAN | 1986 | 1988 | 4 |
| BENNETT | 1983 | 1987 | 3 |
| CURTIS | 1985 | 1986 | 2 |
| DALE | 1988 | 1989 | 1 |
| EMERY | 1981 | 1984 | 1 |

**Leighton City Football Club's results — 1989-90 season**

| When played | Played against | Result | Scorers |
|---|---|---|---|
| August 25th | ATHLETIC (H) | won 2-1 | Allan, Bennett |
| September 1st | WANDERERS (H) | lost 2-3 | Curtis, Bennett |
| September 8th | ALBION (A) | lost 3-4 | Emery, Bennett, Allan |
| September 15th | TOWN (A) | drew 2-2 | Allan, Dale |
| September 22nd | RANGERS (H) | lost 2-4 | Curtis, Allan |
| September 29th | PARK (A) | drew 0-0 | |
| October 6th | CELTIC (H) | lost 0-2 | |
| October 13th | BOROUGH (A) | lost 0-1 | |

H = played at home   A = played away

*Use the information in the first table to ask and answer these questions about each player.*
There are two ways of answering the questions, one with **for** and one with **since:**

1   How long has he been playing for the club?
2   How long has he been playing for the first team?
e.g. **Allan has been playing for the club for — years/since 1986.**
　　 **He's been playing for the first team for — years/since 1988.**

133

## Verb forms

3   How many goals has he scored this season?
4   How long is it since he scored a goal?
e.g. **He's scored 4 goals this season.**
   **Emery hasn't scored for — weeks/since September 8th.**

Use the information in the second table to answer these questions about Leighton City Football Club. There are two ways of answering the questions, one with **for** and one with **since**:

5   How many games has the club won this season?
6   How many have they lost?
7   How many have they drawn?
8   How long is it since they won a game/drew a game/scored a goal?
   e.g. **They haven't won a game for — weeks/since August 25th.**

## 85 Present Perfect with *ever* and *never*

Compare these sentences:

   **I've never been** in a casino **before.**
   It's **the first time I've ever been** in a casino.

Rewrite these sentences, using the alternative form with **ever** or **never,** as in the examples above:

1   I've never played bridge before.
2   It's the first time he's ever spoken to me.
3   It's the first time they've ever invited us to lunch.
4   We've never flown before.
5   It's the first time she's ever won a prize.
6   He's never written a novel before.
7   You've never complained about it before.
8   It's the first time I've ever asked you for money.
9   It's the first time we've ever had bad weather here.
10  She's never arrived late before.

## 86 *ago* and *for*

Compare these sentences:

   Bob last **saw** Rose **two weeks ago**.
   Bob **hasn't seen** Rose **for two weeks**.

These two sentences give the same information in two different ways.
**Two weeks ago** is a fixed point in the past; we always use the Past Simple with **ago**.
**For two weeks** continues up to the present time and we use the Present Perfect.

(For **been** as the Past Participle of **go**, see Practice 82.)

*Verb forms*

For and during are prepositions and are followed by a noun. **For** refers to a total period of time, e.g. **I waited for two hours.** **During** refers to a point of time within a period, e.g. **It rained very hard during the night.**

*Compare the two examples above, and then change each of the following from one kind of sentence to the other kind:*

1. Mr Ball last spoke to Mrs Beal two months ago.
2. Joe hasn't played tennis for five weeks.
3. Ellen hasn't been to the cinema for 3 or 4 months.
4. George last came to see us ten days ago.
5. Hilda hasn't read a newspaper for several weeks.
6. It last rained about 6 weeks ago.

## 87 Present Perfect with **for**; **since** with Past Simple

*Compare these sentences:*

We **haven't had** fish **for** a long time.
It's a long time **since** we **had** fish.

*Rewrite these sentences, using the alternative form with **for** or **since**, as in the examples above:*

1. It's a long time since we played tennis.
2. We haven't heard from her for a long time.
3. It's a long time since we had a party.
4. He hasn't written to me for a long time.
5. It's ages since her boy-friend took her out.
6. My wife hasn't rung me up at the office for ages.
7. It's years since he did any useful work.
8. It's six months since they paid us a visit.
9. You haven't bought me anything for ages.
10. It's a long time since I saw them.

## 88 Past Perfect Simple

a

*Notice the verb forms used in these sentences:*

Mrs Fletcher **locked** the door and **went** to bed.
When her husband **came** home, he **found** she **had locked** the door and **had gone** to bed.

We use the Past Perfect tense (**had** + Past Participle) when we want to talk about something that had happened before the main action in the past.

*Use the Past Perfect to complete these sentences:*

1. While Ida was answering the phone, the soup boiled over and the gas went out. When Ida got back to the kitchen, she found the soup _____.

## Verb forms

2. While Harry was in the shop, someone stole his car. When Harry came out of the shop, he found that someone _____ .
3. Moira left the front door open when she went to get the car out of the garage. While she was in the garage, the cat got out and climbed onto the roof. When Moira came out of the garage, she found the cat _____ .
4. Horace took Ellen to the cinema, but left her in the queue while he went to buy some cigarettes. While he was away, Marvin turned up and took Ellen into the cinema to see the film. When Horace returned, he found that Marvin _____ .

### b with **because**

Compare these sentences:

He played football for two hours in the morning and felt very tired in the afternoon.

He **felt** very tired in the afternoon because he **had played** football for two hours in the morning.

Rewrite these sentences, using the alternative form with **because** and the Past Perfect, as in the example above:

1. He won the match and celebrated his victory with his friends.
2. She didn't sleep much on the plane so she went to bed early that night.
3. He was bitten by a snake and had to go to hospital.
4. They left the door unlocked and a thief got into the house.
5. He didn't do all the questions so he failed the exam.

## 89 Second Conditional

Notice the verb forms used in these sentences:

- A  If I **were (was)** rich, I **wouldn't work**. I**'d live** in a castle.
- B  If you lived in a castle, you**'d be** lonely.
- A  No, I **wouldn't**. If I **lived** in a castle, I **could have** a lot of servants and I **could invite** all my friends.
- B  **Would you invite** me? (if you lived in a castle)
- A  Well, I **might**. (invite you if I lived in a castle)

Note that **could** is used here to mean **would be able to**. **Might** is used to mean **perhaps...would**.

Complete the dialogue with the correct forms of the verbs in brackets. Use **could** and **might** where appropriate:

- A  I wish I lived on a desert island, like Robinson Crusoe. If I __1__ (live) on a desert island, I __2__ (go) to the beach every day. I __3__ (lie) on the beach and __4__ (swim) when I felt like it.
- B  What __5__ you eat? __6__ (not be) hungry?

*Verb forms*

A  Oh, I ___7___ (pick) bananas from the trees, and if I ___8___ (make) a fishing rod, I ___9___ (catch) fish.

B  But if you ___10___ (want) to catch fish, you ___11___ (need) a boat. You ___12___ (have to) build one. And there ___13___ (be) sharks in the water. It ___14___ (be) dangerous.

A  Oh, I ___15___ (not worry) about them. I ___16___ (keep) a look-out for them.

B  But the biggest problem ___17___ (be) water. What ___18___ you (drink)?

A  Oh, that ___19___ (be) all right. There ___20___ (be) a stream on the island.

B  There ___21___ (not be). Some islands haven't got streams.

A  My island ___22___ (have) a stream. If it ___23___ (not have) one I ___24___ (not go) there.

## 90 **wish** with Past Simple

*Look at the passage below and notice the verb forms used after* **wish:**

David is a lonely little boy in a big city. He would like his life to be different. He would like to be able to do things he cannot do. He says, '**I wish we lived** at the seaside. **I wish I could go** swimming every day.'

a  *Change these statements into David's wishes, beginning* **I wish:**

e.g. He would like to be able to go horse-riding.
**I wish I could go horse-riding.**

1  He would like to have a puppy.
2  He would like to be able to go to school on his bicycle.
3  He would like to be sixteen.
4  He would like to be able to play football every day.
5  He would like to work in a zoo.

## 91 Third Conditional

*Notice the verb forms in these sentences:*

If he **had done** better in his exams, he **would have become** a doctor. In fact, he's now a very successful businessman.

*Read this story:*

The other day I was talking to my friend Bernard. He teaches English in Spain. I asked him how he became an English teacher. He said:

## Verb forms

'It's a long story. If a number of things in my life had been different, I wouldn't have come here and I wouldn't have become an English teacher. When I was at school, I wanted to become a pilot in the Air Force but my eyesight wasn't good enough. So I went to university and studied physics. I wanted to stay at university and do research. But my degree wasn't good enough. So I got a job with an engineering company.

I liked the job and I expected to stay there for a long time, but then they appointed a new managing director. I didn't get on with him, so I applied for another job.

I would probably have got the job, but on my way to the interview I met an old friend who worked in a travel agency. He offered me a job in Spain and I accepted it because I've always liked Spain.

After two years, the agency wanted to send me to Greece, but then I met my wife, so I stayed. We got married but I didn't earn enough money to keep a family so I started giving English lessons at a school.

The owner of the school wanted to retire so he offered me a full-time job as Director. I liked teaching more than working at the travel agency, so I took it. And that's how I became an English teacher.'

*Using the information in the story, say how Bernard's life might have been different, as in the example below:*

e.g. **If he had had good eyesight, he would have become a pilot in the Air Force,**

How would Bernard's life have been different?
1 if he had had good eyesight?
2 if his university degree had been better?
3 if the engineering company hadn't appointed a new managing director?
4 if Bernard had got on with him?
5 if he hadn't met his friend from the travel agency?
6 if he hadn't liked Spain?
7 if he hadn't met his wife?
8 if he had earned more money in the agency?
9 if the owner of the school hadn't wanted to retire?
10 if he hadn't liked teaching more than working at the travel agency?

# 92 Imperatives

*Look at these sentences:*

A Do I take a number 17 bus to get to the station?
B No, **don't take** a number 17; **take** a number 23.

For the positive form of the Imperative (i.e. instruction or command) we use the infinitive form of the verb, e.g. **take**.
For the negative form of the Imperative we add **don't** to the infinitive form, e.g. **don't take**.

# Verb forms

*Complete the following with a suitable instruction in each space:*

1. A  Do I turn left for the post office?
   B  No, _____ left; _____ right.
2. A  Must I come on Friday morning?
   B  No, _____ on Friday morning; _____ on Friday afternoon.
3. A  Shall I take this parcel to Mrs Beam?
   B  No, _____ it to Mrs Beam; _____ it to Mr Timms.
4. A  Do you want me to buy large apples?
   B  No, _____ large apples; _____ small ones.

## 93  Alternatives to the imperative

*Notice how we can say the same thing more politely:*
    **Get me** a sandwich.
    **Get me** a sandwich, **will you?**
    **Will you get me** a sandwich, **please**?
    **Would you mind getting** me a sandwich?

*Look at these passages. Change the verbs in the imperative to the alternative form given in the example at the beginning of each passage:*

    a  Colin Hammond is a very busy man, and is rather rude when his wife rings him at the office. He doesn't have time to talk to her. He says:
    e.g. **Ring me back later, will you?**

There are a few things I must tell you, though. I didn't have time to pay the gas bill. *Go round and pay it.* And I won't be able to play tennis with Jack Frost this evening. *Ring him and tell him I can't play.* Oh, yes, and *take the dog for a walk.* And *have a look at Brian's homework.* And I'll be home late to dinner, so *leave it in the oven.*
    b  He is a little more polite with his secretary. In the same situation, he says to her:
    e.g. **Will you ring me back later, please?**

I've got to go out and see a customer. *Book a table at the Ritz.* And don't forget that I'm going to Birmingham tomorrow. *Find out the times of the trains.* And we must send out those letters this evening. *Type them before you go.* Oh, yes, and I can't see Mr Brown tomorrow. *Cancel my appointment with him.* And another thing — *ring my wife and tell her I'll be late home.*
    c  He is more polite with his colleagues. In the same situation he says:
    e.g. **Would you mind ringing me back later?**

I'm afraid I can't see you this morning. *Come up this afternoon.* I haven't had time to read the report you wrote. *Bring it with you.* And *make a note of the main points.* I need a list of last month's sales figures for the board meeting tomorrow. *Get it for me.* And I'll be at the board meeting all morning, so *deal with everything while I'm away.*

*Verb forms*

## 94 Imperative and **Why (not) do this?**, **Why do/ don't you do this?**

*Compare B's responses each time:*

    A  He does what he likes. He doesn't take any notice of what I say.
    B  **Why argue** with him, then?
        **Why do you argue** with him, then?
        **Don't argue** with him, then.

    A  We haven't had fish for some time.
    B  Then **why not have** fish?
        Then **why don't we have** fish?
        **Have** some fish, then.

*For each response of B, give two alternative forms; as in the examples above:*

1  A  He always criticises my work and it upsets me.
    B  Why take any notice, then?

2  A  I know smoking's bad for me.
    B  Why do you smoke, then?

3  A  That programme always irritates me.
    B  Then don't watch it

4  A  I don't think I'm going to enjoy my holiday.
    B  Why are you going, then?

5  A  They've done the job so badly it will have to be done again.
    B  Why are you going to pay them, then?

6  A  I've been working very hard and I feel tired.
    B  Then why don't you have a rest?

7  A  I feel very lonely.
    B  Come round to my house, then.

8  A  I'm sure I've been asked to pay too much income tax.
    B  Why not write to the tax inspector and complain, then?

9  A  I haven't seen her for ages. I wonder how she is.
    B  Ring her up, then.

10  A  I've got a headache.
     B  Then why not take an aspirin?

## 95 **Don't...** and **Be careful not to...**

*Compare these sentences:*

    Be careful! **Don't take** any risks!
    **Be careful not to take** any risks.

    The only advice I can give is: **Don't bet** on horses!
    The only advice I can give you is **not to bet** on horses.

*Verb forms*

*Rewrite these sentences, using the alternative form, as in the examples above:*
1. Take care! Don't lose the money!
2. The most important thing to remember in this situation is: Don't panic!
3. I warn you. Don't do that again!
4. Under the circumstances, the best advice I can give you is not to pay any attention to them.
5. The wisest course of action is: Don't give them any opportunity to complain!

# 96  let's

*Look at these sentences:*

A **Let's go** to a concert this evening.
B No, **let's not go** to a concert. **Let's go** to a film.

**Let's** goes with an infinitive, without **to**, e.g. **let's go, let's play, let's not wait**. We use **let's** to suggest that the speaker and the listener(s) can do something together. It is a stronger suggestion than **shall we?**, which is a question. **Let's not** is the negative form. **Let's sit outside** means 'I suggest that you and I sit outside'. **Let's not stay here** means 'I suggest that you and I do not stay here'.

*Complete the following with* **let's** *or* **let's not**:
1. A  Would you like to go to the cinema with me?
   B  No, _____ go to the cinema; _____ go for a walk instead.
2. A  Shall we go out for a meal?
   B  Yes, _____ go to that new Indian restaurant.
3. A  How about a game of Monopoly?
   B  No, _____ play Monopoly; _____ play bridge instead.
4. A  Shall we paint the windows green?
   B  No, _____ paint them green; _____ paint them blue.
5. A  Shall we go out for a walk?
   B  Yes, _____ go to the park.

# Questions

## 97 Question tags

*Notice the use of the verbs in these statements and question tags:*

    *A*   Jeremy **is** twenty-five, **isn't he?**
    *B*   Yes, he is.

    *A*   Tina **can't** speak Polish, **can she?**
    *B*   No, she can't.

    *A*   Guy **lives** in Barnsley, **doesn't he?**
    *B*   Yes, he does.

When we make a statement and want to ask the listener if he or she agrees with the statement, we can use a question tag. In question tags we only use an auxiliary or a modal verb, e.g. **am, is, are, have, has, had, can, could, will, would, do, does, did;** the subject is a pronoun: **I, you, he, she, we, you, they.** Normally the tag is negative when the statement is positive, and the tag is positive when the statement is negative.

*Add question tags to the following statements:*

  1  *A*   You're from Switzerland, _____ ?
      *B*   Yes, I am.

  2  *A*   Paul hasn't told anybody, _____ ?
      *B*   No, he hasn't.

  3  *A*   They said it was wrong, _____ ?
      *B*   Yes, they did.

  4  *A*   You got to work late again, _____ ?
      *B*   Yes, I did.

  5  *A*   We don't need any money, _____ ?
      *B*   No, we don't.

  6  *A*   The engineers can't work at the weekend, _____ ?
      *B*   No, they can't.

  7  *A*   You'd like an ice cream, _____ ?
      *B*   Yes, I would.

  8  *A*   The children won't leave before 8 o'clock, _____ ?
      *B*   No, they won't.

  9  *A*   You'd better say you're sorry, _____ ?
      *B*   Yes, I had.

10  *A*   Your cousin doesn't play bridge, _____ ?
      *B*   No, he doesn't.

# 98 Question words

Look at these questions and answers; try and fill in the missing answer yourself:

| A | B |
|---|---|
| **What's** it **like**? | It's beautiful. |
| **Where** is it? | In the cupboard. |
| **Which** cupboard? | The one in the hall. |
| **Whose** is it? | It's mine. |
| **Who** made it? | My brother did. |
| **When** did he make it? | Last term at school. |
| **How old** is he? | He's sixteen (years old). |
| **How long** did it take him? | About three weeks. |
| **How much** did the wood cost? | It was quite cheap. |
| **How** does it work? | With batteries. |
| **How many** batteries has it got? | Four. |
| **How far** can it fly? | About 50 metres. |
| **Why** did he give it to you? | Because it was my birthday. |
| **What** is it? | |
| | |
| **How tall** is she? | She's about six feet (tall). |
| **What** are they doing? | They're playing chess. |
| **How** are you? | Very well, thank you. |

Use the correct question words in the following:

1.   A   _____ oil do we need?
        B   Oh, one litre will be enough.

2.   A   _____ are you late?
        B   Because the bus was late.

3.   A   _____ of these pictures do you like best?
        B   The one by Picasso.

4.   A   _____ is Brighton from London?
        B   About 80 kilometres.

5.   A   _____ are you making?
        B   A bookshelf for my bedroom.

6.   A   _____ is your wife?
        B   Two years older than me.

7.   A   _____ are the plates?
        B   In the cupboard, of course.

8.   A   _____ are you?
        B   Very well, thanks.

9.   A   _____ men are there in a rugby team?
        B   Sometimes thirteen, sometimes fifteen.

10.  A   _____ wrote the letter?
        B   I did.

# Questions

11  A _____ are you staying?
    B  About three weeks.
12  A _____ her new boyfriend?
    B  Very handsome, but not very intelligent.
13  A _____ was the concert?
    B  Last Saturday.
14  A _____ jacket is this?
    B  It's Ron's.
15  A _____ did the meal cost?
    B  Just over £5.
16  A _____ did you break it?
    B  With a stone.
17  A _____ time is it?
    B  10 o'clock.
18  A _____ was she dressed?
    B  Very smartly.

# 99  Who? and What? as subject

*Notice how the subject of* **B** *answers the question word in* **A**:
    A  **Who** killed President Kennedy?
    B  **Lee Harvey Oswald** killed President Kennedy.
    A  **What** caused the fire?
    B  **A broken gas pipe** caused the fire.

In these questions **who** and **what** are the subject of the verb. Notice the word order, and notice that you do not use **did, does** or **do**.

*Rewrite these sentences as questions beginning with* **Who** *or* **What**:
    e.g. My aunt made this cake.
         Question: **Who** made this cake.?
1  Nothing happened.
   Question: _____?
2  Tom's girlfriend lives in that house.
   Question: _____ in that house?
3  Shakespeare wrote *Macbeth*.
   Question: _____ *Macbeth*?
4  A guide will meet them at the station.
   Question: _____ them at the station?
5  Janet went to Spain last summer.
   Question: _____ to Spain last summer?
6  Pat is making that noise.
   Question: _____ that noise?
7  The bad weather caused the accident.
   Question: _____ the accident?
8  A big tree has fallen across the road.
   Question: _____ across the road?

# Introductory *there* and *it*

## 100 there is/are

a  Notice when we use the singular and when we use the plural:

> **There is** some grass in the garden.
> **There is** a tree in the garden.
> **There are** a lot of flowers in the garden.

We use **there is** with mass nouns, e.g. **grass, milk, air, cheese.**
For questions we use **is there?**
e.g. **What is there in the garden?**
    **Is there some grass in the garden? Yes, there is.**

We also use **there is** with singular count nouns, e.g. **a tree, a dog, an egg, a bed,**
e.g. **Is there a tree in the garden? Yes, there is.**

We use **there are** with plural count nouns, e.g. **flowers, books, cars, pens.**
For questions we use **are there?**
e.g. **How many flowers are there in the garden?**
    **Are there many flowers in the garden? Yes, there are.**

*Put* **there is, is there, there are** *or* **are there** *in the following:*

1  _____ a pen under that book? Yes, _____ .
2  What _____ in the corner of the room? _____ a bed.
3  How many chairs _____ in the corridor? _____ four.
4  _____ some water on the floor.
5  _____ many people at the bus stop? No, _____ only one old lady.
6  _____ three bottles of milk outside.
7  _____ some milk in the blue jug.
8  _____ a dictionary in here? Yes, in fact _____ two.

b  **there is/are:** various tenses

Notice the different tenses in these sentences:

> **There was** a concert last Saturday.
> **There are** two buses on Sundays.
> **There has been** only one storm this year.
> **There will be** a meeting next Thursday.

We can use **there is/are** in various tenses (e.g. Past Simple: **there was/were;** Present Perfect: **there has/have been;** future: **there will be)** in the same way as other verbs.

*Put* **there is, there are, there was, there were, there has been, there have been** *or* **there will be** *in the following:*

1  _____ several fast trains to Brighton every day.
2  _____ a lot of work at the factory next month.

*Introductory **there** and **it***

    3 _____ six fires in this area in the last six months.
    4 _____ no houses here when I was young.
    5 _____ a lot of trouble in the last few days.
    6 _____ a party for young children yesterday.

## 101  there is/are, it is, they are

*Compare these sentences:*

**There is** a tree in the garden. **It is** very tall.
**There are** some flowers in the garden. **They are** very pretty.

When we talk about the position of something that we haven't talked about before, we usually say: **there is ...** or **there are ...**

When it is clear what we are talking about, we can then say something more about it with **it is** or **they are**.

Notice that we use **it is** to talk about the weather,
e.g. It **is cold today**.
    It **is a nice day for a picnic.**
    It **was raining**.

We also use **it is** for distances, e.g. **How far is it to the nearest hospital?** or **How many miles is it to the nearest hospital? It's about two miles (to the nearest hospital.)**

**Put there is, there are, it is** *or* **they are** *in the following:*

  1 _____ a lake in the park. _____ long but not very wide.
  2 _____ two good programmes on TV this week. _____ both about animals.
  3 My cousin has a new camera. _____ from Germany.
  4 Look! _____ two cats in that tree.
  5 How many kilometres _____ from here to the nearest town?
  6 _____ very warm today.
  7 _____ is a petrol station at the end of this road. _____ open on Sundays.
  8 _____ some nuts in this cake. _____ from my sister's garden.
  9 A _____ a long way to the station?
     B No, _____ about half a mile.
10 We bought some biscuits yesterday. _____ in that tin.
11 _____ raining in the valley, but _____ clear on the hills.
12 A I think _____ something behind that door.
     B Yes, _____ my tennis racquet.
13 _____ three letters for you. _____ on that table.
14 _____ a post office in the village. _____ opposite the church.

*Introductory* **there** *and* **it**

## 102   **there is/are** as alternatives

The constructions with **there is/there are** are usually more common than the alternative constructions. Note that the alternative constructions never begin with **it** or **they**.

### a   Some food is left, there is some food left

Compare the sentences on the left with those on the right, which use **there is/are**:

| Some food is left. | There is some food left. |
| A little food is left. | There is a little food left. |
| Not much food is left. | There is not much food left. |
| A lot of food is left. | There is a lot of food left. |
| A great deal of food is left. | There is a great deal of food left. |
| A few people are outside. | There are a few people outside. |
| Several people are outside. | There are several people outside. |
| Twenty people are outside. | There are twenty people outside. |
| A lot of people are outside. | There are a lot of people outside. |
| Hundreds of people are outside. | There are hundreds of people outside. |

Rewrite these sentences, using **there is/are, there was/were** or **there will be**:
1. Seventeen watches are in the suitcase.
2. Only a few people are in the audience.
3. In those days, not many cars were on the road.
4. Nothing in the law is against it.
5. A few biscuits are in the tin.
6. Thousands of people will be there.

### b   there is/are and exist

Compare these sentences:

**There is** often **bad feeling** between employers and employees.
**Bad feeling** often **exists** between employers and employees.

Rewrite these sentences, using the correct form of **there is/are,** as in the example above:
1. Evidence exists that he is guilty.
2. People like that have always existed.
3. No ghosts exist in this house.
4. Little satisfaction exists in winning games by cheating.
5. No proof that he had done it existed.

## 103   its, it's, it is

Note the spelling in these sentences:

The dog is looking for **its** master.
**It's** a lovely day.
The weather forecast said it would be a nice day today, and **it is**.

*Introductory **there** and **it***

Note that we use the short form **it's,** instead of **it is,** in spoken English except at the end of the clause,
e.g. **It's** a long way
I don't know how far **it is.**

Complete this dialogue, using **its, it's** or **it is**:

Mother     __1__    time for the cat to have __2__ dinner. Put the milk in __3__ saucer.
Susan     I don't know where __4__ .
Mother     __5__ in the cupboard in the kitchen where the plates are. At least, I think __6__ . Have a look, and if __7__ not there, tell me.
Susan     I can't find it. Oh, yes, here __8__ . Does the cat know __9__ dinner's ready?
Mother     Of course it does. __10__ always hungry.

# 104   It takes (two hours) to ...

Look at this question and answer:
A   How long **does it take** the train to get to London?
B   **It takes** the train **two hours** to get to London.
C   **Does it take long** to make these models?
D   Yes, **it takes a long time**.

This means that if the train starts its journey at 9 o'clock, it arrives in London at 11 o'clock.

Complete the following questions and statements:
1   Vera leaves home at 7.30 and she gets to work at 8.30.
    A   How long does it _____ Vera _____ to work?
    B   An hour.
2   This bus leaves at 9.30 and gets to Buxton at 10 o'clock. So it _____ this bus half an hour _____ Buxton.
3   That plane leaves Heathrow at 11 o'clock and gets to Athens at 2 o'clock.
    A   How _____ does it _____ that plane _____ Athens?
    B   Three hours.
4   This train leaves at 4 o'clock and gets to Edinburgh at 9 o'clock. So it _____ this train five hours _____ Edinburgh.
5   A   Does _____ to become a dancer?
    B   Yes, it takes _____ . In fact, it _____ years.

# Gerunds and infinitives

## 105  Verb + gerund, verb + infinitive

### a  Verb + gerund

Look at this sentence:

> I **enjoy working** here.
> **Enjoy** is followed by a gerund. Other verbs that always take a gerund are:
> **avoid, dislike, finish, (can't) help, (not) mind, practise, (can't) stand.**

Use one of these verbs to complete each of the following sentences. Do not use any verb more than once:

1.  People wear safety belts to _____ being injured in accidents.
2.  Would you _____ opening the window? It's very hot in here.
3.  I _____ listening to classical music but I can't _____ queuing for hours outside concert halls to get a ticket.
4.  When I _____ writing this book, I'm going to have a long holiday.
5.  My aunt is very lonely. I can't _____ feeling sorry for her. But she _____ people visiting her without a good reason.
6.  You must _____ answering this kind of question for the examination.

### b  Verb + gerund or infinitive with to

A number of verbs can take a gerund or an infinitive with **to.** In many cases the meaning changes depending on whether a gerund or an infinitive follows the verb. Here is a list of the most common verbs of this type:

**hate**    I **hate living** in London.
            I'd **hate to live** on a boat.

In the Conditional form **hate** takes the infinitive, but the gerund is the usual form.

> I **hate to interrupt** you when you're working.

When the meaning is, as here, 'I'm sorry to interrupt you', **hate** takes the infinitive.

**like**    I **like to dance.**
            I **like dancing.**

Both forms can be used, but the gerund is slightly more usual when we are speaking generally to mean 'enjoy' or 'find agreeable'.

> I **don't like waiting** on railway stations.

In the negative, when the meaning is the same as **dislike** the gerund is more common than the infinitive.

> I **don't like to disturb** you.

When the meaning is, as here, 'I'm sorry to disturb you', **don't like** takes the infinitive. (Compare **hate**, above.)

## Gerunds and infinitives

      I'**d like to help** you.

      In the Conditional, **like** takes the infinitive.

**love**   I **love to walk**
      I **love walking.**

The uses of **love** are the same as those of **like**.

**remember** I **remember/haven't forgotten smoking** my first cigarette.
**and**
**forget**   I **remembered/didn't forget to post** the letter.

**Remember** with a gerund means 'have the memory of', after the event; **remember** with the infinitive means 'not to forget', before or at the time of the event.

(**Remind** means 'make someone remember' and takes the infinitive, so **remind me to**...means 'don't let me forget to...', e.g. **Remind me to post the letter.**)

**stop**   He **stopped talking.** (He was silent.)
      He **stopped** (in the street) **to talk** to a friend.

Here both gerund and infinitive can be used, but with very different meanings. The first sentence means 'He was silent'. The second sentence means 'He stopped walking because he wanted to talk to his friend'.

**try**    I **tried to understand** it. (I made the effort, and perhaps I understood it, perhaps I didn't.)
      I **tried smoking** a cigarette for the first time. (I experimented to see if I would like it, and I actually smoked it.)

*Use the correct forms of the verbs in brackets to complete these sentences. If you think both gerund and infinitive forms are possible, write both forms:*

1 I'd hate (be) a teacher at that school.
2 I like (listen) to Mozart's music.
3 I like (read) the paper on the way to work in the mornings.
4 I'd like to (play) tennis tomorrow.
5 I don't like (stay) in bed late.
6 I remember (go) to the opera for the first time when I was ten.
7 Did you remember (book) the tickets for the opera?
8 I've tried (give up) smoking several times but I've never succeeded.
9 Why don't you try (smoke) a pipe? It would be better for you.
10 I forgot (include) 'forget' in this exercise, but then my co-author reminded me (put) it in.

## Gerunds and infinitives

## 106 Verbs of the senses + infinitive or -ing

*Compare these sentences:*

I **saw** the bomb **fall**.
I **watched** the rain **falling**.

We use the infinitive without **to**, e.g. **fall**, for a completed action; we use the participle, e.g. **falling**, for an incomplete or continuing action. The word order is the same in both cases.

*Choose the more appropriate form for the verbs in brackets in this story:*

There was a fire in our street yesterday morning. I woke up early. I pulled open the curtains and suddenly saw smoke (1. pour) out of the house opposite. Then I heard the fire engines (2. ring) their bells and saw the first one (3. turn) the corner and (4. stop) outside the burning house. Then I saw a woman (5. stand) at the upstairs window. I watched her (6. open) the window and could see her (7. wave) at the firemen. I opened my bedroom window. Now I could hear more fire engines (8. arrive) and smell the smoke (9. come) from the burning house. Then I saw the firemen (10. carry) a large blanket into the front garden and (11. get) ready to catch the woman. Then I heard the chief fireman (12. shout) 'Jump'. For a long time, I watched the woman (13. hesitate) and the firemen (14. wait) underneath, (15. hold) the blanket. Then, suddenly, she made up her mind and I saw her (16. Jump) safely into the blanket and heard the firemen and the neighbours (17. shout) 'Hurray'.

## 107 Preposition + gerund

*Look at this sentence:*

He's very **interested in gardening**.

The verb form after a preposition is always the gerund. The only exceptions are **but** and **except**,
e.g. There's nothing we can do **but/except wait**.

*Complete these sentences with an appropriate verb from the list in the* **-ing** *form:* **do, drive, leave, live, lose, play, sit, speak, spend, use.** *Use each verb once only:*

1 Before _____ the office, there's something I'd like you to do for me.
2 They didn't say a word. They just sat in the corner without _____ .
3 He's very fond of _____ the piano.
4 He returned to England after _____ several years abroad.
5 I'm a good driver but I wouldn't be capable of _____ a racing car.
6 I like this town. I've never thought of _____ anywhere else.
7 Why don't you do something, instead of _____ there in the armchair?
8 He solved the problem by _____ a different method.

*Gerunds and infinitives*

9  I must put this money away in a safe place. I'm afraid of _____ it.
10  My fee for _____ this job will be £10.

## 108  make and let + infinitive

Look at these sentences:
- A  **Let them go!** They haven't done anything wrong.
- B  Yes, they have. They've broken my window and I'm going to **make them pay** for the damage.

**Make** and **let** are the only verbs immediately followed by the infinitive without **to**, apart from auxiliaries (**will, may, could**, etc.), and **help**, which can be used with or without **to**.

Complete these sentences with an appropriate verb from the list: **behave, do, eat, go, read, stay, take, talk, wait, watch.** Use each verb once only:

- A  You shouldn't let Ian ___1___ so many sweets, and you let him ___2___ up too late, too. You should make him ___3___ to bed earlier. And another thing, you let him ___4___ too much television. You ought to make him ___5___ his homework. When I was young, my father made us ___6___ properly at the dinner table, too. He didn't let us ___7___ with our mouths full. And he made us ___8___ until everyone had finished before we left the table.
- B  Oh, Mother! You'll tell me next that I shouldn't let Bob ___9___ his newspaper at breakfast.
- A  No, you shouldn't. Your husband's just as bad as your son. You ought to make him ___10___ you shopping in the car on Saturday afternoons, instead of going to the football match, and...

## 109  for him to do

Notice how the following two sentences express similar information in different ways:
- A  John must do a lot of work today.
- B  Yes, there's a lot of work **for him to do**.

Complete the following in the same way, putting one word only in each space:

1. A  Mary must do a lot of homework today.
   B  Yes, there's a lot of homework for _____ to _____ .
2. A  Mr and Mrs Trim must do a lot of housework today.
   B  Yes, there's a lot of housework for _____ to _____ .
3. A  You and I must do a lot of things today.
   B  Yes, there are a lot of things for _____ to _____ .
4. A  You must do a lot of exercises today.
   B  Yes, there are a lot of exercises for _____ to _____ .

*Gerunds and infinitives*

## 110 Verb + object + infinitive

*Look at these sentences:*

    A  What do you **want me to do?**
    B  I'**d like you to help** me carry this box.

Here is a list of common verbs that are followed by an object and an infinitive with **to:**
**advise, allow, ask, cause, expect, force, help, invite, leave, order, pay, teach, tell, want, warn, would like.**

*Write down what John Stewart wants his secretary to do, and what Anne would like Erika to do:*

    e.g. **John Stewart wants his secretary to type the letters he has dictated.**
         **Anne would like Erika to wash up all the glasses,**

1  John Stewart, a businessman, is going out to lunch with a customer. Before leaving the office, he asks his secretary, Miss Jones, to do a number of things:

Come in, Miss Jones. I'm going out now but I want you to do a few things for me while I'm out. First, would you type the letters I've dictated. Sign them for me and put them in the post. Then make an appointment for me with Mr Adams for Wednesday morning. After that, would you book my flight to Paris for Thursday, please, and also find me a hotel in Paris for two nights. Oh, yes, and put off the board meeting until I return from Paris. Telephone my wife, would you, and tell her I'll be late home. And before you go, could you please file the papers on my desk.

2  Erika is helping Anne clear up after a party. Anne tells her what she can do:

First, wash up all the glasses, and leave them on the draining board in the kitchen. Then wrap the sandwiches in greaseproof paper and put them in the fridge. Empty the ashtrays in the dustbin, would you, and put the empty bottles in those cardboard boxes next to it. Then take the unopened bottles to the cellar. Oh, yes, you could hoover the carpet and dust the furniture. And after that, you can help me move the furniture back into the dining room.

## 111 Question word + infinitive

*Look at these sentences:*

         Tell me **how to do** it.
         He doesn't know **where to go**.
         I'm not sure **how much to ask** for it.

## Gerunds and infinitives

We use this construction instead of more complicated ones like:
Tell me how I should do it.
He doesn't know where he has to go.
I'm not sure how much I should ask for it.

*In the following passage choose the appropriate question words (the first letter of each one is given to help you), and change the words in italics into an infinitive:*

e.g. I don't know w_____ *I must be* there.
I don't know **when to be** there.

I was once travelling from Spain to Switzerland, but I missed my train at the French border. I didn't know w___1___ *I should do* or w___2___ *I should ask* for advice. I wasn't sure whether I should wait 12 hours for another direct train or try to find out h___3___ *I could get* to Geneva by a different route. Eventually a man at the station told me w___4___ train *I ought to catch* and w___5___ *I had to go* to catch it. Meanwhile my friend in Geneva didn't know w___6___ *he should do*, either, when my original train arrived without me. He wasn't sure whether he ought to stay at the station or not. He didn't know h___7___ *he could get* in touch with me. He finally decided to leave a message for me, telling me w___8___ *I had to go* to contact him and w___9___ telephone number *I could ring*.

# Passive

## 112 was born; is/was called

### a was born

Look at the verbs in these sentences:

Mahatma Gandhi **was born** in 1869.
Many Australians and New Zealanders **were born** in Britain.

Look at this table. It shows the names of my cousins and the year when each was born.

| Christine | 1949 | Marjory | 1944 | Barry | 1951 |
| Joan | 1952 | Sheila | 1942 | Terry | 1956 |
| Brian | 1944 | Dorothy | 1942 | Jenny | 1954 |

Christine **was born** in 1949.
Brian and Marjory **were born** in 1944.

Write similar sentences about:
1. Joan
2. Sheila and Dorothy
3. Barry
4. Terry
5. Jenny

### b is/was called

Look at the verbs in these sentences:

He **is called** Bill. (His name is Bill.)
The film **was called** *Casablanca*. (The name of the film was *Casablanca*.)

Rewrite the following sentences; use **is/are called** or **was/were called** in each one:
1. Their names are Shirley and Pat.
2. The name of the book was *Tom Sawyer*.
3. Her name is Tina Rowland.
4. The names of their sons were Bill and Ben.

## 113 made of/from/with/by

Notice the preposition used in each sentence:

The table is **made of** wood. (It is still recognisably wood.)
Wine is **made from** grapes. (We cannot see the grapes in the wine.)
The cake was **made with** flour, butter, eggs, sugar and fruit. (a number of different ingredients.)
The furniture was **made by** my grandfather. (My grandfather made it.)

# Passive

*Supply the correct preposition in each sentence:*

1. Knives are made _____ stainless steel.
2. Whisky is made _____ barley or rye.
3. The model boats are made _____ retired sailors.
4. Trifle is a dessert made _____ cake, custard, fruit and cream.
5. The dial on the telephone is made _____ plastic.
6. Artificial silk is a fibre made _____ a kind of plastic.
7. The wastepaper basket was made _____ Plastics Limited.
8. Paper is made _____ trees.
9. What's it made _____ ? Gold, or platinum?
10. A What have you put in it?
    B I made it _____ pineapple juice, lemonade and coconut milk.

## 114 Active and passive

Compare the active and passive forms of different tenses in the table below. Then convert the active sentences to passive, using **(by...)** only where indicated:

| Tense | Active | Passive |
| --- | --- | --- |
| Present Simple | They **sell** bread here. | Bread **is sold** here. |
| Present Continuous | They **are building** a house. | A house **is being built**. |
| Future Simple | They'**ll do** it tomorrow. | It **will be done** tomorrow. |
| Past Simple | Goya **painted** it. | It **was painted by** Goya. |
| Past Continuous | They **were playing** games. | Games **were being played**. |
| Present Perfect | They **have sold** the house. | The house **has been sold**. |
| Modals | You **can buy tickets** here. | Tickets **can be bought** here. |
|  | People **must obey** the law. | The law **must be obeyed**. |

1. They make shoes in Northampton.
2. Someone has broken the window.
3. The Queen will open the old people's home. **(by ...)**
4. Someone wrote this book in the fifteenth century.
5. Shakespeare wrote *Hamlet*. **(by...)**
6. You must pay the bill immediately.

7   They are repairing the roof.
8   You can play this game indoors or outdoors.
9   They were laying the tables when we arrived at the restaurant.
10  A friend of mine sang the song. **(by ...)**

## 115   Infinitive forms

*Compare these sentences:*

Would you like **to mention your uncle** in your will? (active)
Would you like **your uncle to be mentioned** in your will? (passive)

*Rewrite these sentences, using the alternative form, as in the examples above:*

1   They want to replace the manager.
2   I think we should tell everyone about it.
3   She would like them to invite her, too.
4   I don't like it when people put me in situations like this.
5   I asked them to inform me about the situation.

## 116   Double object verbs

### a   Direct object

*Compare these sentences:*

**Someone gave** the money to John. (active)
**The money was given** to John. (passive)

We prefer the Passive when we are not especially interested in the doer of the action (e.g. **someone**), but rather in the object (e.g. **the money**).

*Rewrite these sentences in the Passive, as in the example above:*

1   At the end of the lesson, someone reads a story to the children.
2   Someone sold the shop to a friend of mine.
3   They have to pay back the loan to the bank.

### b   Indirect object

*Compare these sentences:*

**Someone gave** John the money. (active)
**John was given** the money. (passive)

When we are more interested in the person to whom the action was done, i.e. the indirect object of the Active sentence, we can begin the Passive sentence with the indirect object (e.g. **John**). Other verbs which can be used in this form are: **ask, leave** (in a will), **lend, owe, pay, promise, send, show**.

# Passive

*Rewrite these sentences in the Passive, beginning with the indirect object, as in the example above:*

1. People often ask Roy questions about his work.
2. Someone showed me how to do it.
3. Nobody owed me any money.
4. I think they pay Harry too much.
5. They promised Sarah a rise.

## c  Direct and indirect object

*Compare these sentences:*

**John was given** the money. (passive)
**The money was given** to John. (passive)

Both of these sentences are Passive. In the first sentence we are more interested in **John**, and in the second sentence we are more concerned with **the money**.

*Rewrite the sections in italics in the following conversation. Change the subject of each sentence from a person to a thing, as in the example above:*

Mr Matthews, the bank manager, is worried about a loan the bank made to a young couple to buy a house.

*Mr Matthews*   I think *they were lent the money* without enough guarantee. After all, *they were given the down-payment* as a wedding present. They haven't got any money themselves.

*Assistant Manager*   Oh, that's all right. *We've been paid the whole amount. I was shown the letter* yesterday. *We were sent the cheque* last week. Apparently, *they were left the entire sum* in someone's will.

# 117   Causative: **have/get something done**

## Intentional

*Compare these sentences:*

I **painted my house** last month.
I **had my house painted** last month.
I **got my house painted** last month.

The first sentence means that I did the work myself; the second and third sentences mean that someone painted it for me.

158

# Passive

Get something done suggests a little more effort than **have something done**, such as making a journey. So we may say when we leave home:

**I'm going to the photographer's to get my photograph taken**, but when we arrive, we say: **I've come to have my photograph taken.**

*The people in these sentences are all going to* **get something done.** *Write down what each person says to her husband/his wife before he/she leaves, using the words in brackets:*

e.g. Lucy is going to the hairdresser's. (cut and perm my hair)
**I'm going to the hairdresser's to get my hair cut and permed.**

1. Paula is going to the dry-cleaner's. (clean this dress)
2. Harry is going to the barber's. (cut my hair )
3. Peter is going to the TV shop. (repair this TV set)
4. Margaret is going to the jeweller's. (repair this watch)

*The people in these sentences have just arrived at a shop or similar place where they want to* **have something done.** *Write down what each person says, using the words in brackets:*

e.g. Betty is at the dressmaker's. (alter this skirt)
**I've come to have this skirt altered,**

5. Anne is at the optician's. (test my eyes)
6. Bob is at the tailor's. (make a suit)
7. Frank is at a typing agency. (type this report)
8. Sarah is at the post office. (register this parcel)

# Reported speech

## 118  Direct and reported speech

*Compare these sentences:*

He said, 'I don't like onions.' (direct)
He said **he didn't like onions**. (reported)

She said, 'I visited my aunt yesterday.' (direct)
She said **that she had visited her aunt the day before**. (reported)

Notice that when we change direct speech to reported speech, expressions of time and place (e.g. **yesterday**) often change. The tense will change also if the verb introducing the reported speech is in the past tense (e.g. **said**). Use this list of rules for reference when you do the exercises below. (See also Practice 146 on **say** and **tell**, and Practice 120 on Reported questions.)

### Tense changes

| Direct | Reported |
|---|---|
| 'I'm working very hard.' | He said he was working... |
| 'I earn £100 a week.' | He said he earned... |
| 'I'm going to change my job.' | He said he was going to... |
| 'I'll finish it soon.' | He said he would finish it... |
| 'I've never seen her before.' | He said he had never seen her... |
| 'I didn't break it.' | He said he hadn't broken it. |
| 'I can run faster than her.' | He said he could run faster... |
| 'It may be too late.' | He said it might be... |

### Time and place changes

| Direct | Reported |
|---|---|
| here | there |
| this | that |
| now | then |
| yesterday | the day before |
| tomorrow | the day after |
| last week | the week before |
| next week | the week after |
| ago | before |

1  Read this report of a conversation and then write what Janet and Mary actually said:
   e.g. *Janet*  **I'm going to the cinema...**

Janet told Mary that she was going to the cinema that evening with her husband. He was taking her to see *Rain Man*. They were going to have dinner after the show. She was afraid there might be a queue so they were going to get to the cinema in good time to make sure they got in. She said she was very fond of Dustin Hoffman. In her opinion, he was the best actor in the world. She told Mary that she would tell her all about the film when she saw her the day after. Mary hoped they would both enjoy the film.

2  Put this conversation into reported speech:
e.g. **Mary said they were going on holiday the week after...**

*Mary*  We're going on holiday next week. Ian and the children are looking forward to it. We're going to drive to the west of England and rent a caravan. Ian needs a rest, but he doesn't mind driving, and once we get to the caravan site we'll just stay there for a fortnight and put our feet up. The children will have plenty to do on the beach. The only trouble is that we can't rely on the weather at this time of year, but we'll have to take a chance on it and hope everything will be all right.

*Janet*  I hope you'll enjoy your holiday. I'll see you when you get back and you can tell me all about it.

## 119 Tense changes: Present Simple and Future

Notice the tense changes from direct to reported speech in these sentences:

*John*  I'm sure everything will be all right.
John **was** sure everything **would be** all right.

*Jim*  When the boss comes in, I'll ask him about it.
Jim decided that when the boss **came** in, he **would ask** him about it.

*Sheila*  If you don't keep your eyes on the road, you'll have an accident.
Sheila was afraid that if he **didn't keep** his eyes on the road, he**'d have** an accident.

In reported speech the Present changes to the Past, and **will** changes to **would**.

Note that the same changes referred to in Practice 118 apply here, e.g. **may** changes to **might, can to could, will have to** to **would have to,** etc.

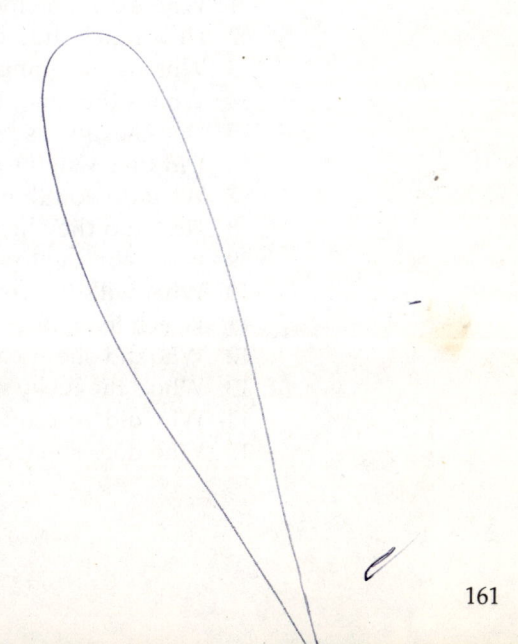

## Reported speech

Change the following to reported speech. Change the tenses in the same way as in the examples. Try not to use **said** all the time:

e.g. *Lucy*   I don't suppose he'll have any problems.
**Lucy didn't suppose that he would have any problems.**

e.g. *Simon*   I'm very worried about my mother.
**Simon was very worried about his mother.**

1  *Doctor Andrews*   I believe that the operation will be successful.
2  *Martin*   I hope that we will meet again.
3  *Mr Grenfell*   I'm afraid that if we don't deliver the goods on time, we'll lose the order.
4  *Linda*   I've made up my mind. I won't accept the job unless they pay me my travelling expenses.
5  *Mrs Roberts*   I'm sure that when you see the report you'll reach the same conclusion.

## 120  Reported speech: questions

Look at the word order in these questions:

**Where are they going?** (direct question)
I wonder **where they are going.** (reported question)

**How much does it cost?** (direct question)
Ask him **how much it costs.** (reported question)

**Did she go with him?** (direct question)
I wonder **if she went with him.** (reported question)

Change the direct questions to reported questions, beginning with the words in brackets:

e.g. Does she want any tea? (Ask her)
**Ask her if she wants any tea.**

1  Where does he live? (Tell me)
2  How much did you pay for it? (I'd like to know)
3  What is she going to do next? (I wonder)
4  What's the time? (Ask that policeman)
5  Does he always behave like that? (I wonder)
6  Did they win the game? (I wonder)
7  What do you think about your chances in the game? (Tell me)
8  How did they hear about it? (I wonder)
9  Is she coming to the party? (Ask her)
10  What will the weather be like tomorrow? (I wonder)
11  Which team does he play for? (Ask him)
12  Who did she speak to? (Ask her)
13  Who's the lucky man? (I wonder)
14  Why did you say that? (Tell me)
15  Who does she think she is? (Ask her)

# 121 Reported imperatives

## a tell someone to do something

*Compare these sentences:*

        Carol   **Don't buy** that red shirt, Roger. It doesn't suit you. **Buy** the white one.
        Carol **told Roger not to buy** the red shirt because it didn't suit him. She **told him to buy** the white one.

Notice how the infinitive with **to** is used in reported commands.

*Change sentences 1-8 to reported speech:*

(The next day Carol was driving a car and Roger was giving her some advice.)

1. Follow the main road as far as the traffic lights.
2. Slow down at the zebra crossing.
3. Look in the mirror.
4. Don't drive so fast.
5. Be careful of that cyclist. (Use **a**)
6. Don't overtake that bus. (Use **a**)
7. Turn left at the traffic lights.
8. Don't turn right.

## b ask someone to do something

*Compare these sentences:*

    *Mr Crump*   Students, will you listen to me, please?
                    Mr Crump **asked the students to listen** to him.
    *Mr Crump*   Please don't smoke in the classroom, Alexander.
                    He **asked Alexander not to smoke** in the classroom.

Notice that a polite request with **please** is usually introduced by **ask** in reported speech.

*Change sentences 1-6 to reported speech:*

(Mr Crump was giving his students some work to do in class.)

1. Will you open your books, please?
2. Will you turn to page 37?
3. Please don't interrupt, Charlotte.
4. Will you do exercise 53, please?
5. Would you mind not talking, Alexander? (Do not use **mind**)
6. Hand your books to me when you have finished, please.

# Clauses

## 122 neither...nor

Notice the use of **neither...nor, either, neither** and **nor** in these sentences:

The Town Council **didn't know** the answer to Harry's question.
The Ministry **didn't know, either, (Neither/nor did** the Ministry.)
**Neither** the Town Council **nor** the Ministry **knew** the answer to Harry's question.

Rewrite each of the following statements twice, using two alternative forms, as in the examples above:

1. Lendl didn't win the tennis tournament. McEnroe didn't, either. Becker won it.
2. Allan didn't play in the match. Nor did Bennett. In the end, the manager chose Johnny Biggs.
3. Neither Mark nor Lawrence was best man at the wedding. Richard did not want to upset either of them, so Sally's brother was best man.
4. Harris didn't steal the money. Morley didn't either. The thief was Mr Carter's nephew.
5. Happy Jack didn't win the race. Nor did Mountain Rose. The winner was London Pride.

## 123 Future time clauses with **when, if, before, after, until**

Make sure you understand the meaning of each sentence:

I will go **when** he arrives.                **When** he arrives, I will go.
I will go **if** he arrives.                  **If** he arrives, I will go.
I will go **after** he arrives.               **After** he arrives, I will go.
I will go **before** he arrives.              **Before** he arrives, I will go.
I will stay **until** he arrives.
I will play the **next time** she comes.      **The next time** she comes, I will play.
I will go **as soon as** she comes.           **As soon as** she comes, I will go.

Note that the verb after **when, if, before, after** or **until** is Present Simple, but in the other part of the sentence we use the Future with **will**.

Complete the following sentences with the correct forms of the verbs in brackets:

1. If it _____ tomorrow, I _____ at home. (rain, stay)
2. They _____ the job after we _____ them the money. (finish, give)
3. We _____ here until she _____ (wait, call)
4. When the children _____ here, they _____ thirsty. (get, be)
5. We _____ that film the next time it _____ . (see, come)
6. They _____ the house if we _____ for the paint. (paint, pay)
7. I _____ out when my headache _____ a bit better. (go, be)

# Clauses

8  Jack and Jill _____ all the food before the guests _____ . (prepare, arrive)
9  If you _____ me the letter, I _____ it to the post for you. (give, take)
10  As soon as she _____ here, we _____ supper. (get, have)

## 124  the more...the more

Look at these sentences:

**The more** he works, **the more tired** he gets.
**The bigger** the car, **the more expensive** it is to run.
**The less** you argue, **the better** it will be for you.

Note the form: **the** + comparative...**the** + comparative

*Put the adjectives and adverbs in brackets into the comparative form to complete these sentences, as in the examples above:*

1  The _____ the students, the _____ it is to teach them. The _____ they are, the _____ they understand. (good, easy, intelligent, soon)
2  The _____ you eat, the _____ you get, and the _____ you get, the _____ you are to have a heart attack. (much, fat, fat, likely)
3  The _____ the whisky is matured, the _____ it tastes, but, on the other hand, the _____ the care needed to mature it, the _____ it is. (long, good, great, expensive)
4  The _____ he gets, the _____ he becomes. He's got a bad back and the trouble is that the _____ exercise he gets, the _____ it becomes. (old, irritable, little, bad)
5  The _____ I think about it, the _____ I understand why he behaved like that. I sometimes think that the _____ you treat people, the _____ they respond to you and the _____ they are. (much, little, good, bad, ungrateful)

## 125  what, the thing that

### a  what is interesting, the interesting thing

Compare these sentences:

**What is interesting** about this is that it was proved by two different methods.
**The interesting thing** about this is that it was proved by two different methods.

*Change one form to the other in these sentences:*

1  The surprising thing is that it took them so long to find out.
2  What is exciting about it is that it's never happened before.

165

# Clauses

3 What is unfortunate is that we didn't realise the mistake until it was too late.
4 The depressing thing in Britain is the weather.

## b  what interests me, the thing that interests me

*Compare these sentences:*

What interests me in their research is the method they used.
The thing that interests me in their research is the method they used.

*Change one form to the other in these sentences:*

1 The thing that worries me is my father's reaction.
2 What pleases me about it is that the problem was solved without any arguments.
3 The thing that matters most is your own health.
4 What annoys me is that they are so rude.

## c  what I like, the thing I like

*Compare these sentences:*

What I like about it is the simplicity of the design.
The thing I like about it is the simplicity of the design.

*Change one form to the other in these sentences:*

1 The thing I hate about Monday mornings is having to go back to work.
2 What I disapprove of is their lack of consideration for other people.
3 The thing I complain about is their selfishness.
4 The thing I can't understand is how they made the mistake in the first place.

## d  what and that

*Compare these sentences:*

What interests him is money.
What he cares about is money.
The only thing that interests him is money.
Money is the only thing (that) he cares about.

*Use **what** or **that** in each space in the following dialogue:*

Harvey, a theatre director in a small provincial town, is talking to Judy, an actress.

Judy   The play went quite well. The only thing ___1___ bothered me was the size of the audience. And the only part of the play ___2___ interested them was the end.

*Harvey*      __3__ you must understand is that people in this town don't come to the theatre to think. The only thing __4__ keeps their attention is something exciting. __5__ they like is a good story. The play __6__ has drawn the biggest audience this year was a murder mystery.

*Judy*      That's __7__ upsets me. And __8__ I learnt at drama school doesn't help me. When I got this job I thought it was the best thing __9__ had ever happened to me, but now the only thought __10__ comes into my head on the stage is: When will it be over? That is __11__ depresses me so much.

*Harvey*      __12__ is worrying me is that if we don't get a bigger audience we'll have to close the theatre. The only solution __13__ occurs to me is to give them __14__ they want. It's a pity but __15__ draws the crowds in London isn't popular here.

# 126   however, whatever, whoever, wherever

Compare the sentences below, which have the same meaning in each case:

**It doesn't matter how efficient** they are. They're certain to make mistakes sooner or later.
**However efficient** they are, they're certain to make ...

I'm going to ask for my money back. **I don't care what** they say about it.
I'm going to ask for my money back, **whatever** they say ...

**It doesn't matter who** they are. They must obey the rules.
**Whoever** they are, they must obey the rules.

**I don't care where** she goes. I'll follow her.
**Wherever** she goes, I'll follow her.

Make single sentences from the pairs of sentences below, using **however, whatever, wherever** or **whoever**:

1. I'm going to complain. I don't care what he says.
2. I don't care who is father is. He has to pass the same test as everyone else.
3. We need that material. It doesn't matter how expensive it is.
4. He won't find it easy. It doesn't matter how intelligent he is.
5. I don't care where he lives. We'll find him.
6. You can't come in. I don't care who you are.
7. It doesn't matter where you are. I'll keep in touch with you.
8. It doesn't matter what you do. They won't take any notice.

## Clauses

## 127 Infinitive of purpose and **for**

*Compare the two answers to the question:*
- A Why did Bob go to the shops?
- B Bob went to the shops **for some bread**.
  Bob went to the shops **to buy some bread**.

We use **for** when we mention the thing alone, e.g. **for some bread**; we use **to** when we mention the action, e.g. **to buy some bread**.

*Put **for** or **to** in the following:*
1. Wendy drove into town _____ see her boyfriend.
2. Penny went to the market _____ some fruit.
3. Mr Smith came _____ talk to my wife.
4. Alan has gone to the club _____ play squash.
5. Pat went to the library _____ a book about Plato.
6. Harry cycled over to his cousins' _____ tell them the news.
7. We'll need some strong wood _____ make the shelves.
8. We'll need some strong wood _____ the shelves.

## 128 **so as to/in order to, so that, because; avoid, prevent**

### a to, so as to, in order to, so that, because

*Compare these sentences:*

He changed his job **to be** free to referee football matches.
He changed his job **so as to be** free to referee football matches.
He changed his job **in order to be** free to referee football matches.
He changed his job **so that he would be** free to referee football matches.
He changed his job **because he wanted to be** free to referee football matches.

All are acceptable English. However, we normally use **to** in simple statements,
e.g. **He went to the station to meet his friend**,

We use **so as to** and **in order to** in more formal circumstances; the **in order to/so as to** clause usually comes first.
e.g. **In order to/So as to deal with the growing problem of unemployment, we have set up a number of Employment Centres in the city.**

**So that** or **because** are essential when there is a change of subject,
e.g. **We have set up Employment Centres so that people will know where to go for advice.**
**We have set up Employment Centres because we want people to know where to go for advice.**

# Clauses

*Use* **so as to** *or* **in order to** *instead of* **because/if** *in the following sentences. Put the clause with* **in order to** *or* **so as to** *first:*

    e.g. They are building a lot of hotels because they want to develop their tourist trade.
    **In order to develop their tourist trade they are building a lot of hotels.**

1   The Ministry has published a road safety booklet because it wants to inform people about changes in the Highway Code.
2   We have designed training courses because we want to improve the standard of hotel management.
3   We have opened a number of branch offices because we want to provide a better service to our customers.
4   He employed a different method because he wanted to test his findings.
5   Please hand your passport application to this office a month before you intend to travel abroad if you want to avoid delay.

## b  so as not to, in order not to, so that...not, to avoid, because...not

*Compare these sentences:*

    He came in quietly **in order not to wake** the baby.
    He came in quietly **so as not to wake** the baby.
    He came in quietly **so that he would not wake** the baby.
    He came in quietly **to avoid waking** the baby.
    He came in quietly **because he didn't want to wake** the baby.

    Note that the simple infinitive with **to** is not possible with the negative.

*Rewrite each sentence in two ways, using* **in order not to, so as not to, so that...not** *or* **to avoid**:

    e.g. Check everything you write, so as not to make silly mistakes.
    **Check everything you write, to avoid making silly mistakes.**
    **Check everything you write, so that you don't make silly mistakes.**

1   If you work in a chemical laboratory, you should wear gloves so that you will not expose your skin to harmful substances.
2   Some dentists wear masks so as not to catch germs from their patients.
3   The thief wore gloves to avoid leaving fingerprints.
4   He put his keys on a key-ring so as not to lose them.
5   We process all the waste products from the factory so that we won't pollute the river.

## c  so that...not, to prevent, because...not

*Compare the following sentences:*

    The cinema has two exits **so that people will not be trapped** inside.
    The cinema has two exits **to prevent people from being trapped** inside.
    The cinema has two exits **because we don't want people to be trapped** inside.

*Clauses*

Rewrite each sentence in two ways, using **so that...not,** and **to prevent** instead of **because...not,** as in the examples above:

1. We are doing research because we don't want our competitors to gain an advantage over us.
2. We tell women who work in the factory to wear hairnets because we don't want their hair to be caught in the machines.
3. He cleaned the bicycle carefully because he didn't want it to get rusty.
4. They have put broken glass on top of the walls because they don't want thieves to get in.
5. 'The Samaritans' provide lonely people with telephone numbers to ring when they are depressed because they don't want them to commit suicide.

## 129  unless

**Unless** means 'if...not and only if...not'. Its real opposite is **provided/ providing (that)**, which means 'if...and only if', but in most cases **unless**= 'if...not'.

Look at these examples:

She'll fail the exam **if she doesn't** work harder.
She'll fail the exam **unless she works** harder.

Use **unless** in place of **if...not** in the following sentences:

1. Don't wake me up if it isn't really necessary.
2. The dog won't bite you if you don't annoy him.
3. If they don't deliver the goods tomorrow, I'm going to cancel the order.
4. You can't rent a car if you don't show your licence.
5. We'll play tennis this afternoon if it doesn't rain.

## 130  in case

**In case** means 'because...may'. It is normally followed by the present tense when it refers to the future.

Look at these examples:

I'm going to leave some food for her in the fridge. She may come home late.
I'm going to leave some food for her in the fridge, **in case** she **comes** home late.

Rewrite these sentences, using **in case** and the appropriate verb in the Present Simple tense:

1. Take an umbrella. It may rain.
2. You'd better write this down. You may forget it.

3   He has taken out an insurance policy. He may have an accident.
4   We'd better take a map. We may lose our way.
5   You'd better explain the rules to them yourself. They may not understand them.
6   Leave a message on his desk because he may not remember our appointment.

## 131  while, meanwhile

**While** is a conjunction meaning 'during the time that...'.
**Meanwhile** is an adverb meaning 'during the same period of time'.

Look at these examples:
**While** we're waiting for them, we'll have a drink.
They'll be here in about ten minutes, and **meanwhile** we'll have a drink.

Complete the sentences, using **while** or **meanwhile**:
1  She often listens to the radio _____ she does her housework.
2  I was doing the housework, and _____ the children were watching the TV.
   I did the housework _____ the children watched the TV.
3  He cooked the lunch _____ his wife was at her mother's.
   'You go round to your mother's, and _____ I'll cook the lunch.'
4  I can't give any definite information about your flight _____ the weather is so bad.
   I won't be able to give you information about your flight for an hour. _____ , would you mind waiting in the lounge?
5  The sergeant stayed at his desk in the police station to answer the phone. _____ , Inspector Smith was at the scene of the crime.
   The sergeant stayed at his desk in the police station to answer the phone _____ the inspector was at the scene of the crime.

## 132  the reason for/why...

Compare these sentences:
Tommy's unhappy home life is **the reason for his bad behaviour** at school.
Tommy's unhappy home life is **the reason for his/him behaving badly** at school.
Tommy's unhappy home life is **the reason why he behaves badly** at school.

The **reason for** is used with a noun or gerund form. **The reason why** is followed by a clause (subject and verb).

## Clauses

*Rewrite these sentences in two ways, using the alternative forms given in the examples above. Use the Past Simple tense with **why** or a gerund with **for**:*

1. The reason for the increase in taxes was that the Government needed more money.
2. I cannot see any good reason for the changes they made to the rules.
3. The reason for my visit to them was to find out what they thought about the idea.
4. Can you give me any reason for their absence yesterday?
5. Didn't she give any reason for his strange behaviour?
6. The reason for the attack on the embassy is not yet clear.
7. The reasons for my decision to resign were obvious.
8. I cannot suggest any good reason for the students' failure.

## 133 although/even though, in spite of; however, nevertheless, all the same

*Compare these sentences:*

**Although he was tired**, he went on working
**Even though he was tired**, he went on working.

**In spite of being tired**, he went on working.
**In spite of his tiredness**, he went on working.

He felt tired. **However**, he went on working.
He felt tired. **Nevertheless**, he went on working.
He felt tired. **All the same**, he went on working.

**Although** is followed by a subject and verb, **in spite of** by a gerund or a noun.

If we use **however, nevertheless** or **all the same**, two sentences are necessary.
All three could come at the end of the sentence,
e.g. **He went on working, however.**

We usually prefer to use a less formal construction, with **though**,
e.g. **He went on working, though.**

*1 Rewrite the sentences with **although** into sentences using **in spite of**, and vice versa. Use an appropriate noun after **in spite of** if you know one; if not, use a gerund form:*

1. In spite of being an experienced driver, he drove carelessly.
2. Although he was strong, he could not break down the door.
3. In spite of being able to speak several languages, he's a terrible teacher. (Use **can**.)
4. Although they protest, the Government won't do anything.
5. Although she was very distressed, she smiled bravely.
6. In spite of his laziness, he is very intelligent.

7   In spite of her rudeness, I still like her.
8   In spite of his wealth, he still lives in that old house.
9   Although he played well, he lost the game.
10  The plane took off on time, although it was foggy.

2  Rewrite the above, using two sentences with **though** at the end of the second sentence:
   e.g. **He was an experienced driver. He drove carelessly, though.**

## 134 Defining relative clauses

Use this table for reference:

|  | Subject Pronoun | Object Pronoun |
|---|---|---|
| Person | who/that | _____ [1](whom/[2]that) |
| Thing | that/which | _____ (that/which) |
| Possessive | whose | whose |
| Prepositional |  | _____ + preposition (preposition + whom/which) |

Note: [1] _____ = no pronoun is used.
      [2] **Whom** is used in more formal, usually written, language.

Defining relative clauses identify the person or thing we are talking about. Relative clauses <u>must</u> be included when they refer to the subject of the verb, because they qualify the meaning of the sentence,
   e.g. The man **who came with her** was her uncle.
       The house **that fell down** was very old.

When these clauses refer to the object of the sentence, the relative pronoun is usually omitted (contact clause),
   e.g. The girl **(whom/that)** he married came from Manchester.
       The car **(that/which)** they bought was very expensive.

However, the possessive form is always used,
   e.g. That's the man **whose dog** bit me.
       That's the man **whose dog** I ran over.

Usually, we avoid pronouns in prepositional clauses either by putting the preposition at the end in a contact clause,
   e.g. Those are the people we had lunch with.
       That's the house I was born in.

## Clauses

or by using **where** or **when** as relative adverbs in references to place and time,

e.g. That's the house **where** I was born.
  Do you know **when** your train leaves?

Note that with **when** we omit 'the time'.
Sometimes we also omit 'the place', 'the shop' etc with **where**,
e.g. That's **where** I buy my vegetables.

*Complete the sentences, using the appropriate relative pronoun,* **only when a pronoun is essential,** *or by using* **where** *or* **when:**

1. That's the man _____ spoke to me on the bus last night.
   That's the man _____ I spoke to on the bus last night.
2. She's the girl _____ handbag was stolen.
   She's the girl _____ car I bought.
3. That's the town _____ I grew up in.
   That's the town _____ I grew up.
4. That's the book _____ has interested me most.
   That's the book _____ I lent you.
5. The office _____ I work was built by people _____ wanted to save money, so they didn't install the lift _____ was obviously needed. Or perhaps lifts weren't invented (at the time) _____ they built it. Anyway, a man _____ I was talking to yesterday, the man _____ office is above mine, says he has counted the stairs _____ he has to climb every day, and it comes to over 600!

# 135 Non-defining relative clauses

*Use this table for reference:*

|  | Subject Pronoun | Object Pronoun |
| --- | --- | --- |
| Person | who | whom |
| Thing | which | which |
| Possessive | whose | whose |
| Prepositional |  | preposition + whom/which |

Non-defining relative clauses do not identify the people or things we are talking about, but give us additional information. They are not very common in conversation and are used more in written English, as they are rather formal.

# Clauses

*Compare these sentences:*

Bob Jones works in the same office as me. He has just got married.
Bob Jones, **who works in the same office as me**, has just got married.

Clauses like this are placed between commas if the person or thing is the subject of the main clause, but if it is the object, the relative clause appears at the end.

I'm going to see my friend, Bob Jones. He has just got married.
I'm going to see my friend, Bob Jones, **who has just got married**.

The use of a proper name (Bob Jones) always indicates that the clause following is not a defining relative because the name itself is a definition, unless the speaker knows two people called Bob Jones (I don't mean **the Bob Jones who works in the same office as you**. I mean someone I was at school with).

Japan exports a lot of cars. Some of them are imported by Britain.
Japan exports a lot of cars, **some of which are imported by Britain**.

The police have arrested two men. Both of them are now in prison.
The police have arrested two men, **both of whom are now in prison.**

As in defining relative clauses, we put prepositions at the end in less formal style,
e.g. I mentioned the exam, which she didn't want to talk about.

*In each case, join the sentences together to make a non-defining clause, replacing the word in italic type with the correct relative pronoun:*

1. Jane Brown is coming to stay with me. *She* was in my class at school.
   Jane Brown is coming to stay with me. I met *her* at school.
   I'm going to stay with Jane Brown. *She* was at school with me.
   I'm going to stay with Jane Brown. I met *her* at school.
2. His case was too heavy for him. *It* weighed 50 kilos.
   He couldn't carry his case. *It* was too heavy for him.
3. Thousands of people came to the concert. Most of *them* were under 18.
4. After the game the police arrested 30 'hooligans'. All of *them* were Chelsea supporters.
5. In the tomb they found hundreds of old coins. Some of *them* were very valuable.
6. Oil is the country's main source of income. Most of *it* is exported.
7. Mary Simmons has become managing director. *Her* grandfather founded the firm.
   The company has a new managing director, Mary Simmons. Her grandfather founded the firm.

## 136 Co-ordinating relative clauses

*Compare these sentences:*

Someone stole her car, **which** was in her garage.
Someone stole her car, **which** made her very angry.

In the first sentence the relative clause is non-defining; **which** refers to 'her car', and gives us some additional information about it.
'What was in her garage'? 'her car'.

In the second sentence the relative clause is co-ordinate; **which** refers to the whole of the main clause, the fact that the car was stolen, not 'her car'.
'What made her angry'? Not 'her car', but the fact that it was stolen.

*Underline the part of the sentence the word* **which** *refers to, and make a question to which the section you have underlined is the answer, as in the examples above:*

1. He is proud of his Rolls-Royce, which cost him a lot of money.
   He is proud of his Rolls-Royce, which is only natural.
2. I caught the last train, which was lucky.
   I caught the last train, which left at 11.30.
3. He lives in Bath, which is a beautiful city.
   He lives in Bath, which means he has a long journey to work every day.
4. He was born on February 29th, which only occurs once every four years.
   He only has a birthday once every four years, which must be annoying.
5. She has just published her first novel, which has been a great success, and she's only 19, which makes it even more remarkable.

# Word order

## 137 all, both, the whole

### a all, both

Compare the word order in these sentences:

The girls are **both** ill.
They are **both** ill.
It was **all** very interesting.

The girls **both** like pop music.
They **both** like pop music.
It **all** happened very quickly.

With the verb **be, both** and **all** go after **am, is, are, was** and **were**. With other verbs, **both** and **all** go before the verb.

We use **both** only for two things or people; we cannot use **all** for two things or people.

Put **both** or **all** in the correct place in the following:
1. The children in Tom's class are interested in football.
2. Sara and I play the guitar.
3. The houses in this town are quite old.
4. Mr and Mrs Proctor are dentists.
5. Mr and Mrs Proctor play bridge very well.
6. You and Shirley like ice cream, don't you?

Now rewrite the sentences with a pronoun (**we, you, they,** etc.) instead of the subject and with **both** or **all**:
e.g. 1 **They are all interested in football.**

### b the whole

Compare these sentences:

I read the story from beginning to end.
I read **the whole** story.

We lay in the sun from morning to evening.
We lay in the sun **the whole** day.

He painted all of the room green.
He painted **the whole** room green.

**The whole** means the same as **all of the**, but with a singular noun (**story, day, room**) we usually use **the whole**.

Complete the following using **the whole** and a suitable noun so that the second sentence means the same as the first:
1. The film was good from beginning to end. _____ was good.
2. The house was dirty from top to bottom. _____ was dirty.
3. I worked hard from Monday to Saturday. I worked hard _____ .
4. Every part of the house was full of people. _____ was full of people.

*Word order*

## 138 enough

*Compare the word order in these sentences:*

    Those curtains aren't **long enough**.
    This train isn't going **quickly enough**.
    There's **enough sugar** in the packet.

**Enough** goes after an adjective or an adverb,
e.g. **good enough, long enough; well enough, quickly enough**.

**Enough** goes before a noun or adjective + noun,
e.g. **enough food, enough knives; enough good ideas**.

*Put* **enough** *in the following:*

1 This bag isn't big.
2 Is there hot water for a bath?
3 I think there are eggs for two omelettes.
4 This tea isn't sweet.
5 You don't work hard.

## 139 Direct and indirect object

### a Give the book to me

*Notice the position of the indirect object:*

    A  Shall I put the book and the magazine on the shelf?
    B  No, **give** the book **to me**, and **take** the magazine **to your father**.

We use this word order, with the indirect object **(to me, to your father)** after the direct object **(the book, the magazine)**, when the person **(me, your father)** is emphasised.

*Put a direct object and an indirect object in each space, using the words in brackets:*

1  A  Who are these cards for?
    B  Send _____ , and send _____ .
       (the big one, Tony; the little one, Aunt Maud)
2  A  What shall I do with the glasses and the bottle?
    B  Take _____ , and give _____ .
       (the glasses, your sister; the bottle, your mother)
3  A  What must I do with these two tickets?
    B  Hand _____ , and show _____ .
       (the green one, the ticket collector; the yellow one, the inspector)

## b  Give me the book

*Notice the position of the indirect object:*

I would like something to read. **Give me** the book, please.

We use this word order, with the indirect object **(me)** before the direct object **(the book)**, when the thing **(the book)** is emphasised.

*Put a suitable pronoun (**me, them,** etc.) as the indirect object in each space:*

1. They think the tea is very strong. Give _____ the hot water.
2. John is thirsty. Bring _____ a drink.
3. The girls are still hungry. Pass _____ some more sandwiches.
4. We are interested in stamps. Show _____ your collection.
5. I haven't got enough money Lend _____ £5.
6. The children are bored. Read _____ a story.
7. Esther doesn't know we're on holiday. Send _____ a postcard.
8. It's my turn to play. Throw _____ the ball.

# 140  Phrasal verbs

*Compare the word order in these sentences:*

Put your coat **on**.
Put **on** your coat.
Put it **on**.

When the object is a pronoun **(it, them)**, the pronoun must come between the two parts of the verb.

Notice the position of **all** with a similar phrasal verb:
**Please put them all back.**

*Change the object to a pronoun in the following, and make sure that the word order is right:*

e.g. Mr Ford cut down the tree yesterday.
**Mr Ford cut it down yesterday.**

1. Mrs Frost took off her gloves.
2. Have you turned the television off?
3. We put on our swimsuits as quickly as possible.
4. Can you blow out the candle, please?
5. The soldiers blew up the bridge.
6. Can you bring the chairs in, please?
7. Fill in all these forms.
8. Did they pay back all the money.

# Lexis

## 141 Nationality words

*Look at these sentences:*

    A  Does he come from England?
    B  Yes, he's **an Englishman**. His wife's **English**, as well.

We normally use a nationality noun, e.g. **Englishman, Spaniard, Dane**, etc. only for men or boys. For women or girls we usually use the adjective, e.g. **English, Spanish, Danish**.

In many cases, the noun is the same as the adjective, e.g. **American, German, Chinese**.

Note that although we do not usually use nationality nouns for women, we can use nationality nouns or adjectives for men, e.g. **Pedro is a Spaniard. He's Spanish**.

*Complete the following in the same way:*

1.  A  Does he come from the United States?
    B  Yes, he's an _____ . His wife's _____ , as well.

2.  A  Does he come from Greece?
    B  Yes, he's a _____ . His wife's _____ , as well.

3.  A  Does he come from Germany?
    B  Yes, he's a _____ . His wife's _____ , as well.

4.  A  Does he come from Spain?
    B  Yes, he's a _____ . His wife's _____ , as well.

5.  A  Does he come from Denmark?
    B  Yes, he's a _____ . His wife's _____ , as well.

6.  A  Does he come from France?
    B  Yes, he's a _____ . His wife's _____ , as well.

7.  A  Does he come from Poland?
    B  Yes, he's a _____ . His wife's _____ , as well.

8.  A  Does he come from Italy?
    B  Yes, he's an _____ . His wife's _____ , as well.

*Write similar examples for some other countries that you know.*

## 142 Mass (uncountable) nouns

These fall into three main groups:

1  abstract nouns, such as **courage, despair, honesty**.

2   mass nouns describing materials, food etc., such as **coal, meat, water**; subjects for study, such as **music, biology**; games and sports, such as **golf, swimming**. Sometimes words may have more than one meaning, and are countable in some cases, uncountable in others; for example, **paper** (material), **a paper** (= a newspaper).
3   words that are countable in some other languages, but not in English, such as **advice, applause, behaviour, commerce, damage, equipment, evidence, furniture, hair, harm, information, insurance, knowledge, lightning, luggage, merchandise, money, news, nonsense, practice, produce, progress, research, rubbish, scenery, thunder, trouble, weather, work.**

*Use words from the list in Group 3 once only to complete the following passage:*

We had a wonderful holiday. The ___1___ was very good, although there was a storm on the first day, with ___2___ and ___3___ . The only problem was that we were carrying a lot of ___4___ ; three cases as well as the camping ___5___ . If you are thinking of going on a holiday like that, my ___6___ is to travel light. The ___7___ was lovely and we soon forgot about the rest of the world. It didn't worry us that we never listened to the ___8___ . Of course, we were careful not to cause the farmers any ___9___ . They get very angry with people who leave all their ___10___ behind them.

## 143  I'm cold, thirsty etc.

*Look at these sentences:*

Jane **was cold**. I'**m thirsty**.
You'**re wrong**. Ted **is nineteen** (years old).

We use **be** with **cold, warm, hot, thirsty, hungry, right** and **wrong**, and also with age, e.g. **She's twenty-one.**

*Complete the following with an adjective from the list above and the correct form of the verb* **be**:

e.g. I'm **hungry**. I want something to eat.
1   John _____ . Can he have a cake, please?
2   A   Mick says New York is the capital of the United States.
    B   Well, he _____ , because Washington DC is.
3   Can I have a drink, please? I _____ very _____ .
4   Victor doesn't want to sit in the sun; he says he _____ too _____ .
5   A   You aren't English, are you?
    B   You _____ quite _____ . I'm Swedish.
6   _____ you _____ ? Well, come and sit near the fire.
7   A   How old _____ you?
    B   I _____ ten but I _____ eleven next month.

# Lexis

## 144 look, sound, taste, seem

*Look at these sentences:*

The cake **looked** delicious, but it **tasted** terrible.
That dog **seems** friendly but it bites when it's afraid.

The verbs **look, sound, taste** and **seem** go with an adjective,
e.g. **look nice, sound happy, taste salty, seem pleasant**.

We use these verbs to talk about the way something appears to us.
We use **look** for the way something appears to our eyes,
e.g. **That building looks old.**
We use **sound** for the way something appears to our ears,
e.g. **This cassette sounds interesting.**
We use **taste** for the way something appears to our tongue,
e.g. **The soup tasted delicious.**
We use **seem** for appearance in general,
e.g. **The idea seems interesting.**

*Put the correct form of* **look, sound, taste** *or* **seem** *in the following, and complete each sentence with one of the adjectives below:*

a distant             e pleasant
b young               f weak
c interesting         g pretty
d strong

1  That's a nice dress. It _____ very _____ on you.
2  I only heard a little of the play but it _____ _____ .
3  This coffee _____ _____ but it _____ very _____ .
4  At first Mr Peters _____ _____ , but in fact he's not very nice.
5  The phone isn't working very well. Everybody's voice _____ _____ .
6  From a distance she _____ quite _____ , but she's older than my mother.

## 145 make and do

*Look at these sentences:*

I have to **make a confession**. I haven't **done my homework**.
She's **done her best**. But she's still **made** a lot of **mistakes**.
I've **made a discovery**. **Doing** your own car **repairs** can be quite easy.

# Lexis

As a general rule we can say **do** tends to relate to actions, **make** to causing, creating or constructing. However, here is a list of some common expressions, excluding phrasal verbs, for reference:

**do**

| | | | |
|---|---|---|---|
| better | an exercise | a job | a service |
| one's best | a favour | justice (to) | wonders |
| business | good | a kindness | work |
| damage | harm | an operation | worse |
| one's duty | homework | repairs | one's worst |
| evil | an injury | right | wrong |

**make**

| | | | |
|---|---|---|---|
| an appointment | an effort | money | a success (of) |
| arrangements | enquiries | the most (of) | sure (of) |
| attacks (on) | one's escape | a movement | a trip |
| the best (of) | an excuse (for) | an offer | trouble (for) |
| certain (of, about) | faces (at) | peace | use (of) |
| a change | a fool (of) | preparations | a voyage |
| a choice | friends (with) | a profit | war (on) |
| a complaint | fun (of) | progress | way (for) |
| a confession | a fuss (about) | a report (on, to) | welcome |
| a decision | a guess | a request | work (for others) |
| a demand | haste | room (for) | |
| a difference (to) | a journey | a search (for) | |
| a discovery | a mistake | a speech | |

*Complete the exercise without looking at this list. Then check your answers against the list. Use an appropriate form of* **do** *or* **make:**

1. A  If you don't _____ an effort, you won't improve your English.
   B  Well, I'm _____ my best. I always _____ my homework.
   A  Yes, but you _____ too many mistakes. Still I suppose you're _____ some progress.

2. Would you mind _____ me a favour? I've got to _____ a speech on Thursday. I want to _____ certain that it's all right. Would you look at it and _____ any changes you think are necessary. I've never _____ anything like this before and I don't want to _____ a fool of myself. But I think I've _____ justice to the subject.

3. A  He's the worst boss I've ever had. He's incapable of _____ a decision, and I'm tired of _____ excuses for him.
   B  He means well, though. He doesn't _____ any harm, does he?
   A  He doesn't _____ any good, either. I don't know how the company _____ a profit if all their managers are like him. I could _____ his job better myself.

# Lexis

## 146  say and tell

### a  say and tell with reported statements

*Look at these sentences:*

  *Paul* There is a letter for you.
  Paul **said** there was a letter for me.
  Paul **told me** there was a letter for me.

These sentences mean the same, but the uses of the verbs **tell** and **say** are different.
**Say** means 'speak words'. It has no object.

**Tell** usually means 'inform a person' and with this meaning always has a personal object (e.g. me),
e.g. **Paul** Hello.
   Paul said hello.
**Tell** cannot be used. Paul is not giving information. In addition, there is no personal object here.
**Tell** can have other meanings,
e.g. **He told a story/the truth,** (Here **tell** means 'relate'.)
  **They're so alike that I can't tell one from another.** (Here **tell** means 'distinguish between'.)
Finally, **tell** is used in a special idiom to mean 'read the time from the clock',
e.g. **He's only three. He can't tell the time yet.**

*Complete these sentences with the correct form of* **say** *or* **tell**:

1 I _told_ you that I couldn't come to the party.
  I _said_ that I couldn't come to the party.
2 He didn't _say_ 'Hello' or _tell_ me his name.
3 What does the notice _say_? I can't read it.
4 This leaflet is supposed to explain the new tax system but it doesn't _tell_ me anything.
5 I'm sorry. I wasn't listening. Did you _say_ something?
6 You'd better _say_ that I'm busy.
  You'd better _tell_ him that I'm busy.
7 They didn't _tell_ me anything. They just sat there without _saying_ a word.
8 I don't think you're _telling_ the truth.

### b  say and tell with reported commands

*Compare these sentences:*

  *Paul* Don't do that again.
  Paul **said that I shouldn't** do it again.
  Paul **told me not to** do it again.

Note that a reported command with **say** is followed by **that** and the auxiliary **should (not)**. The reported command with **tell** takes an infinitive.

Complete these sentences with the correct form of **say** or **tell**:
1. I _told_ you not to bet on the numbers. Now we'll lose our money.
   I _said_ that you shouldn't bet on the numbers.
2. I _told_ him to keep quiet.
   I _told_ him not to make so much noise.
3. He _said_ that we should be more careful.
   He _told_ us to be more careful.
4. They _told_ me not to _say_ anything about it.
   They _said_ that I shouldn't _tell_ anyone about it.
   They _told_ me not to _tell_ anyone about it.
   They _said_ that I shouldn't _say_ anything about it.

### c  say and tell: passive

Note the passive forms:
People say it's a good film.
**It's said** to be a good film
People have told me that it's a good film.
**I've been told** that it's a good film.

Complete these sentences with the correct form of **say** or **tell**:
1. I've been _told_ that there is trouble at the factory.
   It's been _said_ that there is trouble at the factory.
2. It's _said_ to be a very interesting book.
   I've been _told_ that it's a very interesting book.
3. I was _told_ to report here.
4. He's an expert. He's _said_ to know everything about the subject.
   He's an expert. It's _said_ that he knows everything about the subject.
   He's an expert. I've been _told_ to ask his advice on the subject.

# 147  arrive, get to, reach

Study the examples of the constructions used with these verbs:
They **arrived** (**at** the station, **in** England) last night.
They have been talking about the project for a long time and have finally **arrived at** a decision.
What time does the train **arrive** (**at** the station, **in** London)?
When I **got to** the station, the train had already left.
What time does the train **reach** the station/London?
They have taken a long time to **reach** a decision.

# Lexis

The choice between **at** and **in** following **arrive** depends on the size of the place from the speaker's point of view. **In** is normally used for countries, cities. Note that there is no preposition in '**arrive** home'.
**Get to** implies more difficulty than the others. For example, a journey may be slower, longer, have problems.
**Reach** has no preposition and is directly followed by the object.

*Complete the following sentences, using the correct form of* **arrive, get** *or* **reach:**

1. What time did the plane _____ ?
   What time did the plane _____ at the airport?
   What time did the plane _____ the airport?
2. The plane _____ to New York an hour late.
   The plane _____ New York an hour late.
   The plane _____ in New York an hour late.
3. Let me know when you _____ a decision.
   Let me know when you _____ at a decision.
4. When you _____ the age of 50, you'll think differently.
   When you _____ to my age, you'll think differently.
   Not many people _____ at the age of 100.
5. I'm waiting for my cousin to _____ .

## 148 raise and rise

**Raise** means 'lift, put up, cause to go up'. It is a regular verb (**raise, raised, raised, raising**) and always has an object.
**Rise** means 'come up, go up'. It is irregular (rise, rose, risen, rising) and never has an object.

*Look at these examples:*

He **raised** his hand, asking for silence.
The manufacturers **are going to raise their prices**.
The sun **rises** later in winter.
Prices **have risen** since last year.

*Complete the sentences, using the correct forms of* **raise** *or* **rise:**

1. It's very hot and the temperature is still _____ .
2. The workers are going on strike because the management has refused to _____ their wages.
3. _____ your hand if you want to ask a question.
4. The sales of ice cream _____ last summer because it was very hot, but we don't expect them to _____ this year because the company has _____ its prices.
5. The number of passes in the exam has _____ since last year but we hope to _____ the standard even further.

# 149 I (don't) think so, I hope so/not

Look at the answers to these questions:

    A  Is she coming to dinner?
    B  **I think so.** (or **I don't think so.**)
    A  Is her friend coming too?
    B  **I hope so.** (or **I hope not.**)

Here, **I think so** means 'I think she is coming'.
**I hope so** here means 'I hope her friend is coming'.

Put one of these four expressions in each of the following:

1  A  Do you think the film will be interesting?
    B  I don't know, but _____ .
2  A  Does Freda play tennis?
    B  No, _____ .
3  A  Will you fail the exam, do you think?
    B  I don't know, but _____ .
4  A  Has the post come?
    B  Yes, _____ .

# 150 likely, probably

Compare the use of tenses in these sentences:

They **will probably leave** the hotel.
They **are likely to leave** the hotel.
He **will probably not arrive** on Wednesday.
He **is not likely to arrive** on Wednesday.

Rewrite these sentences, either with **probably** or **likely,** as in the examples above:

1. They'll probably go to England next summer.
2. It's likely to rain tomorrow.
3. The tourist industry will probably grow quite fast next year.
4. The price of hotels will probably go up.
5. The guests will probably receive bad service.
6. They will probably not come back.
7. He is likely to change his mind.
8. They will probably spend more than they can afford.
9. He is not likely to argue.
10. The weather will probably be disappointing.

# Structural Appendix

1. **Because**

    We use **because** to give a reason:
    **We stayed at home because it was raining.**
    We use **why** to ask a question, or when such a question is reported:
    **Why do leaves fall in the autumn?**
    **They asked me why leaves fall in the autumn.**

2. **But, though**

    **We stayed but it got cold towards the end.**
    **We stayed, though it got cold towards the end.**
    **But** and **though** cannot be followed by **that**.

3. **Close to, next to**

    We can also say **(very) close to** or **next to** something:
    **The bus stop is close to my house.**
    **The bank is next to the post office.**
    We cannot say **very next**.

4. **The date**

    There are two ways of saying the date; both use ordinal numbers:
    **It is the fifteenth of December**, or
    **It is December the fifteenth.**
    When we write the date, we often use
    **15th December**, or
    **15 December**.

5. **Else**

    **Else** has a similar meaning to **other**; we use **else**, but not **other**, in certain contexts: with question words **what, who, where, how**, and with words made from **some-, any-** and **no-** combined with **-one, -body, -thing, -where**:
    You saw Bill. **Who else did you see?**
    **I didn't see anybody else.**

6. **Fish**

    Notice that the singular form **fish** is normal with both singular and plural uses:
    **We caught one fish.**
    **We caught four fish.**

7. **For**

    We always say 'a present **for** someone'. If we want to say that the present belongs to someone, we can say, for example, **my sister's present**.

8. **Good, well**

    We can say, in a letter for example, **it was good** (or **nice**) **to hear from you**.
    We cannot use **well** (in place of **good**) or **listen** (in place of **hear**) in this sort of sentence.

9. **Half**

    If there is no other number, we usually use **half** before **a** or **an**:
    **half a pound, half a mile, half an hour.**
    If there is a number before **half** we say, for example:
    **one and a half hours**
    **three and a half tons.**

## Structural appendix

### 10 Health

In talking about health we say:
**I'm fine**, or
**I'm very well**,
but not
**I'm good**, or
**I'm very fine**, or
**I'm best**.

### 11 Interested, interesting

If a film or book or song or talk is **interesting**, then the people are **interested**; similarly, if a film is **boring**, the people are **bored**. The same goes for other pairs like **exciting/excited, fascinating/fascinated, pleasing/pleased** etc.

### 12 Like

With the verb **like**, we use **a lot** and **much**:
I like him a lot.
I don't like fruit very much.

### 13 Nouns

When there are two nouns together, e.g. **hockey team, pea soup, ground floor**, it is the second noun that is the head word. So a **hockey team** is a sort of **team**, not a sort of **hockey**; and **pea soup** is a sort of **soup**, not a sort of **pea**; and the **ground floor** in a house is one of the **floors**. The others are **first floor, second floor** etc.

### 14 Numerals

In counting, we say **a hundred** (100), **two hundred** (200), **a thousand** (1000), **two thousand** (2000); when we do not know exactly what the number is we can say **hundreds of, thousands of**:
Three hundred people saw the game.
Hundreds of people saw the game.

### 15 Sorry

**Sorry** is an adjective, usually used to express sympathy for people or to apologise:
**I am sorry you are not well.**
In Test 14, question 1, **sadly** and **unhappily** are adverbs. We cannot use them after **be**.

### 16 Time

In talking about the time, we say:
**What time is it?** or
**What is the time?**
A clock or a watch gives you the time; a watch is small enough to carry with you, but a clock is bigger and stays in one place.
An hour is sixty minutes.

### 17 Too

We use **too** to express excess. **Too** goes with **much** and **many** as well as with adjectives and adverbs:
**too much milk, too many problems;**
**too long, too sweet, too fast.**

*Structural appendix*

---

We also use **too** to mean **as well** or **also**:
**I've seen the Queen, too.**

## 18 With

When we describe someone's features we use **with**:
**a girl with dark hair**
**a man with a moustache**
**a woman with blue eyes**
We also use **with** for an expression with tools: instruments and money:
**cut it with a knife/a razor**
**draw with a pencil/a pen**

## 19 Will

**What will you do with the money you won?**
In English we cannot use **will** and **must** together; we get this meaning by using **will have to**.

## 20 Would like

We use **would like** to ask for something and to offer something:
**What would you like to drink?**
**I'd like a lemonade, please.**
**Just** means 'at this moment' in these sentences. With this meaning it is not used with the present simple or past simple tenses.

# Lexical Appendix

1 **Abroad, on the Continent, foreign, overseas**

**Abroad** = 'in/ to a foreign country':
**He was born in England but he lives abroad.**
**Foreign** is an adjective (see definition above).
Since Britain is an island, **on the Continent** refers to Europe, and all foreign countries are **overseas**. **Overseas** is an adverb, like **abroad**, and has the same meaning except that one must cross the sea to reach the foreign country referred to.

2 **Alone, lonely, only, single**

**Only** is an adjective, adverb and conjunction; **alone** is an adverb; **lonely** and **single** are adjectives.
**Only** (adjective) = 'with no others':
**She is the only person here.**
**Lonely** = 'with no friends' (of a person); 'with no people' (of a place).
**Single** = 'not married' (of a person); 'one' (emphatic, of a thing):
**He cannot give me a single reason for his actions.**
**Alone** = 'without other people':
**She is alone in the room.** (compare **only**).

3 **Ask, talk**

We use **ask** in reference to questions, as in these examples:
**I asked (him) a question.**
**I asked (her) her name/I asked (her) what her name was.**
**(What is your name)?**
The verb has a different meaning with the following constructions:
**I asked (him) for some money.**
**I asked him to lend me some money.**
**(Please lend me some money/**
**Will you lend me some money, please)?**
**Talk** is 'to communicate with words'
**I want to talk to you.**
For **say** and **tell**, see Exercise 146.

4 **Bad, wrong**

**Bad** = 'not good', **wrong** = 'not correct'.
**There was a bad programme on television.**
**The student gave the wrong answer.**
**There is something wrong with a thing/person** means something is not working correctly.

5 **Bear, carry**

**Carry** is normally used for 'move from one place to another, holding the person/thing in one's hands'. **Bear** is now only used with this meaning poetically. Compare:
**The case is too heavy. She can't carry it.**
**The pain is too great. I can't bear (stand) it.**

6 **Beat, win**

Compare these sentences and their structure:
**Steffi Graf beat Navratilova (in the final).**
**Steffi Graf won (the match, the cup, the championship).**
**Beat** has an object, usually personal; **win** never has a personal object.

*Lexical appendix*

## 7 Become, get

These verbs can mean the same thing when followed by an adjective:
**It's becoming (getting) dark.**
With a noun **become** suggests a change of state:
**He's become a member of the club.**
**Get** has many meanings. In Test 11, question 10, it means 'earn, obtain'.

## 8 Bring, take

**Bring** means 'towards the speaker', or 'from another place here'; **take** means 'away from the speaker, to another place'.
**Bring it here/Take it over there.**
**He brought me a present for my birthday.**
**It was my aunt's birthday, so I took her a present.**

## 9 Carry, wear

**Carry** (see 4) suggests holding something in one's hands; **wear** means 'be dressed in, have on'. Compare:
**He is carrying an umbrella.**
**He is wearing a jacket/a watch** (attached to his body).

## 10 Come, get, go

We use **come** for movement towards where we are, **go** for movement away from where we are, so we say:
**Come here!**
**Go over there!**
**Get** has many meanings. With places, **get to** means the same as **arrive at/in** (see Exercise 147).
**We go to work by bus. We get there about eight o'clock.**
When we talk about entering or leaving a vehicle, we use **get in/into, get out** and **get on/off**. We use **in/into** and **out** when there are doors which close:
**Get in! Get into the car!**
**She got out (of the train) at the last station.**
**He got on his bicycle.**

**He got off the bus** (because buses traditionally did not have closing doors in Britain) **at the last stop.**

## 11 Depend on

The verb has two main meanings with this preposition:
(1) = vary according to,
The cost of the ticket **depends on** the length of the journey.
(2) = trust, rely on,
I can **depend on** her to do the job well.

## 12 Do, make

A large number of expressions are used with these verbs, but the basic difference is that **do** refers to actions, **make** to creating, constructing:
**I'm going to do some work.**
**I've made a cake.**

192

## 13 Drive, ride

**Drive** = 'to guide a vehicle, take someone in a vehicle'. We use **ride** when we have one leg on either side of the vehicle (motor cycle, bicycle) or for a horse. Compare:
Can you drive a car/Can you ride a horse (bicycle)?

## 14 Expect, hope, wait (for)

**Expect** refers to what we think will happen (good or bad); **hope** refers to what we want to happen in the future (good); **wait** is an activity, while the others indicate a state of mind. Compare the sentences and note the constructions used:
I expect (to get) a letter from them soon.
I expect that it will rain tonight. There are a lot of clouds.
I am hoping for success (I hope to succeed).
I hope that it will be a fine day tomorrow.
She waited (for the bus) for half an hour.
When **wait** has an object, it must be followed by **for**:
What are you waiting for? The bus.

## 15 Fault, mistake

**Fault** usually refers to a defect in a person's character, or to a technical problem with a machine. It is also found with the meaning of 'responsibility for which one can be blamed'. It is not used with **make** or **do**.
She has a lot of faults.
There is a fault in the machine.
Don't blame me for what happened! It wasn't my fault.
**Mistake** is an error in action
You've made a lot of mistakes in your composition.

## 16 Flat, floor, ground

**Flat** (noun) (USA: apartment) = rooms in a house, usually on the same floor; **flat** (adjective) = level.
I live in a flat.
The land near the sea is flat.
**Floor** = (1) the surface inside a building; (2) a level in a house, block of flats:
There is a carpet on the floor.
She lives on the second floor.
**Ground** = the surface outside.
There is snow on the ground.
It can also be used adjectivally to mean 'the level nearest the ground', so the level of a house 'on the ground' is the 'ground floor' (USA: first floor). Compare these combinations:
The house stands on flat ground.
His flat is on the ground floor.

## 17 Follow, keep

**Follow** usually means 'go, come after'; **Keep** (on) can mean 'continue'; **follow** is not followed by a gerund.
Follow me, and I'll show you the way.
Keep on/Keep going until you get to the traffic lights, and then turn right.

*Lexical appendix*

### 18 Fond of

To be **fond of** = have a liking for, like.
Look at these examples:
**He is fond of ice cream.** (He has a liking for it, likes it)
**I'm very fond of her.** (I like her very much, I feel affectionately towards her)
This is not as strong in feeling as 'I love her'.

### 19 Go away, go out

**Go away** = go to another place
**Go out** = leave the house, office, place where you are etc.
Look at these examples:
**Go away!** I never want to see you again.
They've **gone away** on holiday.
She's **gone out** (shopping). She'll be back in half an hour.

### 20 Have, take

We usually use **have**, not **take**, when referring to meals:
**What time do you have lunch?**

### 21 Hear, listen

**Listen** is active, we have to make an effort.
**Hear** can be the result of listening, but it is a passive action and does not need any effort:
**We were listening to the teacher but we could hear a lot of noise outside.**

### 22 Hold, keep

**Hold** = have in the hand, possess; **keep** = retain, not let go of. In Test 19, question 10, the contrast is between giving half the money to other people, and not giving them the other half (keeping it).

### 23 Hot, warm

We cannot use **hot** when we are talking about clothes because **hot** suggests unpleasant heat; **warm** suggests pleasant heat. Compare:
**Be careful! The plate is very hot.**
**I'm cold. I must put on my warm coat.**

### 24 Interest, interested in

**In** is always used as the preposition following these words.
**He showed a lot of interest in my work.**
**He is interested in buying the house.**

### 25 Job, work

**Job** is countable, **work** is not. Compare:
**He is looking for work/a job.**
**I must do some work/I have a few jobs to do.**

### 26 Journey, travel

**Journey** is countable, **travel** is not.
**Travel** is rather literary, so **travelling** is the usual noun.
**I am fond of travelling.**
**I am going on a journey.**
But note the phrase: **travel agent**.

*Lexical appendix*

27 **Large, long, tall**

**Large** refers to size, not length; **long** refers to length; **tall** refers to height, so we use it of people, trees and buildings, but not of clothes.

28 **Look, see**

**Look** is active, making an effort; **see** refers to a passive action or the result of looking:
**Look! Can you see that bird in the tree?**
**Yes, I can see it.**

29 **Look, seem**

**Look** refers to outward appearance (face, clothes etc); **seem** refers to outward appearance expressing feelings, qualities etc. In many cases, both could be used:
**He looks/seems intelligent.**
The difference is clear when it refers to dress, for example, as in Test 20, question 5. Here the writer means his sister 'looked nice', when dressed as the queen.
In Test 18, question 2, **seem** is correct because the writer cannot see Fred's face.

30 **On holiday**

**On holiday** = not at work, not at school etc.
Look at these examples:
He's not in the office this week. He's (gone) **on holiday**.
**The restaurant is closed because the staff are on holiday.**
The plural form, **holidays**, is only used in sentences like:
**The holidays (from school) begin on July 10th.**

31 **On the radio, on TV etc.**

**On** is the correct preposition to use when referring to performances seen or heard: **on television, on the radio, on the stage, on the screen**.
**On** refers to the medium used, **in** to the place where the performance takes place: **in the studio, in the theatre, in the cinema.**

32 **Own, proper**

**Own** (adjective) = belonging to oneself and not to anyone else.
**Proper** = correct, suitable for a purpose.
Compare these sentences:
**All the students have their own books. There is one book for each student.**
**I can't teach these students to speak without the proper equipment. I need a tape-recorder so they can hear good models.**

33 **Pass, spend**

**Pass** and **spend** can both be used with 'time'. The difference is that **we pass time to avoid being bored**; the usual verb to use is therefore **spend**:
**He had no books so he passed the time doing crossword puzzles.**
**Where did you spend your holidays (a period of time)?**
**Spend** can also be used for money. It is followed by **on** when we mention the thing that was bought, or the reason why time was spent.
**He spends his time collecting stamps.**
**He spends all his money/time on his stamp collection.**

## Lexical appendix

### 34 Put on, take off

We use these expressions with reference to clothes.
**Take off your wet clothes (Take your wet clothes off)** and **put on these dry ones (put these dry ones on).**

### 35 Replace, substitute

These verbs mean 'put someone (something) in the place of the person/thing there at present', but the constructions are different.
Compare these sentences and note the word order:
I've **replaced** the old machine **with** this new one.
I've **substituted** this new machine **for** the old one.
When used with people, **replace** implies a permanent change, **substitute ... for** a temporary one:
Jones has replaced Smith as manager.
Jones is substituting for Smith while Smith is on holiday.

### 36 Rest, stay

**Rest** means 'not do anything', because of being tired, ill etc.
**Stay** means 'live in a place for a time' or 'not move'.
He's resting on the sofa. He's tired.
I stayed at my friends' house for a week.
Stay still and keep quiet! Grandfather is resting.

### 37 Time expressions

To refer to the evening of the day before today, we can say **yesterday evening** or **last night**. To refer to the evening at the end of today, we can say **this evening** or **tonight**. We use **at night** more generally:
I never go out at night.
**In the night** is also possible here, but is less usual.
In English the day is divided into **morning** (sunrise to about midday); **afternoon** (about midday to sunset or about 6 p.m.); **evening** (from sunset or about 6 p.m. to about 10 p.m.); **night**.
'**It's time** (for me) to...' means 'I must, because of the time'. So when we say 'It's time (for us) to go home', it means 'We must go home, because it is late/we have work to do etc'.

### 38 Want, would, would you like?

**Want** and **would like** are followed by the infinitive with **to**; **will** is followed by the infinitive without **to**:
I want to go home.
Would you like to have some tea?
When John comes, we will go home.
**Want** is not normally found in continuous forms.
**Do you want...?** is not as polite as **would you like...?**, so it is not used for polite invitations.
**Would** is an auxiliary verb indicating the conditional tense; it has no meaning without an accompanying verb.

Look at these sentences:
'**Do they want** to have dinner early?' (The cook, for example, is speaking to the waiter about guests in a hotel)
'Yes. They **want** to have it at 6.30'.

'**Would you like** to have dinner early'? (The waiter is speaking to the guests).
'Yes. We **would like** to have it at 6.30'.
'**Would** you like steak for dinner or **would** you prefer fish'?

## 39   Worth

To be **worth** = to be of the value of.
**The house is worth £100,000.**
To be **worth** + gerund = to deserve.
**The film is worth seeing.** You would enjoy it.

# Index

a, an 1,2
abroad LA 1
alone LA 2
a lot of 6
adjectives 18-20,28-34
adverbials 36-41
adverbs, formation of 35
after 123
ago 86
all 3,137
all day 3
all the same 133
along 43
already 37
although, even though 133
always 41,75
another 12-13,21
any 7-8,11
anybody, anyone 16
anything 17
anywhere 17
apostrophe, use of 24,26
arrive 147
as 28,36,46-7,80
as/so ... as 128
as far as 46
ask LA 3
as soon as 123
at 42-3
auxiliaries 48-64
avoid 105,128
bad LA 4
be 65,67
be able to 49
bear LA 5
beat LA 6
be capable of 49
because 128,SA 1
become LA 7
been 81-2,114
before 123
belong to 27
best 30-1,36
better 29-30,36
both 137
bring LA 8
but SA 2
by 113
by air, etc. 43
can 48-49,114
carry LA 9
causative use of have 117
clauses 122-136
close to SA 3
come LA 10
comparatives 28-31,36
compound nouns SA 13
compound verbs 116
conditional 89-91
could 50,89-91
count nouns 6-8
the date SA 4
depend on LA 11
determiners 1-8
did you have to 55

direct object 116,139
do 55,64,68,73-4,LA 12
double possessives, a friend
 of mine 25
drive LA 13
each other, one another 13
either...or 122
else 17,SA 5
(big) enough 34
enough 138
ever 83,85
every 3,14
every day 3
everyone, everybody 14
everything 14
exclamations 2
expect LA 14
expressions of frequency 41,75
expressions of time 3,40-1,44
fast 36
fault LA 15
few, a few 8
first 41
fish SA 6
flat LA 16
floor LA 16
follow LA 17
fond of LA 18
for 86-7,107,109,127,132
foreign LA 1
frequency adverbs 41
from 45,107,128
future 71,119
future time clauses 123
genitive 24-26
gerunds 105-7
get 117
get to 147
going to 71
go LA 10
go away LA 19
go out LA 19
gone 81-2
good SA 8
ground LA 16
had 68,88,114,117-8
had better 61
had to 54
half SA 9
hard 36
have 68,81,114,LA 20
have (got) 68
have lunch (breakfast/
 dinner) 68
have to 52,54-55
health SA 10
hear LA 21
help 105,110,128
hold LA 22
hope LA 14
hot LA 23
how 120
how? 98
how much/many? 98
however 126,133

I (don't) think so 149
I hope so not, etc. 149
I'm cold, thirsty, etc. 143
if 89-91,120,123
imperatives 92-4
in 42,44
in case 130
in order to 128
in spite of 133
indirect object 110,116,139
infinitives 105-6,108-11,115
inside 42
interest LA 24
interesting SA 11
interested LA 24
into 43
introductory there and it 100-4
is called 112
it 9,11
it takes ... 104
its 18-19,103
job LA 25
journey LA 26
keep LA 22
large LA 27
last 41
(the) least 30
let 108
let's 96
lexis 141-50
like 47,105,SA 12
likely 150
listen to 45,LA 21
little, a little 8
lonely LA 2
long LA 27
look 144,LA 28-9
look at 45
make 145
many 6
mass nouns 142
may 51
may have 51
meanwhile 131
might 51
might have 51
mine, etc. 19
mistake LA 15
modals 48-58
more 29
(the) most 31
most of 31
much 6,31,33
much (bigger, etc.) 31,33
must 52-3
must have 58
my, etc. 18-19
myself, etc. 21-2
nationality words 141
need to 52
needn't 52
negative commands 7,94-6
negative statements 6-7,16-17,38,52,
 73,78,81,97
negative words 15-17

# Index

Neither/nor do I, I don't, either 63-4,122
next to SA 3
never 75,85
nevertheless 133
no 7,15
nobody/no one 15-16
none 15
nothing 15
numerals SA 14
of 6,11,15,113,137
of (possessive) 24-6
off 43
often 75,85
on 42,44,LA 30-1
on holiday LA 30
on the radio LA 31
on to 43
once 40
one (ones) 10
only LA 2
others, the other(s) 12
ought to 57
out 42
outside 42
out of 43
overseas LA 1
own LA 32
participles 38,69,81,41
**pass LA 33**
passives 112-117
past continuous 80,84
past perfect 88
past simple 77-80,83,87,119
**people 142**
personal pronouns 9
phrasal verbs 140
**play squash (football, tennis, cards) 4**
**play the piano (violin) 4**
plural (agreement)6-9,66,72-4
positive commands 92-4
positive statements 33-4
possessive adjectives 18-20
possessive pronouns 19-20
possessives 18-20,25
prepositional verbs 45
prepositions of movement 43
prepositions of position 42
prepositions of time 44
prepositional phrases 42-7
present continuous 69,71,75
present perfect 81-7
present perfect continuous 84
present simple 72-5,119
**prevent 128**
**probably 150**
pronouns 9-17,19-22
**proper LA 32**
**put on LA 34**
question tags 97
question words 98-9
questions 97-99
**raise 148**
**reach 147**

reflexives 21-3
relative clauses 134-6
replace LA 35
reported speech 118-121
rest LA 36
ride LA 13
rise 148
say 146
seem 144
shall 59
short answers 63
should 56
should have 58,91
simple verbs 38,41
since 87
single LA 2
singular (agreement) 6-9,14,66,72-4,104,137
so (...that) 33
so as to 128
So do I, I do, too, etc. 64
so much, many 7,33
so that 128
some 7-8,11
somebody, someone 16
something 17
sometimes 41,75
somewhere 17
sorry SA 15
sound 144
spend LA 33
stay LA 36
still 38
subject verb/agreement 7,14,18,19,66,100-102,109,112,116,139
substitute LA 35
such, such an (...that) 33
superlatives 30-31
take LA 8
take off LA 34
talk about, talk to 45
tall LA 27
taste 144
teach (speak, learn) Arabic/French, etc. 4
tell 146
than 28-31,36
that 134-6
the grocer's, etc. 26
the more...the more 124
the reason for/why 132
the same...as 28
the, use and omission of 4
the whole 137
them 11
they 9
this, that, these, those 5
though SA 2
through 43
(three) times 40
there is/are 100-2
time SA 16
time expressions LA 37
to 4,43,95,104-5,127
too 64, SA 17

too (big) 34,SA 17
too (...for/to) 34
travel LA 26
twice 40
two-part verbs 45,140
unless 129
until 123
used to 60
usually 41,75
verb forms 65-96
verbs not used in continuous 76
very 39
wait for 45
want LA 38
warm LA 23
was born 112
wear LA 9
well SA 8
what (the thing that) 125
what...! what an...! 2
what? 98-9
whatever 126
when 120,123,134-6
when? 98
where 111,120,134-6
where? 98
wherever 126
which 111,120,134-6
which? 98
while 131
who 111,120,134-5
who? 98-9
whoever 126
whom 134-6
whose 120,134-5
whose? 20,98
why 111,120,132,134-5,SA 1
why? 94,98
will 59,119,123,SA 19
win LA 6
wish 90
with 113,SA 18
word order 32,37-41,137-40
work LA 25
worse 30-1
worst 30-1
worth LA 39
would 89,91,119
would like SA 20
would you like LA 38
would rather 62,LA38
wrong LA 4
yet 37

**Thomas Nelson and Sons Ltd**
Nelson House  Mayfield Road
Walton-on-Thames  Surrey
KT12 5PL  UK

51 York Place
Edinburgh
EH1 3JD  UK

**Thomas Nelson (Hong Kong) Ltd**
Toppan Building 10/F
22A  Westlands Road
Quarry Bay  Hong Kong

This edition contains material first published by Thomas Nelson and Sons Ltd in Test Your English 1, 1977, Test Your English 2, 1978, Practise Your English 1, 1982 and Practise Your English 2, 1982.

© W.S. Fowler and Norman Coe 1977, 1978, 1982

Test and Practise Your English 1 (Beginners to Intermediate) first published by Thomas Nelson and Sons Ltd 1990.

© W.S. Fowler and Norman Coe 1990

ISBN 0-17-555749-7
NPN 9 8 7 6 5 4 3 2 1

All Rights Reserved. This publication is protected in the United Kingdom by the Copyright Act 1956 and in other countries by comparable legislation. No part of it may be reproduced or recorded by any means without the permission of the publisher. This prohibition extends (with certain very limited exceptions) to photocopying and similar processes, and written permission to make a copy or copies must therefore be obtained from the publisher in advance. It is advisable to consult the publisher if there is any doubt regarding the legality of any proposed copying.

Printed and bound in Hong Kong